William Thomas Charley

The Legal Profession

Viewed in the Light of its Past History, its Present State and Projected Law Reforms

William Thomas Charley

The Legal Profession
Viewed in the Light of its Past History, its Present State and Projected Law Reforms

ISBN/EAN: 9783337297442

Printed in Europe, USA, Canada, Australia, Japan

Cover: Foto ©Suzi / pixelio.de

More available books at **www.hansebooks.com**

THE LEGAL PROFESSION:

VIEWED IN THE LIGHT OF

ITS PAST HISTORY

ITS PRESENT STATE

AND

PROJECTED LAW REFORMS.

EDITED BY

DOCTOR-IN-JURE-CIVILI,

OF THE OUTER CIRCLE, ESQUIRE,

APPRENTICE-AT-LAW.

"Miscuit Utile Dulci (?)."

LONDON:
WILLIAM RIDGWAY, 169, PICCADILLY. W.
1873.

PREFACE.

THE *dramatis personæ* will, in the following pages, speak for themselves. The Editor has little more to do than to bow to the audience, utter this brief Prologue, give the signal to draw aside the curtain, and then gracefully retire into the obscurity from which he emerged.

The scene-shifting has been arranged on the "fair play" system, so that opposite views of "Law Life" may be presented, alternately, to the audience. The Bar, "the other branch of the Profession," and the Public, are all three pulling, at present, in different directions. The Editor hopes that, in the following pages, the several representatives of these important interests will faithfully reproduce the sentiments of their respective constituencies.

The Editor is not aware of any grievance connected with the Legal Profession that is not ventilated by the *dramatis personæ*. If there be any such, the *Law Times* will probably let him hear of it.

The Editor believes that the Legal Profession is "treading upon the verge of a great region of change": and he will be deeply thankful if, out of the materials furnished by this little volume, which contains, he believes, a digest (however imperfect) of all the learning upon the subject, the slightest inkling be obtained of a satisfactory re-adjustment of the relations of the two branches of the Profession towards each other and towards the Public. Reconstruction out of the existing elements he believes to be possible. "Destructions," he fervently hopes, will "come to a perpetual end." Nothing is sacred nowadays. It is proposed to substitute for the Inns of Court a body as "shadowy" as the University of London, whose only resident member, it is currently rumoured, is the hall-porter. The House of Lords and " any other Court" must " cease to exist." Wild schemes for making "every man his own lawyer" are not without influential support. The Public is to be its own " Minister of Justice :" " free trade in law" is to be established : and lawyers are to be abated as a nuisance that ought never to have been allowed to exist. The fratricidal struggle going on under their eyes in the bosom of the Profession must be highly gratifying to the "free traders," who are not, it may be observed, unrepresented in "another place." It cannot, indeed, be denied that, although Barristers and Attorneys have many interests in common, many interests of one branch of the Profession clash with the interests of the other. Shall might make right? or shall a spirit of compromise pervade our discussions?

The existence of the Legal Profession, the Editor

humbly suggests to the "lay reader," is essential to the maintenance of the rights and liberties of the people.

We can still apply to the unsullied ermine of Westminster Hall the language of Lord Erskine, who, in his maiden speech, addressing Lord Mansfield, said :—" That torrent of corruption, which has unhappily overwhelmed every other part of the Constitution, is, by the blessing of God, stopped here by the sacred independence of the Judges." That eight Judges should have devoted three whole days to the hearing of Mr. Edwin James's appeal,* is a remarkable proof of the desire of the existing Bench that the silk of the Senior Bar should be unsullied, also.

The Attorneys and Solicitors of England are, likewise, a highly independent body of gentlemen, and their system of discipline, education, and representation of professional interests is by no means contemptible. To an Attorney or Solicitor, writhing under a sense of social wrong inflicted upon his order, it must be some consolation to peruse the Pamphlets, dealing with the subject-matter of this volume in an incisive manner, that have issued from the Press in recent years. If some of the *Dramatis Personæ* should occasionally deal in an incisive manner with some of these Pamphlets, the Editor trusts that the authors will kindly pardon

* The appeal has been, as the Profession, generally, expected, dismissed.

the presumption ; he will be happy to give these excellent persons their revenge.

The "Great Central Bar" of England is, no doubt, very dependent on the Attorneys, but it "forms a real and principal check on the abuse of patronage by the Government;" and "the only real practical check on the Judges" is "the habitual respect which they all pay to" its "opinion."* The Editor cannot express the sentiments that he feels for the Bar of England in terms more appropriate than those contained in the closing sentences of Mr. Shaw Lefevre's remarkable Essay on "The Discipline of the Bar."†

"In conclusion, I have only to say, that it must not be supposed, because I have pointed out some of the weak points in the organization of the Bar, and have had occasion to advert to the practices of some of its obscurer members, that I would either wish or venture to speak slightingly of its members as a whole. I believe the Bar of England was never more full of men of the highest honour, probity, and learning. The generation has hardly yet passed away in which it gave us such men as Romilly and Brougham, Denman, Lyndhurst, and Campbell, and it has now among its ranks men who will be no unworthy successors to these."

* Per Mr. Justice Blackburn, 2nd Report of the Judicature Commission, p. 26.
† Paper read before the Law Amendment Society, p. 42.

TABLE OF CONTENTS.

	PAGE
Preface	i—vi
INTRODUCTORY	1—18

What was thought of the Second Report of the Judicature Commission

§ 1. By the Junior Bar	1
§ 2. By the Mercantile Community . .	8
§ 3. By certain Attorneys and Solicitors . .	13

THE LEGAL PROFESSION . . .	19—346
§ 1. The Wrongs of Attorneys . . .	19
§ 2. The Honour and Dignity of the Bar .	24
§ 3. The Right of Audience in the Superior Courts	33
§ 4. Audi alteram partem	47
A Sketch of the early history of Legal Practitioners	48
Section I. Serjeants-at-law . .	48
Section II. Apprentices-at-Bar .	58
Section III. Attorneys-at-law .	68
Section IV. The Year-Books .	91
§ 5. The Office of Judge promoted by the Attorneys against the Inns of Court . .	127
§ 6. How to get from the Temple to Chancery Lane	144
§ 7. Client Jilting. A Suitor's Grievance .	157
§ 8. Etiquette for Gentlemen . . .	164
(I.) Instruction of Counsel by Attorney . .	165
(II.) Touting	187
(III.) A. B. (Barrister) and Co. . .	206
(IV.) Caste-iron	212
(V.) Precedence	214
(VI.) Fees	215

	PAGE
§ 9. The Incorporated Law Society	232
§ 10. No taxation without representation	261
§ 11. Exclusion of Attorneys from Legal Appointments	274
§ 12. How not to become an Inner or Outer Barrister	278
§ 13. Discipline	289
§ 14. Doe on the demise of Sir Roundell Palmer v. The Inns of Court	306
§ 15. A Moot Point	319
§ 16. Amalgamation	321
§ 17. Woo'd an' married an' a	344
§ 18. A gloomy prospect	345
APPENDIX	347—351

ERRATA.

Page 43 *(foot-note), for* " Legibus" *read* "Laudibus."
,, 51 *(et alibi), for* " Reeve's" *read* " Reeves.' "
,, 93. *for* " tortuously" *read* " tortiously."
,, 97. *for* " Douis" *read* " Donis."
,, 158 *(foot-note), for* " dont" *read* " doit."
,, 264 *(foot-note), insert* the word " as" *before* " to."
,, 269. *four lines from bottom, after* " Society" *dele* the comma.
,, 299 *(foot-note), for* "74" *read* "72."
,, 348. *for* " Peurice" *read* " Penrice."

INTRODUCTORY.

WHAT WAS THOUGHT OF THE SECOND REPORT OF THE JUDICATURE COMMISSION.

SCENE.—*Westminster Hall. Marchmont and Singleton of the Utter Bar, Esquires, meeting.*

SINGLETON.—Have you read the Second Report of the Judicature Commission?

MARCHMONT.—I have, Singleton, to my sorrow. It gives us, Barristers, I think, the *coup de grace.* We have long had a second charge on the right of audience—the ancient legal fee being vested in the Serjeants. In the general shipwreck, however, of the profession, the legal fee has, somehow, drifted away, and I see clearly that the Attorneys and Solicitors, having a third charge, are bent upon tacking the "tabula in naufragio," and squeezing out the Bar, as a mesne incumbrancer. The Report of the Judicature Commission deprives us of all hope of getting in the legal fee!

SINGLETON.—Marchmont, you're incorrigible; you "sing at grave-making."

MARCHMONT.—" Custom hath made it in me a property of easiness."

SINGLETON.—Is there, then, no hope? Compromise—give and take—is the good old English method of settling vexed questions. Let's try and negociate a compromise. The other branch of the Profession is not satisfied, and we are not satisfied. Why not come to terms? There can be no harm, surely, in trying: and if the worst does come to the worst, why, we can—What can we do Marchmont, if the worst comes to the worst?

MARCHMONT. — Emigrate, like Edwin James, Q.C., M.P., to America: disappear, like the *scintilla juris*, *in nubibus:* jump, like Ginx's Baby, off Vauxhall Bridge ; or live in a common lodging house with vermin, and die like poor Haddy,* of starvation in the Union Workhouse.

* SAD END OF A BARRISTER.—Last evening Dr. Lankester held an inquiry at the workhouse of the Strand Union, Cleveland-street, on the body of Mr. John Haddy, son of a Wesleyan Minister, and a barrister-at-law, aged 47, who had died in the workhouse under the following extraordinary circumstances :—

Mr. Hugh Weightman said he resided at No. 1, Mitre-court, Temple, and was a barrister and Master of Arts. About nine months ago while passing up Fleet-street, being attracted by an announcement in the window of the Temple Discussion Forum that a discussion would be opened by a colonist, he went in, and saw the deceased, who was the colonist referred to. He entered into conversation with him, and deceased informed him that he was born at the Cape of Good Hope, that he was the son of a Wesleyan Minister, and had come to

England to be called to the Bar. Finding that deceased was in bad circumstances, witness gave him the money for his night's lodging, and afterwards found that he was in distressed and destitute circumstances almost impossible to imagine. Since that period he had frequently met him at the same place, and had assisted him in a similar manner. He had been called to the Bar, and was a most profound scholar, and perfect master of most of the living and also the dead languages. He had no chambers, and no one knew where he lived, but he had his letters addressed to the lodge of the gardener of the Middle Temple. He last saw deceased at the Temple Discussion Forum on the evening of Friday week, when he appeared in a prostrate condition. He had not seen him since.

Wm. Wotten, of 12, Hanover-court, Long-acre, said deceased formerly lodged there, but not for the last six weeks prior to Saturday week, when he came again. It was a common lodging-house. He remained in bed the whole of Sunday and till Monday morning, and during the interval some of the lodgers gave him some gruel, tea, toast, &c., as he was ill and destitute. On Monday morning witness went to Dr. Brooks, the divisional police surgeon, and told him deceased's condition, and he ordered him to be taken to the Strand Union, and he was removed there in a cab. On arriving at the workhouse deceased described himself as a writer on the press and a barrister. He was then admitted.

John Bowman, relieving officer of No. 1 District of the Strand Union, said he gave the order for deceased's admission. He was in a dreadful state and covered with vermin.

Mr. John Anderson, medical officer to the Strand Union, said deceased was brought there on the 19th of November in a prostrate condition. He was in a filthy state, and had great difficulty in breathing. He at once ordered him beef tea and brandy and water, and then to be very carefully washed. He expired in about five hours after his admission. The *post-mortem* examination showed that the right lung was destroyed by inflammation, and glued to the wall of the chest. The pleura was inflamed, and, although the stomach was quite healthy, *it was perfectly empty.* The cause of death was pleuro-pneumonia, and he believed that the death was accelerated by removal in the cab. Had he been carried in a recumbent instead of upright position his life might have been saved. There was no evidence of drinking.

Mr. Weightman, upon this point, said the deceased, on every occasion he had seen him, was a most abstemious man. A letter which had been sent addressed to deceased at the gardener's lodge was produced, from a lady in South Brent, Devonshire, telling deceased to take private lodgings, and she would send him assistance.

The Coroner having offered some remarks upon the singular and sad features the case presented, the Jury returned a verdict, "That the deceased died from inflammation of the lungs, accelerated by removal from his lodgings to the workhouse in a cab in a sitting position."—*Standard, November 26th,* 1872.

A WASTED LIFE AND A WRETCHED DEATH.

Seldom has a sadder story been told at a coroner's inquest than that of Mr. John Haddy. This unfortunate gentleman, who died in the workhouse of the Strand Union, was no ordinary pauper. He had struggled long and desperately with unfavouring fortune. What little we know about him we learn from a member of his own profession, who found him when his troubles were gathering round him, who supplied his necessities, and who, though a mere casual acquaintance, would probably have saved him from his melancholy fate if he had but guessed the depth of misery to which he had sunk. Nine months ago Mr. Hugh Weightman, a barrister of the Inner Temple, was passing the Temple Discussion Forum. A handbill in the window announced that "A Colonist" would begin the discussion of the evening. Mr. Weightman went in, got into conversation with "the Colonist," found that he was a barrister, *and one of the many to whom his profession failed to furnish the means of living.* The leader of the debate was in very low water. He had no clients, nor hope of obtaining any. He had no chambers, for he could not pay their rent. He had no friends, for he was a native of the Cape of Good Hope, and apparently knew little or nothing of any dweller in the great City whose streets he paced from day to day. The son of a Wesleyan minister at the Cape, he had come to England to keep his terms for the bar.

Of his means at this time we know nothing, except that he must have been much above want, or he could not have paid the ordinary fees upon entering the Middle Temple, at which he was called to the bar so far back as June, 1856. He was then thirty-one years of age, rather older than most of his companions on "call night," but still less advanced in life than many who have made their way at the bar in spite of similar disadvantages. But poor Mr. Haddy was not destined to point an encouraging moral for the benefit of high-spirited pursuers of knowledge under difficulties. After the lapse of sixteen years he was as briefless and more hopeless than ever. The eloquence that might have persuaded juries was wasted in a tavern, where ability was unrewarded, save by occasional gifts from those who traced the gentleman in his disguise, and discovered the poverty he would fain have concealed. He put himself in no man's way, and asked for no man's help, though he was not so proud as to refuse it when tendered. His health gave way, so that when his benefactor saw him on Friday week " he appeared in an almost prostrate condition." Then, weary and heart-worn, he went back to a common lodging-house in Long Acre, in which he had formerly resided. When he took to his bed he was dependent on the charity of inmates almost as poor, but scarcely so miserable as himself, for such little medical comforts as gruel, tea, and toast, till on Monday morning the landlord deemed it advisable to have him removed to the workhouse.

There he had all the attention his condition required, but he rapidly sank, and five hours after his admission the broken-down barrister expired.

There is something unutterably painful in this picture. Only those who are pauperised in spirit as well as pocket can contemplate without feelings of horror the possibility of such an end. How acute, therefore, must have been the mental misery of this unhappy gentleman, whose misfortunes appear to have been in no way due to any misconduct of his own Mr. Weightman bore testimony to his excellent scholarship, his strictly temperate habits, and his general propriety of conduct. Connected with two learned and liberal professions he might have been sure of help if he had but made his necessities known. But he shrank from asking alms. He was ashamed to beg when his pen and his tongue failed to find him means of living.

The disease from which he died makes it only too probable that, lodging no one knows where and existing no one knows how, his health was undermined by exposure and privation when he went back to his old lodgings in a bye street, to be supported for a few days by the volunteered kindness of his social inferiors. When they saw he wanted more care and skill than they could give, he was carried in a cab to an asylum which he would never have sought, though he must have foreseen and dreaded the approach of the day when he would have no other roof to cover him. But the step which might have saved his life was taken too late. *In brief, Mr. Haddy died of want*, and this when the help he so sorely needed was being pressed upon him. After his death a letter from a lady in Devonshire was found at the Temple gardener's lodge, in which the writer urged him to take private lodgings, and promised to send him assistance. No one can be blamed for the miscarriage of this missive, nor is it any reproach to his professional brethren that they failed to relieve miseries of which they knew nothing. Still it is to be regretted that a man who had suffered so much went out of the world without knowing that there were some ready to pity and to befriend him. The assurance might have prolonged though it probably could not have saved his life. And it would certainly in some measure have mitigated the misery of living and dying thus " ALONE IN LONDON."—*Evening Standard,* Nov. 27, 1872.

[In consequence of this sad case, a " Barristers' Benevolent Society" has recently been formed. Mr. Edmund Macrory, Barrister-at-law, of No. 7, Fig Tree Court, Temple, to whose efforts its formation is due, is Hon. Sec. The Attorney-General (Sir John Coleridge) and ex-Attorney-General Sir John Karslake have come forward nobly in this good cause.—*Note by Editor.*]

§ 2. THE MERCANTILE COMMUNITY.

"Have you read the Second Report of the Judicature Commission?" enquired a Liverpool broker of a Manchester merchant, whom he met on 'Change.

"I have not," replied he of Manchester. "I agree entirely with Mr. Norwood, the excellent Member for Hull, who, in addressing the Associated Chambers of Commerce at Southampton, in September last, used these forcible words — (I quote from memory, but the words impressed themselves upon my mind)—'It is hopeless to expect any aid from the Judicature Commission, in the constitution of which commercial interests have been ignored.'* I didn't think it worth while to waste time in reading the Report."

"We had, however," said the Liverpool broker, "one great ally on the Judicature Commission— Mr. Ayrton, the first Commissioner of Works."

"And so we have come to this, that the commercial interests of the Empire depend upon Mr. Ayrton for protection!" said the Manchester merchant, laughing: "If we are to judge by his progress with the New Law Courts, it is like placing the world on the back of a tortoise."

"Come, come," said he of Liverpool, "Spare our solitary champion! I made a note of his

* *Morning Post*, Sept. 25th, 1872; Report of Meeting of Sept. 24th.

opinion. Ah! here it is. 'In signing the Report, I desire to record my opinion, that no adequate provision is recommended for the large and increasing number of commercial cases, which either require immediate and summary decision, or which are of such a nature that it is found inconvenient to try them in the ordinary Courts, and by their ordinary procedure.' . . . 'This subject,' he adds, 'having been investigated by a Select Committee of the House of Commons' —(of which, by the way, Mr. Ayrton was himself the Chairman)—' they have made a Report, recommending the establishment of Tribunals of Commerce in connection with the County Courts.'"

" A fact, which the other Commissioners had forgotten, I suppose," said the Manchester merchant.

" Perhaps their Commission only extended to existing Courts," said the Liverpool broker. " By the bye, I noticed, that, at the Annual Meeting of the Associated Chambers of Commerce, of which you spoke just now, Mr. Whitwell, the active Member for Kendal, and Mr. Norwood, were invited to introduce a Bill, next Session, for the establishment of Chambers of Commerce. A Bill with a similar object was before the House last Session. The Bill, I presume, will be founded on the Report of the Select Committee, which recommended the establishment of Tribunals of Commerce on the Hamburg principle, in populous centres—the President to be a member of the legal profession, and the other members to be two unpaid mercantile assessors. A not dissimilar arrangement exists in Admiralty cases, where the County Court Judge is assisted by nautical assessors. The president should be, if practicable, the County Court Judge, and the mercantile assessors would rank with Justices of the Peace. The procedure would necessarily be of the simplest character. Cheapness and expedition are the results anticipated from the establishment of these tribunals. As they would be invested with *coercive* and *exclusive* jurisdiction in all Commercial cases, it is evident that their establishment would effect a complete revolution in the Legal profession, and deliver the merchants of Great Britain out of the hands of those Philistines, the Lawyers. We might then indulge in litigation, without involving ourselves in endless delays and extravagant charges. —I see that the new Lord Mayor of London, Sir Sydney Waterlow, has taken action in the Common Council of the City, with a view to the establishment of a Tribunal of Commerce in the City—in 'the very centre of the World of Commerce,'—as my Lord Granville styled the City at the Lord Mayor's Show—Banquet, I mean. The Lord Chief Baron, too, in congratulating the new Lord Mayor, said that he would ' entitle himself to the gratitude of his fellow-citizens, if he succeeded in establishing this Tribunal.' "

" I fancy," exclaimed the Manchester merchant,

"that the Attorneys and Barristers, who listened to these remarks, must have wished the Lord Chief Baron at the back of the North Pole."

"No doubt," said the Liverpool broker. "And still more, when he added, that 'the Tribunal would be a great benefit and blessing to the country.' After this, Lawyers may as well leave off sneering at the idea of 'Merchant Judges.'"

"But did the great lights of the Law, who were selected by Her Majesty for the purpose of investigating the subject of reconstructing our Legal system, agree in their Report?" said he of Manchester, earnestly.

The Liverpool broker laughed. "Agree! I should rather think not. You may well despair of Law Reforms from the members of the Legal Profession! The Attorney-General, Lord Selborne's chief coadjutor in the House of Commons, is 'unable to concur' in the Report. The ex-Attorney General's views are diametrically opposed to it. Mr. Justice Blackburn's 'doubts as to the expediency of what is recommended are too great to permit' him 'to join in the Report.' Sir William Erle 'is not prepared to recommend' some of the most important changes proposed in it. Lord Penzance thinks that the changes proposed in the Report are 'far more wide and sweeping than is necessary or expedient.' 'So general a dislocation of the existing system' he can't 'recommend.'*

* See, as to these Opinions, the Report itself, pp. 23 to 27.

How can the Public be expected to view with confidence a Report, condemned by these distinguished ornaments of the Legal Profession ? The public must decide what is best for their own interests. My opinion is, that there should be free trade in law : and that's the opinion of my friend, Mr. J. J. Aston, the Sheriff's Assessor. Abolish *both* Branches of the Legal Profession."

" By all means," said the Manchester merchant; " and the establishment of Tribunals of Commerce will no doubt be a long step in that direction. Good day to you."

" Good day."

§ 3. CERTAIN ATTORNEYS AND SOLICITORS.

"WELL, Smith, long-looked-for come at last. Have you seen it?"

"Seen what?" enquired Smith.

"Why, the Second Report of the Judicature Commission, of course. A queer looking State paper it is, with blanks left for the signatures of six of the best-known Commissioners. Of the remaining eighteen, seven only sign it without mental reservation; but as two of the seven are the late and the present Lord Chancellors, there's some chance of its recommendations being carried into effect."

"Have 'our trusty and well-beloved' William Gandy Bateson and Francis Dobson Lowndes, Esquires, signed it?"

"Yes. The excellent representatives of *our* branch of the Profession have signed it. They qualify their assent, no doubt: but while all the other Commissioners, who qualify their assent, think that the report goes too far, Messieurs Bateson and Lowndes think that it doesn't go ·far enough." *

"The spirit of the age," observed Mr. Smith, " demands cheap law administered at every Englishman's door."

* Second Report of the Judicature Commission, pp. 22, 25.

"Or within a convenient distance from it by rail," added Mr. Jones.

"Yes. Cheap law administered at every Englishman's door, or within a convenient distance from it by rail,"—

"And solely by Attorneys," added Jones.

"Cheap law administered at every Englishman's door, or within a convenient distance from it by rail, and solely by Attorneys," recapitulated Mr. Smith. "And is this what the Report gives us?"

"Well, not exactly; but it is a long step, my friend, in that direction. Imprimis. There are to be County Courts at 'convenient centres,' and at 'certain other towns,'*—(forgive the Commissioners' English!)—easily accessible by rail.† 'The jurisdiction' of the County Courts is to be, *primâ facie*, 'unlimited by the amount claimed,'‡ and to 'be extended to all actions of tort.'§ The Commissioners gleefully announce that, 'these changes will necessarily cause a considerable diminution of Civil business at the Assizes.'|| And they chuckle over the prospect that 'a substantial portion of the Common Jury causes, now tried at Nisi Prius in the Metropolis, will be absorbed by the County Courts.'"¶

"Cheerful, isn't it, for the Barristers?" cried Smith.

---

* Second Report of the Judicature Commissioners, p. 17.
† Ibid. p. 18.　　‡ Ibid. p. 14.　　§ Ibid. p. 15.
|| Ibid. p. 21.　　¶ Ibid. p. 19.

"Just so," said Jones. "But don't you see that what the Barristers lose, the Attorneys gain? The Barristers have no 'right of exclusive or pre-audience' in the County Courts. In the Superior Courts at Westminster, London, and Assize, they have an exclusive right. Every case taken from the Superior Courts and added to the growing list of the County Courts, is another triumph for the Attorneys—another nail knocked in the coffin of the Bar. Attorneys are virtually the sole advocates in the County Courts. So says one of us."*

"But it isn't enough," said Smith, "that we should be Advocates, as well as Attorneys in the County Courts. We want to be County Court Judges.—What do the Commissioners say to that?"

"A good deal," replied Jones. "Registrars are to be empowered, with consent, to 'hear any matter within the jurisdiction of the Court;' and, without consent, to 'hear cases not exceeding £5,'†—that is, as Mr. Justice Quain believes,‡ '80 per cent of the whole.' Being thus endowed, as the Commissioners say, with 'judicial functions,'§ the Registrars will, by an easy transition, receive 'promotion from the office of Registrar to the office of Judge.'"‖

"Well done, ye trusty and well-beloved, *par nobile fratrum*, Messieurs Bateson and Lowndes !" exclaimed Smith, unable to restrain his enthusiasm. "The office of Registrar of the County Courts is

* Mr. Saunders, Attorney-at-law.   † Report, pp. 17, 18.
‡ Ibid. p. 23.   § Ibid. p. 18.   ‖ Ibid. p. 19.

by Act of Parliament 'given exclusively to Attorneys.'"

"The Commissioners talk about 'Barristers' becoming Registrars :* but no Chancellor would think of selecting a Barrister to be a Registrar, except as a set off against the appointment of an Attorney to be a County Court Judge."

"Any more good news?" enquired Smith.

"The County Courts are also to absorb the business of all the other local Courts, which are forthwith to be abolished.† Mr. George Moffat,‡ who signs the Report, makes wry faces over the abolition of the Lord Mayor's Court, the Court of Passage at Liverpool, and the Salford Hundred Court of Record, which, he says, 'are self-supporting, and command a preference with suitors over the County Courts existing within each of their respective localities,' but what of that? As Mr. Stansfield says of the English Church, so the Commissioners say of these Courts, 'no one would now propose to establish them.'§ So it has been decided that they 'must cease to exist as establishments.' That's the correct phrase, I think."

"What a loss that will be to the Bar, and what a gain to the Attorneys!" exclaimed Smith: "In the County Courts, as you observed just now, the attorneys are 'virtually the sole advocates.' In these doomed local Courts the Bar have an ex-

* Report, p. 18.   † Ibid. pp. 18, 19.   ‡ Ibid. p. 25.
§ Ibid. pp. 18, 19.

clusive right of audience. When the County Courts become the only Inferior Courts, 'the so-called lower walks of the profession,' as Mr. Jevons satirically calls them, will be 'virtually the sole Advocates' in every inferior Court throughout the land."

"The Bar must content themselves with airing their social superiority in the Superior Courts," said Jones, laughingly: "and even the Superior Courts will afford them but slender opportunities for the exercise of that privilege, for you will recollect that there will be a 'considerable diminution of Civil business at the Assizes,' and 'a substantial portion of the Common Jury causes, now tried at Nisi Prius in the Metropolis,' will, also, be no longer available. 'Complaints have been made,' it appears, with reference to the 'service of process by the bailiffs of the County Courts;' and so the Commissioners recommend that 'the parties should be at liberty to serve their own process.'* By 'parties,' of course is meant, their Attorneys. This will enable us to swell our costs. Employment is also to be given to a staff of Attorneys in every County Court district, under the name of 'Registrars,' 'Deputies,' or 'Agents.' They are to charge 'fees for issuing summonses, subpœnas, &c.'† Isn't it kind and thoughtful ?"

"Very," replied Mr. Smith. "But what about the rearrangement of Circuits ?"

* Report, p. 16.   † Ibid. p. 19.

"O, Circuits are to be practically abolished," replied Mr. Jones.

"And what is to be substituted for them?" enquired Smith.

"Roving commissions are to be issued to the Judges. 'Two or more' of their Lordships must alight four times a year at St. George's Hall, and four times a year at Strangeways, and settle in both places for indefinite periods.* This will help to realize the expectations of Mr. Saunders. It will 'localize all litigation, except appeals, and will oblige the Bar to break up that central organization, which has been the mainstay of their power and influence, and settle down in batches in the country towns.' Mr. Justice Blackburn declined to sign the Report because he saw clearly that its recommendation would scatter to the four winds 'the great central Bar of England.'†

"Bye, bye, Smith."

"Ta, ta, Jones."

* Report, p. 21. † Ibid. p. 26.

THE LEGAL PROFESSION.

§ 1. THE WRONGS OF ATTORNEYS.

"The existing state of the Legal Profession is unsatisfactory, and needs reform," observed Mr. Robinson Rich, drawing a deep sigh.

A slight shudder passed over the frame of Cornelius Brown. Now Cornelius Brown was the confidential clerk of Rich and Readymoney, Attorneys and Solicitors, of Lincoln's-Inn-Fields, W.C. He shuddered to think of the revered head of that great firm arraigning so unceremoniously the sacred Profession, which it adorned. Cornelius Brown was a disciple of Sir George Jessel, and, like that eminent Conservative, scouted the idea of reforming the Legal Profession. The British Constitution needed "sweeping and severe" reforms —but reform the Legal Profession! never!—So Cornelius Brown sat staring vacantly at the head of the firm, who had just uttered such " flat blasphemy" against the golden image, which Sir George Jessel worships, and could only gasp, in fragmentary astonishment, " Legal Profession . . . unsatisfactory . . . needs reform !"

"Why, yes," said Mr. Rich, unheeding the anguish of poor Brown; "and here is a set of papers on the wrongs of Attorneys, which prove to demonstration the truth of what I say. Mr.

Saunders, in his able paper on 'The Amalgamation'"—(at that fatal word Brown interjected a faint shriek)—"'The Amalgamation,' repeated Mr. Rich, 'of the two Branches of the Legal Profession, considered with a special reference to contemplated Law Reforms,'* tell us, that attorneys are a 'long proscribed caste,' and 'always experience a rankling sense of injustice.' What,' says Mr. Saunders, 'are the Attorney's prospects ? By a long series of encroachments, but by no legislative enactments, the attorney has been deprived of his ancient privilege of pleading in Court, and of being a member of the great Inns . . he has before him, as a reward of the most diligent study and of the highest legal attainments, no prize or distinction whatever; all these being appropriated by the other branch of the Profession.' Mr. Jevons, in his interesting pamphlet, on 'The Relation between the two branches of the Legal Profession,'† says, that 'if the matter is looked at from the side of the interest of the public'—("The public," muttered Brown, contemptuously, "what does Sir George Jessel care, I wonder, about *them !*")—"the conditions under which the Bar and the Attorneys practise need only to be stated to be condemned.' 'The relations of Barristers and the so-called lower walks of the profession

---

* London, Butterworths, 7, Fleet Street, 1870. (See pp. 5, 30, 31.)

† Liverpool: T. Brakell, 7, Cook Street. 1868. (See pp. 7 and 8.)

are not left,' he adds, ' to any natural adjustment, but the members of each branch of the Profession are forced into artificial grooves.' Then there is ' A Sketch of the Early History of Legal Practitioners, and of the Inns of Court and Chancery,'* ' in which,' (I quote Mr. Saunders,†) ' it is clearly shewn, that during the earlier centuries of our judicial system, before its simpler forms of procedure became encumbered with the refinements and subtleties of later times, the Attorneys had the right of pleading before all the Courts both of Westminster and Assize.' Mr. Marshall, the author of the paper in question,* assures us that 'the only practitioners known to the Courts in the 12th century were the Attorneys'—think of that, Mr. Brown. You must brush up your antiquarian lore. Mr. Marshall 'speaks,' also, 'with tolerable confidence on one or two' other 'points.' ' It is not to be doubted,' he says, with some acerbity, ' that all the existing Inns of Court and Chancery were founded for the common benefit of the Legal Profession, for during the whole range of time which extends from the reign of Henry III.'—Mr. Brown, your attention, if you please—' from the reign of Henry III. to the reign of Henry VI. and which covers the establishment of these societies, there was no line of demarcation between the

* Leeds: Charles Goodall, 16, Woodhouse Lane. 1869. (See pp. 5 and 23.)

† P. 10.

several practitioners of the law. The Attorneys, Pleaders, and Apprentices of Edward III.'s time were the common class for whose benefit the legal colleges of the 14th century were set up, and for whose benefit alone any institution of a like nature could have been designed. The Counsel, Men of the law, and Attorneys of Henry VI.'s time—each of whom discharged duties, connected then but now separated—constituted that numerous membership, of which Fortescue speaks with so much pride. It was by the joint contributions of these persons—the students, practisers, and professors of the laws of England—that the houses were supported, the rents paid, and that the societies were enabled to continue their existence for so many ages, and to establish a claim—founded on the fact of long-continued existence—upon the liberality of the Earl of Lincoln, Henry VIII. and James I. Whatever else is doubtful, this is clear; so that the absolute exclusion of seven-eighths of the Profession at the present day, from these Inns, by whatever else recommended, cannot be defended on the plea of the true, ancient, and laudable government of the societies in question.' These are the arguments of eminent Attorneys, who are also able pamphleteers. The paper of Mr. Saunders was read before 'the Metropolitan and Provincial Law Association' at York, in 1869. The paper of Mr. Jevons was read before the Conference of Provincial Law Societies held at Leeds,

in 1868. And Mr. Saunders,* characterizes the
'Sketch' of Mr. Marshall as 'a paper of great research.'
Mr. Marshall's historical researches agree
with those of Mr. John Fraser Macqueen. In a
'lecture'† delivered by him twenty-two years ago,
before the Benchers of Lincoln's Inn, that eminent
Queen's Counsel unhesitatingly affirms that 'in
the time of Edward I. the duty of Barrister, or
advocate, was performed by the Attorney, who
united functions, subsequently severed, but which
peradventure may again, in the present age, be
consolidated.'"

Mr. Robinson Rich, having thus proved his thesis, paused for a reply. But none came.

Mr. Rich looked triumphantly at his vanquished foe. Cornelius Brown was asleep.

* P. 10.
† "A Lecture on the Early History and Academic Discipline of the Inns of Court and Chancery." London: Sweet. 1851.

§ 2. THE HONOUR AND DIGNITY OF THE BAR.

The Honorable Percival Pennyless had known Stephen Starvington at the University :—but Stephen was several years his senior, and when the Hon. P. P. was called to the Bar, his friend was a Barrister of three years standing. Stephen Starvington was very glad to sublet his Chambers in the Temple to his former acquaintance. He wished to retain the Chambers, which were conveniently situated for business, and yet he found it difficult, when Lady-day and Michaelmas came round, to find money to pay the rent.

A thrill of satisfaction shot through the Hon. Percival Pennyless's frame, when he recalled the illustrious names, that had adorned his branch of the Legal Profession ; and when he reflected on the dignity and splendour of the offices, to which its members alone were eligible. As the son of the Earl of Pauperborough, he felt, on being admitted into the Society of the Utter Temple, that he was " the right man in the right place," for had not James I., in the very first year of his reign, declared that " none be from henceforth admitted to the Society of any Inn of Court, who is not a gentleman by descent?"* No " Common Attorney " could there presume to accost him : for Charles II. had

* Order of 9 Jan. 1 Jac. I. Dugdale's Origines, pp. 316, 317.

decreed, that the " Common Attorney " was an
" immaterial person of an inferior nature,"* and
unfit to associate, therefore, with the patrician caste
of Barrister-at-law.

A few days after Percival's call-party, Stephen
and Percival were seated together in Stephen's
Chambers, when Percival, as is the wont of newly-
fledged Barristers, anxious to profit by the experience of his senior in the profession, asked Stephen
to rehearse his previous progress at the Bar.

" Progress!" repeated Stephen Starvington, with
intense bitterness. " My progress has been like
that of a stone—to the bottom; and, as there's
no Attorney to pick me up, I'm likely enough to
remain there for the rest of my natural existence.
Instead of helping a fellow, they'll throw more and
more of their cold water over him.—I've looked to
the public for sympathy and support : but I find
myself isolated—cut off from all contact with the
public by a serried array of 11,000 attorneys and
solicitors. I look to these gentlemen for sympathy
and support. Etiquette whispers severely in my
ear, ' Sir, you are actuated by an unworthy motive,'
—that's the cant phrase,—' remember the honour
and dignity of your Profession !' And so I,
Stephen Starvington, upon whose education at
public Schools and at the University thousands have
been spent, for whom my dear mother and sisters,

* Order of 16 Car. II. : Dugdale's Origines, p. 322.

with all the wealth of maternal and sisterly affection, have made sacrifices that the world will never know, resign myself to my fate, bestowing 'curses, not loud, but deep,' upon that cruel law which says to me, 'You must endure want, and spend your best days in idleness, for the honour and dignity of your Profession!' At the end of my first year I began to realize what it was to be destitute of Attorney 'connection.' Seated in my lonely Chambers, an indescribable feeling of disgust, heart-sickness, and isolation stole over me. I was shut out from the Superior Courts for want of a 'connection.' One day, when complaining of my fate to a friend of mine, a Barrister, he asked, 'Why don't you localize? There are the County Courts, for instance. You can earn a livelihood by practising in them.' And so I went down into the provinces, and became a 'Local.' I had been there six months without getting anything to do, when a shopkeeper, with whom I was in the habit of dealing, told me that he wanted to recover a debt from a customer, and asked me to appear for him in the County Court. The case was called on. I rose and said, as impressively as I could, 'I, Sir, appear for the plaintiff,' looking wistfully, when I had said it, for Counsel on the other side to rise and say, 'And I, Sir, appear for the defendant.' But no, not a single vestige of horse-hair, that 'crown of glory' to the Bar, was to be seen. There were 'bibs,' no doubt, — rendered imperative by the sumptuary laws of Edmund Beales, M.A.—to be seen, a goodly array: and I found myself confronted by one of these. All my professional instincts were alarmed. 'Is it not laid down in the books,' I asked myself, 'that Barristers-at-law have the exclusive right of addressing the Court—of 'audience,' as it is technically termed? What possible right can a 'common Attorney'—'an immaterial person of an inferior nature' (as Charles II. calls him,) possess of exercising the patrician calling of Advocate? of trenching upon *my* prerogative?' And so I broadly hinted that the gentleman with the 'bib' was arrogating to himself privileges, which belonged to another and 'a higher' branch of the Profession The Attorney for the defendant immediately produced chapter and verse for his appearance in the capacity of Advocate. 'I beg to call the attention,' he said, in honeyed accents and with a simper like that of Lord Westbury, 'of my learned friend on the other side'— ('learned friend,' indeed! this is, I thought, 'adding insult to injury')—'to an act passed in the year of our Lord, 1852,' intituled, 'An Act further to arrange and facilitate proceedings in the County Courts,'—15 and 16 of the Queen, cap. 54. If he will turn to the tenth section he will find that the Legislature of his country, in its wisdom, has deprived him of any right of exclusive, or (*sic*) 'pre-audience in this Court.' And, with a triumphant bang, he closed the statute-book. I was quite crest-fallen. I had no 'connection' among Attorneys, and I was, therefore, virtually excluded from practice in the Superior Courts. A 'connection' among the Attorneys was unnecessary in the County Courts. But there the Attorneys met me as rivals, on a footing of *equality*, and so, after holding a brief or two for a tradesman, I found myself virtually 'squeezed out' by the very men, whose patronage was absolutely essential to my success in the Superior Courts, and whom it was my interest not to offend by rivalry. Recollect that the Superior Courts now entirely transfer to or send for trial at the County Courts a large number of actions both of contract and of tort ; so that, while the business of the County Courts is increasing, the business of the Superior Courts is diminishing. From returns laid before the House of Commons, it appears that there were sent down from the Superior Courts in 1870, for trial in the County Courts, 597 cases. In the same year there were 9000 fewer writs issued out of the Superior Courts, than in 1869. In 1868 there were 44,500 fewer writs issued out of the Superior Courts than in 1867. These figures will give you some idea of the steady encroachment of the Attorneys upon the Bar.

" Driven from the County Courts, I betook myself to Quarter Sessions. And even here I found that I had no right of 'exclusive or pre-audience,'

except so far as the Bench chose to give it to me.*
I received the usual allowance of 'soup,' that is to
say, of briefs for the prosecution, doled out to poor
fellows, whose poverty obliges them to haunt
'soup sessions.' My earnings rarely, if ever, exceeded three guineas; and on this amount of ' skilly'
it can hardly be expected that the legal ' casual'
can keep body and soul together till the Recorder
fixes his next ' Soup Sessions.' Soup Sessions are
generally held in cities and boroughs. I determined to try my fortune at the Quarter Sessions
for the County. Here I saw ' the other side of the
picture.' The beerhouse appeals were then pretty
numerous; and I saw the clerk to the clerk of the
Magistrates of a neighbouring district deliver twenty
briefs to a local Barrister, whose practice amounted to
' nil' elsewhere. As I was not in the ' good graces'
of any of the Magistrates' clerks or of the clerks to
Magistrates' clerks, my earnings at the County Sessions figured in my fee-book as ' nil.'

" But, during my short career as a '.Local,' I
learnt something of the ' ways and means' by which
' Locals' rise into practice at Assizes. London men
have little chance at Assizes now. The clerks of
Attorneys have much influence in the distribution
of their masters' patronage. What more natural,
therefore, than that the less fastidious members of

* See Evans, *ex parte*, 9 Q. B. 279: S. C. nom. Reg. *v.*
Denbighshire Justices : 2 New Sess. Cas. 422 : 10 Jur. 542 :
15 L. J. Q. B. 335.

the local Bar should notice these clerks—should enquire earnestly after the state of their healths, and the healths of their families—should nod and wink at them in Court, and be 'hail, fellow! well met!' with them at the corner of every street—should present them with Albert chains, and even grace their marriage-breakfasts with a speech?

'Naturam expellas furcâ, tamen usque recurrit.'

You can't stop the course of nature with a pitchfork. I once ventured to express myself to a brother barrister, a 'Local,' pretty strongly in condemnation of this undue familiarity with Attorneys' clerks. 'Well, my dear fellow,' he replied, 'our bread and butter depends upon it; and what are we to do?' What, indeed! A gentleman 'by descent' and education—who has taken distinguished honours, perhaps, at the University—obliged to tear up by the very roots all vestige of gentlemanly feeling, *and toady Attorneys' clerks for a living!* I would appeal, my dear Pennyless, to every candid mind," exclaimed Starvington, vehemently, " whether the system is not indefensible, which exposes the Local Barrister to such temptations—which places him in so false a position ? Alas for 'the honour and dignity' of the Profession!

" About six months ago, I returned to the Metropolis, fastidious as ever, and determined to vindicate 'the honour and dignity' of the Profession.

A friend of mine had been unfortunate in business, and was desirous that I should hold a brief on his behalf before the Chief Judge in Bankruptcy. The family-solicitor was so good-natured as to humour his client; and behold the vindicator of 'the honour and dignity of his Profession,' in full canonicals, before the Honourable Sir James Bacon, Vice-Chancellor. My breast heaved with emotion, when I reflected upon the august tribunal that I was to have the privilege of addressing. The reward of all my sacrifices was at hand. Sir Roundell Palmer or Sir Richard Baggallay was sure to be opposed to me. Imagine, if you can, my disgust, when I found that a 'Common Attorney'—'an immaterial person of an inferior nature' —(as Charles II. calls him)—was, once more, my opponent. My indignation knew no bounds. I was about to expostulate, when the Attorney who had instructed me, plucked me by the sleeve. 'Calm yourself, my dear Sir,' he whispered in my ear. 'Your opponent is, no doubt, an Attorney;' but he has 'a statutory right of audience:' and you have only a customary right. Mr. Yates Lee, in his recent work on 'Bankruptcy,' page 351, judiciously observes :—' Counsel *may* be employed, in a proper case;' and he refers to a decision of Mr. Serjeant Wheeler, in the Liverpool County Court, (!) in support of that kind indulgence. I have availed myself of the option. But, Sir, the 'Legislature of your country, in its wisdom,'—

'The Legislature of my country is bent on ruining me,' exclaimed I, between my teeth, my mind running upon the speech of my opponent in the County Court—'in its wisdom,' repeated the Attorney, with provoking coolness, 'has passed three enactments, intituled, respectively, The Bankrupt Law Consolidation Act, 1849, (12 & 13 of the Queen, cap. 106),—Sec. 247, the Bankruptcy Act, 1861,—(24 & ·25 of the Queen, cap. 134)—Sec. 212, and the Bankruptcy Act, 1869,— (32 & 33 of the Queen, cap. 71)—Sec. 70,—all of which expressly confer upon Attorneys and Solicitors a statutory right of audience in this Court. 'Every Attorney and Solicitor,' says the chef-d'œuvre of Sir Robert Collier, 'of the Superior Courts, may *be heard*, without being required to employ Counsel. —And let me tell you, my friend,'—(that odious and familiar word again !)—' that you'd better make the most of your present chance. The Solicitors are rapidly acquiring a monopoly, as Advocates, in Bankruptcy cases.' "

The Honourable Percival Pennyless's views of the grandeur of the Bar had, during the history of Stephen Starvington's "progress," been undergoing material modifications.

§ 3. THE RIGHT OF AUDIENCE IN THE SUPERIOR COURTS.

"After all," thought Mr. Robinson Rich, "Brown is not an Attorney. He is only an Attorney's Clerk. 'Attorneys,' says the *Fortnightly Review*,* 'are allowed to grow rich'—kind, isn't it, very? I'm a successful man. Rich and Readymoney is a prosperous concern. We can afford to pay Brown £800 a year: a Queen's Counsel might find it stiff work to pay him £200. And so Brown can't see the need of Reform! Exclusion from West End Clubs and from fashionable society has no terrors for him. The 'Caste' iron hasn't entered into his soul." And the wealthy lawyer laughed bitterly.

The entrance of a third party roused the sleeping Brown, who retired in some confusion, on perceiving that the senior partner had finished his quotations, and that the heads of the great firm of Rich and Readymoney had both "caught him napping." The junior partner—for the new-comer was he—looked wistfully at the retreating figure of Brown.

"Mesmerism, or electro-biology?" enquired Mr. Readymoney, rather abruptly. "Will you show me the passes?"

"Willingly," replied Mr. Rich. "You have only to waive a few 'elegant extracts' from these pamphlets before the mental vision of Mr. Brown, and—hey, presto!—the thing is done."

* Cited by Mr. Saunders, p. 31.

Mr. Readymoney glanced at the titles of the pamphlets. "What an interesting subject," he observed. "Just the one on which I want reliable information. The wrongs, in short, of Attorneys."

"That fellow Brown thinks only of moneymaking, and there are many Attorneys and Solicitors like him," said Mr. Rich, his thoughts reverting to the confidential clerk and his indifference to all Reform in the Legal Profession. " Moneymaking is not to be despised : but there are many things that money can't purchase, and that honourable ' Men of the Law' might aspire to, but from which the members of our branch of the Profession are rigidly shut out. And yet, if there be any virtue in historical precedent, our constitutional right to these things is clear."

" Let's take one point at a time," said Mr. Readymoney.

" First, then," said Mr. Rich, " there's the right of audience in the Superior Courts;—we've a constitutional right to that."

" How do you prove it?" enquired the junior partner.

" By a reference to historical precedent," replied the senior. " Mr. Marshall is my sheet-anchor. Mr. Marshall draws a line right across the latter end of the 13th century. ' Forms and precedents,' and ' men who made these forms their study,' ' prior to' that ' time' ' did not exist.' There were ' practitioners,' no doubt,—' Attorneys,— that is, agents'—but even they were 'not recognized members of the legal system.' I gather, in fact, from Mr. Marshall that for 200 years after the Norman Conquest there was a kind of 'legal chaos,' 'no legal system,' in fact. 'The litigant party discharged the various duties of Attorney, Pleader, and Counsel,' in the 11th and earlier part of the 12th century, and, although Attorneys appeared upon the scene 'in the latter part of the 12th century,' they were merely ' agents,' not lawyers. Attorneys became 'public officers' in 1292. It is true that ' Serjeants' are mentioned seventeen years before in the Statute Westminster I, as legal practitioners—but what of that? Mr. Macqueen, Q.C., makes short work of the Serjeants—'a handful of monopolists,' so contemptible a lot, that Edward I. didn't think it worth while to mention them in his famous precept, ' De Attornatis et Apprenticiis.' "

" Bravo ! Mr. Macqueen," ejaculated Mr. Readymoney.

" Mr. Macqueen's translation of the Order in Parliament of the 20 Edward I. is so neat, and so *free*, withal, that I can't refrain from quoting it :— ' Edward I, with the Sanction of Parliament, issued a commission, which was addressed to the Chief Justice of the Court of Common Pleas, John de Metingham, authorizing him, in conjunction with his colleagues, to look out for, provide, and appoint, from every county, a certain number of *Attorneys*, to practise in the Courts, and a certain number of *pupils.*' "

".Mere schoolboys, of course," observed Mr. Readymoney.

" Of course," said Mr. Rich—" ' a certain number of *pupils* to study the common law, and secure its continuance. The Commission suggested that 140 *Attorneys* might suffice for the purpose in view. But power was granted to increase and diminish the number, as the Justices in their wisdom should see fit ; and it was declared that the persons to be chosen, and those only, should attend the Courts, and conduct the business of the King's subjects therein.' * ' Ordinent certum numerum de attornatis et apprenticiis,' is the version of the Order in Parliament given by Sir William Dugdale, and cited by Mr. Marshall in a foot-note.† This precept establishes, to Mr. Marshall's satisfaction, the right of audience of attorneys before Justices in Itinere, that is to say, before Judges on circuit. The 140 Attorneys selected by the Court of Common Pleas went circuit, appeared in Court, and argued cases, while the ' pupils' looked respectfully, and, no doubt, admiringly, on."

" Was there any Bar-Mess, I wonder, in those days ?" mused Mr. Readymoney.

---

* Inns of Court and Chancery, p. 7. See Rot. Parl. Vol. 1. 20 Ed. I. p. 84 (No. 22).

† Page 6, Referring to Dugdale's Orig. C. 55.

"There was no Bar to make a Mess," said Mr. Rich, flippantly. "If the Order in Parliament of 20 Edward I. is the Magna Charta of the Attorneys, the Statute of Carlisle—15 Edward II. A.D. 1322—is his Declaration of Rights.—' This ordinance is chiefly noteworthy,' says Mr. Marshall, ' for the evidence it furnishes of the right of attorneys to appear before the Judges at Westminster. The possible inference that they appeared for the parties in the modern sense of the term ' appear ' is negatived by what we know of the practice of the time as well as by the probabilities of the case.'*
' Read by the light of the procedure of the time,' he repeats,† ' the Statute of Carlisle furnishes evidence that in the early part of the 14th Century Attorneys were permitted to plead before the Courts at Westminster.' Carlisle, Mr. Readymoney, has produced three great things."

"Which be they ?" enquired the junior partner, irreverently.

"This Statute, Sir Wilfrid Lawson, and ' our old friend, the Permissive Bill.' "

"But what does the Statute say?" enquired the junior partner, sceptically.

" It says," replied Mr. Rich, " I quote Mr. Marshall's translation‡—the Statute, you know, is in Latin—that ' the Barons of the Exchequer and the Justices' are ' not to admit Attorneys—' "

* " Legal Practitioners, page 8.
† Page 9. ‡ Page 8.

" 'Not to admit!'" ejaculated Mr. Readymoney.

"Yes. Are 'not to admit attorneys, except in pleas in banc, and in places where they (*i.e.* the Barons and Justices, I suppose) might be assigned.' 'The object,' adds Mr. Marshall, 'of this Statute was to authorize the Judges of the Exchequer and King's Bench to exercise similar powers, in specified cases,' to those conferred 'in the preceding reign, on the Court of Common Pleas.' Mr. Marshall argues that if the attorney was 'allowed to appear' he must necessarily have been 'allowed to speak.' In a foot-note* he cites three instances, out of 'numerous' ones that, he says, are to be found in the Year-books, of Attorneys exercising 'the right of appearing and arguing before the Justices' on circuit. The Master of the Rolls has published an edition of the Year-books of 20 and 21 Edw. I., 30 and 31 Edw. I., and 32 and 33 Edw. I., with a translation and prefaces by Mr. Horwood, and these will assist us.

"The first case is taken from the Cornish Iter, 30 Edw. I.† It is a writ of entry, brought by Richard Wysard and Catherine, his wife, v. B. After stating the pleadings, the report proceeds:—'On another day, when the inquisition was about to be taken, *B.'s attorney said* that the tenements were taken into the King's hands, therefore, &c. Berrewik J.—The tenements are taken into the King's hands, saving all persons' rights. And he

* P. 6. † The reference is to p. 160, but this is evidently intended for p. 162.

took the inquisition, which decided for Richard and Catherine. Richard said, We pray judgment. Berrewik, J., Await judgment.'"

"A clear case," said Mr. Readymoney, "of B.'s Attorney arguing as Counsel. What is the next reference?"

"It is taken from the Year Book, 31 Edward I. It is the case of William Standish v. John, clerk of Langeton, and it commences thus :— 'Sheweth unto you William, the son of Jordan, of Standish, *by his attorney*, &c., that John the clerk of Langeton tortuously deforces him of the advowson of the chapel of Wigan.'* The third case is taken from the same series of reports, and is twice referred to by Mr. Marshall.† It is the case of Thomas de Grandcourt, a dispute about the levying of a fine, and Mr. Justice Herle observes, 'We have seen cases where *the attorney could not explain the matter in dispute*, the principal has been made to appear.' This Mr. Marshall terms, 'the client himself interposing and addressing the Court in the presence of the Advocate.'"

"And these are Mr. Marshall's three cases?"

"Yes," replied Mr. Rich, "but I was determined to follow up his investigations and satisfy my own mind on the subject: so I looked into the first

* These two cases are cited as from the "Cornish Iter," 30 Edw. I., but they are cases decided in term-time (Mich. term,) 31 Edw. I. p. 338.
† Pp. 6 and 8.

volume of the regular series of published Year-
books; and searched for precedents. I did not
search in vain. I looked hard for the word,
'Attorney,' and came upon quite a treasure of
a case in the first of Edward III.—a case which
proved clearly that Attorneys *did* speak in the
Superior Courts :—' An Attorney comes to the bar,
and says to the Justices, that a man, whose Attorney
he is, had recovered a certain debt in the time of
the other King'—(Edward II. of course)—'against
a man who comes into Court by the Bishop, and
pleads. And before he (the plaintiff) had execution, the King died. And inasmuch as we (the
plaintiff) could not have execution without a fresh
notice, the Court gave us a Scire Facias to the
Sheriff for the possibility that he (the defendant) might have lay fee—which writ the Sheriff has
returned, nihil habet in balliva sua, ubi eum præmunire potuit. Therefore the Attorney prayed
a writ of execution to the Bishop, because he (the
defendant) was a parson.

" 'Stonor, J. If the Sheriff has returned that
he is a Clerk, you may have it, certainly.

" ' *The Attorney*:—Sir, he came by the Bishop,
and of part we have execution, and we should
have had it of the whole, if the King had not died.

" Ludlow* said that in such a case they could
grant it. Et ita fecit.' "

---

* Mr. Serjeant Manning calls him "Lee, J." But see list of
Counsel, 3 Foss's Judges, p. 374 and p. 456.

" This is, indeed," observed Mr. Readymoney, " a valuable precedent."

" Yes," replied Mr. Rich, " and the reporter evidently considered the case so important, that he reported it twice over: first, under Hilary Term,* and then under Trinity!" †

" And Mr. Marshall does not refer to this case ? "

" No ; but he refers‡ to the Year-book 1 Edward III., in which it will, twice over, be found. He refers to that Year-book, however, for another purpose. Mr. Marshall was then on the track of the word ' Apprentice:' I was on the track of the word, ' Attorney,' when I consulted it."

" Ah! how about the Apprentices? " asked Mr. Readymoney. " I think, from the authorities, which you have cited, that it is pretty clear that the Attorneys had a right of audience in the Superior Courts."

" Mr. Marshall," replied Mr. Rich, " contends for more than that; he contends that, with the exception of those contemptible fellows, the Serjeants,—as the poet says, ' Rari nantes in gurgite vasto'—the Attorneys had an *exclusive* right of audience in all the courts of the kingdom. ' Appearing and pleading ' (by which he means arguing cases) ' in Court,' were, he says, ' the ordinary

* This is a fact. Fol. 5, pl. 33.
† Fol. 17 (Ed. 1596, 14), pl. 10.
‡ Page 9.

business of an Attorney.'* In another place he terms it 'their old monopoly.'† However, it is not necessary to carry our contention so far. All that we want is the right to argue cases in open Court at Westminster, in London, and on Circuit. We don't want to oust the Bar, but we do want to share their honours and emoluments."

"We shall soon squeeze them out," said Mr. Readymoney, smiling, "when we obtain the right of instructing ourselves at Westminster, in London, and on Circuit. The Legislature has enabled us to instruct ourselves in the County Courts and in Bankruptcy, and we are squeezing out the Bar from advocacy in the County Courts and in Bankruptcy. ' It will go hard if' we 'do not better the instruction,'" added Mr. Readymoney, laughing.

" But how about the Apprentices? "

" The subject is rather a painful one," replied Mr. Rich, " like the history of all usurpations. I will spare your feelings as much as I can."

" Yes, cut it short," said Mr. Readymoney.

Mr. Rich looked somewhat shocked at the levity of his junior partner, but continued : " These Apprentices, Mr. Marshall‡ says, ' we first hear of in the 20th year of Edward I.' They are mentioned in the precept of that King, addressed to John de Metingham and the other judges of the Common Pleas. Mr. Macqueen, you will recollect, translates the word, ' pupils.' ' Apprenticius,' says Sir

---

* Page 9.   † Page 14.   ‡ Page 6.

William Dugdale,* 'cometh from apprendre, to learn,' and he cites the great Selden in proof of it. Mr. Marshall is a little misty about these 'Apprenticii,' for he says† that they attended circuit *mainly* as a means of education, and that they were '*rather* learners than practitioners.'‡ Mr. Saunders, who takes his antiquarian lore from Mr. Marshall, thus sums up§ the subject. 'The origin and status of the Barrister or Apprenticius, as he was then called, as a separate order, and his gradual appropriation, although apparently at first of inferior standing, of the sole privilege of pleading before the Courts is involved in considerable *obscurity*; but thus much is clear, that, however established such privilege has become by long custom and etiquette, no warrant for it can be found in our Statute-books.' Mr. Marshall devotes much of his 'research' to the elucidation of this difficult subject. I gather from him (1) that for five years, *i.e.*, from the passing of the famous Statute of Carlisle, in the 15th year of Edward II. till the death of that prince, the Attorneys alone competed with the Serjeants in the Courts of King's Bench and Exchequer as Advocates—the Court of Common Pleas being the exclusive domain of the Serjeants. (2) That for 35 years, *i.e.*, from the date of the Order in Parliament of 20 Edward I., A.D. 1292,

---

* Dugd. Orig. c. 55, citing Selden's notes to Fortescue's 'De Legibus,' c. 8.
† Page 7.   ‡ Page 9.   § Pp. 10, 11.

till the death of Edward II., A.D. 1327, the Attorneys outside the metropolis had a 'monopoly,' not merely of issuing processes and conducting causes through the forms of the Courts, but, practically, of the right of audience; the Serjeants only appearing on circuit on behalf of the Crown. The Apprentices during all this time attended the Courts of the metropolis and went circuit, for the purpose of improving their minds in the capacity of 'learners.' Suddenly we find the Apprentices 'employed in the ordinary business of an Attorney,' that is to say, appearing as Advocates in Court, in the metropolis, and, a fortiori, in the provinces. The usurpation of the Apprentices dates from the first year of Edward III., A.D. 1327, for, in that year, 'en bank le Roy,' as Dugdale says,* an Apprentice asked a question of the Court, about a case that was before it.† This, as Selden points out, is 'the ancientest mention' in the books of an 'Apprentice del la ley' appearing as Counsel.‡ What might have happened, if the Apprentice hadn't asked that question, it is impossible to say; but the Apprentices were not slow to follow up this advantage: and in the reign of Henry VI., they even made an effort to deprive the Serjeants of their exclusive right of audience in the Court of

* Dugd. Orig., c. 55.
† Year-books, 1 Edw. III. Fol. 16, pl. 3. (Fol. 13, pl. 3. Ed. 1596.)
‡ Notes to Fortescue's 'de Laudibus,' c. 8.

Common Pleas, by sending one of their number to ask a question of the Justices of that Court. Sir William Dugdale seems to stand amazed at this piece of impudence, and says that it is 'somewhat observable.'* But to return to Mr. Marshall's ' researches.' The Apprentices, when they usurped the right of audience, usurped, also, the rest of the Attorney's practice; so that ' the functions' of the Attorneys and Apprentices became 'identical.' The Conservative tendencies of the ' country party' induced him still to style the Advocate on circuit and in the local courts, ' Attorney;' but in the metropolis the name of the Advocate varied,—first it was ' Apprentice,' that was during the reign of Edward III. During the reigns of the Princes of the House of Lancaster—Henry IV., Henry V., and Henry VI., and also during the reign of Edward IV., Attorney-Advocates and Apprentice-Advocates were indifferently termed in the metropolis ' Homines legis,' ' Consiliarii,' and ' Homines curiæ legis.'† As Mr. Marshall only professes to give us ' a Sketch of the *Early* History of Legal Practitioners,' he does not carry his ' researches ' beyond the reign of Edward IV. The Paston Letters ' go down to the year 1485,'‡ the date of the death of Richard III.; and as Sir William ' Paston transacted business, with which no

* Dugd. Orig., c. 55. Mr. Rich refers to a case reported in the Year-books, 2 Hen. VI. Fol. 5, 3.

† Marshall, pp. 9—14.   ‡ Page 11.

modern Barrister would be permitted to interfere,'*
Mr. Marshall concludes that 'the separation between' the Attorneys and the Apprentices 'had certainly not taken place in the reign of Edward IV.,'† who died A.D. 1483. As Mr. Marshall stops short in his 'researches' at that year, the appropriation by the Apprentice of the *sole* right of audience in the Superior Courts, 'is' left by him, as Mr. Saunders says,‡ 'in considerable obscurity.'"

"Never mind," said Mr. Readymoney, encouragingly. "It is sufficient for our purpose to be able to shew that there was a time, when the Apprentices did not enjoy that right, and when the Attorneys did enjoy it: and that the Apprentices gradually 'appropriated' it—took, stole and carried away what did'nt belong to them." And Mr. Readymoney left the room, repeating the familiar refrain,

" Him as prigs vot isnt his 'n,
Ven he's cotched, he goes to prison ! "

---

* Page 14.   † Page 9.   ‡ Page 11.

§ 4. AUDI ALTERAM PARTEM.

"Do you know, Pennyless, said Stephen Starvington, "that the Attorneys (or perhaps, I ought to say, an ambitious section of them) are not content with obtaining, by pressure upon the Legislature, a virtual monopoly of advocacy in the Inferior Courts? They are 'improving the occasion;' and insist that they have a constitutional right to audience in the Superior Courts. A 'paper of great research' has been written by Mr. Marshall, Attorney-at-law, which deliberately tries to saw this last plank of the English Bar asunder."

"We shall all swim to the bottom like you, eh, Starvington? if he succeeds," replied Pennyless.

"I've drawn up a reply to it," said Stephen.

"Let us have it, by all means," said Pervival, and he threw himself back into a listening attitude.

A SKETCH OF THE EARLY HISTORY OF LEGAL PRACTITIONERS:

By STEPHEN STARVINGTON, Esq.,

BARRISTER-AT-LAW.

SECTION I.

SERJEANTS-AT-LAW.

"OUR judicial course of proceeding, the general language of our jurisprudence, and its terms of art, are all of Norman extraction.* The most ancient depositary of Norman customs is the Custumier du Pays et Duché de Normandie,† written about the year 1180.‡ In the 64th

* 1 Stephens' Blackstone, 44 (Ed. 1853).
† Stephens' Pleading (Note 9), 411 (Ed. 1866).
‡ Beugnot: Preface to "Assizes of Jerusalem," xxxv. The Assizes of Jerusalem were compiled in the middle of the 13th century, not, as stated by Mr. Serjeant Stephen and Mr. Pearce, A.D. 1099. They contain, however, an account of the feudal system as it was imposed, shortly after the conquest of Jerusalem by Godfrey de Bouillon, on the kingdom which he set up in the East. The feudal system was introduced by Godfrey in a much more stringent form into his new kingdom, than by William the Norman, into England.—N.B. Eighteen chapters of the first portion of the Assizes are devoted to the appointment and duties of Pleader and Counsel.

chapter of the Custumier will be found a description of the Norman Advocate under the title 'Conteur,' the Latin equivalent of which is 'Narrator.' 'Il est appelé Conteur que alcun establit à parler et a Conter pour soi en Court.'* The 65th chapter is devoted to the Attorney (Atturne). The adoption at the Conquest of the laws of Normandy, rendered necessary the assistance in England of Advocates from that country.† In England as in Normandy, the Advocates were called Countors.‡ The Curia (or Aula) Regis was at once the Council Chamber and Supreme Court of Justice of William the Conqueror and of his immediate successors upon the English throne. The proceedings of this Supreme Court were carried on in Norman French, a tongue 'not understanded of the' English 'people.' The gradual combination of the laws of Normandy with the English laws, and the introduction into England of many of the forms of the Roman law so materially increased the complexity § of legal science, that it could only be acquired after a long course of study.‖ William the Conqueror ordained that the students should be taught in schools of law adjoining his royal

* " He is called ' Countor,' whom one appoints to speak and count for oneself in court."
† The Judges of England, by Foss: Vol. i. p. 160.
‡ Dictionnaire Analytique: Title " Avocats."
§ Foss's Judges: Vol. i. 160, 161.
‖ Pearce's Inns of Court, 10, 11.

palace.* Suitors were bound to appear in person,† but once before the Court, both plaintiffs and defendants availed themselves of the services of Countors, who might stand by them, advise with them, and speak for them.‡ The Countor (unlike the suitor) was conversant with the law as administered in the Curia Regis, and familiar with the language of the Court. Parties were not allowed to conduct their own causes, and none but the Countors were allowed to be heard. Such, at least, is the opinion of Mr. Serjeant Manning, Mr. Pearce, and Mr. Foss. Permission to the parties to conduct their own causes would frequently have been attended with great confusion.§ When the cause came on in Court, first the writ was read; next, the Advocate for the plaintiff stated his case more fully; which was called 'narrare,' or 'to count;' from whence the opening statement was called the 'narratio,' or 'count,' and the Advocate 'narrator,' or 'countor.' Then the Advocate for the defendant put in his exceptio or plea. And so they went on to reply, rejoin, take issue, or demur, as it seemed advisable on the spur of the moment. All this was transacted *ore tenus* by the Advocates on either side. The Prothonotary (or the Advocates

* Dictionnaire Analytique: Title, "Avocats."
† 3 Stephen's Blackstone: 365 (Ed. 1853).
‡ Note to Doe d. Bennett *v.* Hale, 15 Q.B. 225 (by Serjeant Manning).
§ Manning's Preface to Serviens ad Legem, IX: Foss's Judges: Vol. i. 22, 23. Pearce's Inns of Court, 18.

themselves) minuted it down by the help of a copious use of abbreviations. If the Advocates desired to retract or amend, and obtained leave from the Court to do so, it was done *instanter*. The Court at once overruled, or admitted, the pleas. Pleading had more the appearance of argument, than of form, and was managed very much like the scholastic disputations, which were so fashionable in those days.* The Advocates were styled not only 'countors' or 'narratores' simply, but also Serjeant-countors, or ' Servientes-narratores,' and ' Serjeants ' or ' Servientes,' as well as 'Serjeants-at-law,' or 'Servientes-ad-legem.' William the Conqueror treated the professors of the laws which he had introduced into his new states, with marked distinction. He accorded to them the right of speaking before him with their heads covered.† The covering which they wore, and which effectually concealed the tonsure of clerical serjeants, was called a coif: it was originally a kind of linen helmet, the material being afterwards changed into white silk. Eventually it assumed the form of the black patch at the top of the Serjeant's wig—the distinguishing mark of the degree of the coif (tena).‡ The aristocratic tone, which, in spite of the invasion of modern ideas, still pervades the English Bar, is, perhaps, largely due to the circumstance that the

* Reeve's History of English Law : vol. ii. 267.
† Dictionnaire Analytique, Title, " Avocats."
‡ Foss's Judges, Vol. i. 25.

Advocates practising in the Curia Regis were invested by writ under the great seal, with the estate and dignity of Grand Serjeanty. To the circumstance that all Advocates were originally Serjeants-at-law, and that, therefore, as a matter-of-fact, the selection of Judges by the Crown was necessarily confined to persons who had taken that degree, is, probably, due the curious rule of etiquette, observed at the present day, that every Barrister, selected by the Crown to fill a vacancy on the Common Law Bench, must pass through the preliminary ceremony of being called to the state and degree of Serjeant-at-law. Bracton, who wrote in the reign of Henry III., enumerates as causes of suspicion, upon which an exception to the person of the Judge might be founded, ' Si Justiciarius sit consanguineus, &c., consiliarius vel narrator suus exstiterit in causa illâ, vel in aliâ.'* The elevation of Counsel to the Bench is here distinctly pointed at, and as the Judges were selected from the number of the Serjeants, the presumption is, that the Counsel mentioned by Bracton were ' *Servientes*-narratores,' or Serjeants-at-law. In the 11th year of King John mention is made of Serjeants holding pleas of the Crown.† All Serjeants-at-law were originally ' Servientes regis ad legem,' and assisted both the King himself and his Judges with their counsel. Nor was this all.

* Treatise 'De Exceptionibus,' cap. 15 (412a).
† 1 Maddox's Exchequer, 442 (g).

They were frequently invested with judicial functions, and included in Commissions of Assize and Gaol Delivery. The entry in 11 John carries us back beyond Magna Charta. Sir John Campbell, when arguing against the Serjeants, as Attorney-General, in the celebrated 'Serjeants' Case,'* admitted that Serjeants have existed from time immemorial. This would carry us back-beyond the first year of Richard I., A.D. 1189. Mr. Serjeant Wilde claimed for the office of Serjeant, in his speech on the first day of Michaelmas Term, 1839, to the Court of Common Pleas, a pedigree as ancient as that of 'the law itself.'† Some authors declare that it is as ancient as the Laws of Edward the Confessor;‡ but this is manifestly erroneous, as the feudal rank of Serjeant was as unknown to our Anglo-Saxon forefathers as the Science of Pleading.§ When the Court of Common Pleas, or 'Magnus Bancus,' as it was called, was severed from the Curia Regis, the Serjeants-at-law transferred their attendance to the new Court, in which, until the year 1834, they enjoyed an exclusive right of audience. Mr. Macqueen, however, is in error in supposing‖ that the Serjeants confined themselves exclusively to the Court of Common

* Reported, Manning's Serviens ad Legem (122).
† Reported, Manning's Serviens ad Legem (316).
‡ Whitelock's Memorials, 352, et seq.
§ See Stephen on Pleading. App. No. 11, p. 417. Edn. 1866.
‖ Lecture on Inns of Court and Chancery, 1851, p. 8.

Pleas. I cannot better describe their office than in the language of one of themselves, when impleaded.* 'Thomas le Mareschal dicit quod ipse est communis serviens narrator coram Justiciariis (*i.e.*, in the Court of Common Pleas) *et alibi, ubi melius ad hoc conduci poterit.*'

" The Serjeants had, in addition to their right of exclusive audience in the Court of Common Pleas, a right of pre-audience in the King's Bench and the Exchequer.

" Mr. Macqueen is, in my humble judgment, also in error in calling the Serjeants,† ' a handful of monopolists.' It is impossible to accept the scanty list of names inserted by Sir William Dugdale, under the heading 'Servientes ad Legem,' as an exhaustive list of the Serjeants. His list commences in the 3rd year of Edward I. (1276), but in the preceding reign the Serjeants of the Bench are spoken of as a well-known and somewhat numerous body. Matthew Paris, in his History, gives a lively description of the 'altercation' between Henry III. and Hubert de Burgh, Earl of Kent, A.D. 1239, when the King '*cum omnibus prolocutoribus Banci, quos narratores appellamus,*' was mastered in argument by ' Magister Laurentius of St. Alban's'.‡ The same author, in his 'Lives,'§ speaks of the ' Placitantium Advocati, quos Banci narratores *vul-*

---

* Plac. Abr. 237 : and more fully set out, Manning, 280.
† Page 8.   ‡ Wats's Edition, 1640, 516, 26.
§ 142, 56.

gariter appellamus.' The Rolls of Exchequer, 52 Hen. III. (A.D. 1267), speak of Robert de Colevile narrator de Banco, et ' *socii ejus narratores.*'*

" In proof that the Serjeants were ' a handful,' Mr. Macqueen cites from Mr. Serjeant Manning's 'most learned Report,'† that, two hundred and seventy-five years after the 20th Edw. I. (the time of which he was speaking), ' there was but one Serjeant for a whole term!' From 20 Edward I. (1292), to 10 Elizabeth (1567), is a tolerable leap, for proof. If Mr. Macqueen, however, had glanced at Mr. Serjeant Manning's most learned foot-note,‡ he would have seen that 30 Serjeants were made between 1554, the date of the supposed solitary Serjeant's writ, and the 17th November, 1567, the commencement of the 10th year of Elizabeth; and that the story of Serjeant Bendloes being the sole Serjeant for a whole term involves no less a consequence than the death of all these, four of whom were made Judges subsequent to the year, in which the term of the solitary Serjeant occurred! It will be evident, from this simple narrative, founded on the best authorities, that Mr. Marshall is in error in stating§ that ' we first hear of Serjeants in the third year of Edward I.' The first legislative enactment, in which they are named, was passed, no doubt, in that year.‖ But they are mentioned by historians,

---

* Maddox's Exchequer, c.vii. s. 3 (k) (Vol. i. p. 236).
† Page 138. ‡ Page 138 (a).
§ Page 6. ‖ Westminster I. cap. 29.

and in legal documents, long before that year. Indeed, Mr. Marshall admits as much: for he says, in another place,* that 'we first hear of Serjeants in the period covered by the reigns of *John*, *Henry III*, and *Edward I.*' I have also shewn, I think, on pretty good authority, that, both in Normandy and England, in the 12th century, a class of 'legal practitioners' existed totally distinct from Attorneys. Indeed, although Mr. Marshall insists in one place,† that 'Attorneys were the only practitioners known to the Courts in the 12th century;' in another place,‡ he admits that 'Serjeants are spoken of as practising in the Curia Regis,' and it is generally agreed that the Court of Common Pleas, which the Serjeants were bound to attend,§ was separated from the Curia Regis in the reign of Richard I.‖ The Exchequer is spoken of as a distinct Court in the reign of Henry I.¶ Mr. Marshall** seems to confound 'appearing in person' and pleading in person, which are two very distinct things. On the whole, the line which Mr. Marshall draws across the middle of the 13th, I would feel disposed, though not with equal confidence, to draw across the middle of the 11th century. Mr. Marshall, I think, is hardly justified in leaving the English

* Page 5. † Page 5. ‡ Page 7.
§ Note to Doe d. Bennett, *v.* Hale, 15 Q.B., 225.
‖ 1 Reeves' Hist. Eng. Law, 57.
¶ 1 Maddox's Ex. 179.
** Page 1.

people, for two hundred years, to the tender mercies of Anglo-Norman Kings and Judges, without any assistance whatever from the 'Professors of the Law.'*

* Mr. Marshall styles the Attorneys of the 12th and part of the 13th century '*practitioners*,' but he rightly admits that they were not *lawyers*, i.e., legal practitioners.

SECTION II.

APPRENTICES-AT-BAR.

"'We must remember,' says my Lord Chief Justice Campbell, in the case of Doe d. Bennett v. Hale,* that Serjeants-countors *and other Counsel* existed in England long before the time of Edward I.' Spelman, in his Glossary,† speaks of an 'infesta multitudo' of Advocates as existing prior to the 20th year of Edward I. Sir Edward Coke was clearly of opinion that Apprentices had a right of audience in the Superior Courts prior to the 20th year of Edward I. The Statute Westminster I. (3 Edw. I.), cap. 29, commences thus:—'Si ul Serjeant-countor ou auter face ùl maner de disceit ou de collusion en Cour le Roy.' Coke says‡ that the words, 'ou auter,' 'extend to Apprentices, Attorneys, Clerks of Courts, or any other.' The Statute mentions, however, the distinct classes of offenders, against whom it enacts appropriate punishments. One class consists of Countors; the other class of persons 'other than countors' ('autre que countor.') Both classes were to be liable, for an infringement of the Statute, to imprisonment for a year and a day; but Countors were to be liable

* 15 Q. B., 171.   † Sub. voc. 'Attornatus.'   ‡ 1 Inst. 214.

to the further penalty of being deprived of the right of audience in the Superior Courts: ' et ne soit oyé en Court le Roy a conter pur nulluy.' ' *This* punishment,' says Lord Coke, ' extends as well to the Apprentice as to the Serjeant.' No mention of its applicability to the Attorney! The Apprentice, therefore, in Lord Coke's opinion, had at that time—seventeen years before the Order ' De Attornatis et Apprenticiis ' (of which more anon) a right of audience in the Superior Courts, of which he might be deprived for violating the Statute. The Attorney had no such right, and could not, therefore, be deprived of it. He was liable to the same punishment as an ordinary layman. From the tenor of Coke's remarks, it is evident that the abuses which the Statute was designed to check arose in the reign of Henry III., to which, at all events, we would be justified, on his authority, in carrying back the Apprentices' right of audience in the Superior Courts. Under the strict feudal law, the vassal was bound to act as Counsel for the suitors in his Lord's Court.* This system was broken in upon by the clergy, who soon obtained a practical monopoly of pleading, devoting themselves with ardour to the Legal Profession. ' Nullus clericus nisi Causidicus ' is the language of William of. Malmsbury, in the reign of William Rufus.† The Serjeant-countors

* See the Assizes of Jerusalem, passim.
† Book 4. Fol. 696.

appear to have been originally clergymen.* Stephen de Blois, Archdeacon of Bath, gives an interesting account of a number of clergymen who lived in the house of St. Thomas of Canterbury. The description of them might well apply to the Apprentices. Lord Lyttelton, in his 'Life of Henry II.,'† thus translates this remarkable passage:—' In the house of my master, the Archbishop of Canterbury, there are a set of very learned (literatissimi) men, expert in all the rules (rectitudo) of justice, as well as other parts of prudence and knowledge. It is their constant custom, after prayers and before they dine, to exercise themselves in reading (lectione) in disputations, and in the decision of legal cases. To us all the knotty questions of the kingdom are referred (omnes quæstiones regni nodosæ referuntur ad nos), which, being brought forth into the auditory, where all the company assembles (in commune auditorium), every one, according to his rank, whets his understanding to speak well, without wrangling and obloquy (obtrectatione) and with all the acuteness and subtilty that is in him, declares what he thinks the most prudent and sound advice. And if it pleases God to reveal the best opinion to one of the lowest among us (minori) the whole assembly (universitas) agrees to it without envy or detraction.'

* 1 Foss's Judges, 25.

† Vol. ii. p. 261. See Selden's Notes to Fleta, chap. vii. s. 7.

There is a strong resemblance between these 'disputations' and the 'boltings' and 'mootings' of the Inns of Court, in the palmy days of those legal seminaries. It was in the 2nd year of Henry III. that the clergy were warned not to practise in the Secular Courts.* It seems pretty clear from the case of the Priest-Serjeant, de Bussey,† that before the end of that reign the clergy had generally abandoned to laymen the study of the Common Law and the privileges of Advocates 'in foro seculari.' From that day to this lawyers have been (to use Dr. Johnson's phrase) 'good haters' of the clergy. Nothing delights the heart of a true lawyer so much as to roast a parson. As the clergy withdrew from the secular Courts, how were their places supplied? The answer seems to me to be clear:—by the lay Apprentices, who had settled, as the sages of the law tell us,‡ in the outskirts of the City of London, attracted thither by the settlement of the Common Pleas in the palace of Westminster. Some of these Apprentices were selected to be lay Serjeants, to supply the place of the clerical Serjeants; but the entire severance between the Exchequer and the King's Bench, on the one hand, and the Curia Regis on the other, the existence of

* By Poer, Bishop of Salisbury, in his " Constitutions."
† Matthew Paris, A.D. 1259, (41 Hen. III.) : 984, 56, 57 : 985. 1, 2, 3. 'Principalis Consiliarius' of William of Valentia, who was brother-in-law of Henry III., and uncle of Edward I.
‡ Vide Coke, Spelman, Blackstone, &c.

the rule, which required that only qualified Advocates should presume to count for suitors in all the King's Courts,* and the difficulty, which Serjeants, tied, as they were, to the Court of Common Pleas, must have experienced in following the royal progresses and the Itinerant Justices all over the kingdom, would necessarily suggest the creation of a new class of Advocates; and the selection would naturally fall upon the more advanced class of the lay Apprentices, who were the only persons, besides the Serjeants and Judges, imbued with a scientific knowledge of the Common Law, from the study and practice of which the clergy had withdrawn. The Apprentices could not be called to the state and degree of Serjeant-at-law till they were of sixteen years standing.† It appears to have now become usual for the Judges to admit them to practise as Advocates when of seven years standing. Spelman points,‡ I think, to

* "Et in Curia Regis pro aliquo narrare, non audietur, nisi pro semetipso, si narrator fuerit."—Fleta: B. 2, c. 37. "Et Abellius de Sancto Martino venit et narravit pro episcopo. Et non fuit Advocatus. Ideo in misericordia. Custodiatur."—Archbishop of Canterbury v. Bishop of Rochester: Plac. Abr. 137, 38 Henry III. (Mr. Stephen and Mr. Pearce misquote the passage as occurring 32 Henry III. Steph. Pl. 409: Pearce, I.C. 18.) "Et prædicta Juliana defecit de judicio suo et seizina, quia non habuit narratorem."—1 Rot. Parl. 4: 6 Edward I. (1278).

† 3 Black. Comm. 27: Fortescue de Laud. Leg. Ang. c. 50.
‡ Glossary, s.v. 'Approuticii.'

this old custom where he observes:—'Apud nos utique dicuntur alii apprenticii ad legem, alii OLIM apprenticii-ad-*barras*. Hi, quod post septenne (vel id circiter) studium cancellos fori (quos barras vocant) salutare, atque illic causas agere permitterentur. Illi, quod in facultate juris provectiores lectiones item publicas edidissent.' Selden* also observes, that in the Order 'De Attornatis et Apprenticiis' the name 'Apprenticii' was 'used for practisers'—(not students)—'and Apprenticii-ad-barros are Barristers in the ridiculous verses of Andrew Horn before his Mirror aux Justices:—

> Hanc Legum summam, si quis vult mira tueri,
> Perlegat et sapiens si vult orator haberi:
> Hoc Apprenticiis ad Barros ebore munus
> Gratum juridicis utile mittit opus
> Horn mihi cognomen, Andreas est mihi nomen.'

"Mr. Macqueen mentions† three classes of Apprentices, although, unfortunately, he does not give his authority;—'the junior class,' he says, 'embraced the students or novitiates of the house, who, not being competent to give instruction were,' he presumes, 'content to receive it. The next, or second class of Apprenticii, were those who conducted the educational exercises prescribed. The third, or senior class, were the Apprenticii ad legem, who from their standing and acquirements were permitted by the Judges to practise as Advocates.'

* Selden's Notes to Fortescue, cap. 8.
† Pp. 12, 13.

There are three classes, also, of Apprentices mentioned in the subsidy of 1379, which gave rise to Wat Tyler's rebellion. Barons, Serjeants, and *Grand Apprentices-at-law*—(' Grant Apprentices du loy')—were assessed at 40s. Other Apprentices practising the law ('autres Apprentices, qui pursuent la loy',) and Bachelors were assessed at half the amount—20s. Other *Apprentices of less estate* and *Attorneys*, and also Esquires of less estate were assessed at the now well-known figure of 6s 8d.*

" Spelman thus classifies the three degrees of the Common Law Bar in his day,† contrasting them with corresponding Academical degrees and degrees in the Civil Law:—' In Causidicorum gradationibus inferior est eorum, qui ad barros vocantur; secunda, Apprenticiorum; tertia, Serjantorum, vel Serventium ad Legem:—

(1.) *Academia.*	(2.) *Foro Regni.*	(3.) *Foro Civili.*
3. Doctor.	3. Serviens.	3. Doctor Legum.
2. Magister.	2. Apprenticius ad Legem.	2. Licentiatus.
1. Bacularius.	1. Barrasterius.	1. Lyta.

' Apprenticius' is used as a generic term for the entire Bar in Henry IV.'s precept for summoning the ' Parliamentum Indoctum' :‡—' Nolumus autem

* 3 Rot. Parl. 58.
† 1626. Glossary. s. v. ' Serjans.'
‡ Spelman's Glossary, s. v. Apprenticii. (6 Oct. 6 Henry IV. at Coventry).

quod tu seu aliquis alius Vicecomes regni nostri, aut *Apprenticius*, sive aliquis alius homo ad legem, aliqualiter sit electus.' The Liber Albus of the City of London* describes the Recorder as 'one of the most skilful and virtuous Apprentices-at-law of the whole kingdom.' Mr. Ryley, in a note, defines 'Legis apprenticius' to mean 'a Barrister of less than sixteen years standing and under the degree of Serjeant.' Mr. Ryley must have been thinking of the original Apprentice, who was, indeed, not an Apprentice-at-bar, or Barrister, but a simple student. The Apprentice-at-Law, in the reign of Henry V., when the Liber Albus was written, was not necessarily *under* sixteen years' standing. The title was then applied to *all* Counsel under the degree of Serjeant-at-Law. It is with great diffidence that I dissent from so great an authority as Mr. Serjeant Manning, with whose views for the most part I heartily agree; but I confess that I cannot find any authority (except an obiter dictum of Mr. Reeves† for his assumption, that the Order in Parliament of 20 Edward I. 'de Attornatis et Apprenticiis, *first* conferred on Apprentices the right of audience in the Superior Courts (other than the Court of Common Pleas). There is nothing in the Order itself to sanction this assumption, and the authorities which I have already cited, point to the conclusion, that the Prolytæ, or senior class of

* B 1. P. 1. c. xv.
† Hist. of Eng. Law, vol. 2, 284 ("probably").

Apprentices,* were allowed to practise in the Superior Courts (other than the Court of Common Pleas), as early as the reign of Henry III. This Order in Parliament of 20 Edward I. 'is a Statutory power to the Judges to admit Attorneys, and it cannot apply to advocates in any of the King's Courts.' Such was the opinion of Sir William Follett, reported by Mr. Serjeant Manning himself.† Waterhous, in his lively and garrulous Commentary on Fortescue,‡ referring to this Order, says, 'Though in Edward I.'s time, (anno 20,) Attorneys are named before Apprentices, after which Fleta also so marshals them, yet are those Attorneys not to be named in a day with Apprentices.' How little importance is to be attached to the sequence of the names is evident from a passage in the Liber Albus cited by Mr. Marshall.§ There we find a portion of the Calender of the City papers|| headed, 'De Attornatis, Essoniatoribus et Narratoribus.' Under this heading appear the following entries : — 'Diversæ Ordinationes de Narratoribus, Attornatis et Essoniatoribus:' 'que nulle Attourne, Contour, ne Essoneour estoysent deinz la Barre:' 'quod Narratores, Attornati et Essoniatores sint jurati:' the sequence of the names being different in each case. I cannot

* Selden's Notes to Fortescue, c. 8.
† Serviens ad Legem, 45.
‡ Fortescutus Illustratus, 138.

agree, therefore, with Mr. Marshall that the position in which the names of Serjeants, Attorneys, and Apprentices are placed, 20 Edw. I., is any indication of the 'relation of rank' of these three classes :—or that the circumstance that in the Roll of Parliament, tempore Edw. III.,* a petitioner describes himself as 'Apprentice of the Court of our Lord the King and Attorney,' indicates that the 'relation of rank' of two of these classes, had, in the interval between the 20 Edw. I. and 11 Edw. III., undergone a material change.

* 2 Rot. Parl. 96 b.

SECTION III.

ATTORNEYS-AT-LAW.

"We must pass from the Conquest to the reign of our English Justinian, Edward I., an interval of more than 200 years, for the origin of the right, which Englishmen universally enjoy, of appearing by Attorney. Prior to the year 1285, except in certain cases specially provided for, or by virtue of the King's writ of dedimus potestatem de Attornato faciendo, every suitor was obliged to appear in person.* A general power to appear by Attorney was first given by the Statute Westminster the Second (1 Stat. 13 Edw. I.), cap. 10. From that date suitors were, in most instances, at liberty to appoint either a general Attorney or an Attorney ad lucrandum et perdendum in a particular cause. Mr. Marshall admits† that, prior to the latter end of the 13th Century, Attorneys, in the cases in which it was lawful to appoint them, were merely 'private agents,' not 'Attorneys-at-law.' A father might appoint his son his Attorney, a wife might appoint her husband her Attorney; abbots and priors of Canons regular were received as Attorneys for their convents.‡ The ancient significance of the word, Attorney, is preserved in the expression,

---

* 3 Black: Com. 25. Note to Doe d. Bennett *v.* Hale, 15 Q. B. 225.   † Pp. 5, 6.

'power of Attorney,' which may be given to a person wholly unlearned in the law to act for the person giving it. The expression, 'appear by Attorney,' which seems to puzzle Mr. Marshall so much,* meant simply the substitution for the party in the cause of another person to act, as his 'alter ego,' in his 'turn' or stead. Mr. Marshall thinks † that the circumstance that the party, whether plaintiff or defendant, was bound to appear in person, shews conclusively that he discharged, at first, 'the duties of Attorney, Pleader, and Counsel.' I have shewn that he did not discharge 'the duties of Pleader and Counsel:' and the party could not discharge 'the duties of Attorney,' when the party appeared in person, for the simple reason that there were no 'duties of Attorney' for him to discharge. The only 'duties of Attorney,' prior, at all events, to the year 1285, were to discharge the duties of the party: and the party could not be himself and a substitute for himself, his own 'ego,' and 'alter ego,' at the same time. Glanville does not mention Attorneys eo nomine. He speaks only of 'responsales.'‡ But whether the party appointed a 'responsalis,' or an Attorney, he put him in his place—('posuit talem loco suo') on the tacit understanding that he himself could not

---

* Pp. 8, 9. † P. 1.

‡ Glanville speaks of both parties appointing responsales. Mr. Marshall says that defendants, only, appointed them.

be present during the hearing.* This idea of the Attorney, as a substitute for the party *in his absence* runs through the whole of the early history of the common law. Take, *e.g.*, the reign of Henry V. In the 3 Hen. V. A.D. 1415—more than 120 years after the Order in Parliament of 20 Edw. I.—we find the Commons praying that the Chief Baron of the Exchequer, and each of the puisne Justices of the King's Bench and Common Pleas, as well as each of the King's Serjeants, might have power to enrol Attorneys in any place and in any of the Courts of the King, because 'some who have been or are impleaded or are impleading, were, or are decrepid, some so old, some so sick and detained with such infirmities, some occupied in the service of our Sovereign Lord the King or otherwise about such business, that they for these causes and the like *cannot well come* to the Courts of our Lord the King *in their own person.*' Some had been 'put to great loss' and others 'disinherited to their great hurt,' by proceedings being taken in their absence.†

In the reign of Henry VI, an Act of Parliament was passed (2 Hen. VI. cap. 3), which further illustrates this idea of the Attorney:—'Johan Duc de Bedford, uncle a nostre Seignur le Roy, *qui est*

---

* Glanville: B xi. c. 3. 'Ita intelligitur quilibet alterum loco suo ponere, scilicet si ipsemet interesse non possit.' See Reeves' Hist. of Eng. Law: vol. i. 170.

† 3 Rot. Parl. 80.

dela le mer es parties de France, en le service du Roy, en toutz maners, des plées moevez et amoevers envers ascune person,' &c. 'soit par son Atturne on Atturnez receu a defendre son droit et en mesme la manere ait et enjoie toutz maners benefices et avantages *sicome li fuist present en sa propre personne.*'

"Mr. Maugham, expatiating, like Mr. Marshall, in favour of the right of audience of Attorneys in the Superior Courts,* urges that, if the Attorneys were not permitted to argue in open Court, the party was placed in a worse position by appointing an Attorney, than if he had appeared in person, for then he could have argued in open Court himself. But Mr. Maugham forgot, first, that the advantage of appointing an Attorney consisted in the representation of the party before the Court *in his absence*, which was surely a great gain in those days of slow and difficult travelling : secondly, that although the party appeared in person, it did not follow that he conducted the vivâ voce pleadings in person.—The following passage from the Statute 36 Edw. III. c. 15 ; (1362) will show how little able the party was to *plead* in person :—'Les gentz que pledent ou sout emplez en les Courtes le Roi, et les Courtes d'autres, n'ont entendement ne connaisance de ce qu'est dit pur eulx, ne contre eulx, par lour Serjeantz et autres Pledours.'

"It was, therefore, enacted, that all pleas what-

* Maugham's Law of Attorneys, p. 351. (Ed. 1825.)

ever should be pleaded, defended, debated and adjudged in the English tongue, but that they should be entered and enrolled in Latin. Fabian thus summarises this Statute:—'About this time was an ordinance and Statute made that Serjeants and Prentyses-at-law should plead *their* pleas in their mother tongue.' So little was the suitor or the Attorney regarded as a Pleader.* Fabian adds, 'But that stode but a short whyle.' Counsel went back, no doubt, to their forensic lingo. If the suitors could not understand what their Counsel said, how little able must they have been to address the Court in Norman-French themselves! The Attorney stood in precisely the same position as the party. In the Placitorum Abbreviatio† such entries as these constantly occur:— 'Rogerus de Scales ponit loco suo Robertum de Scales, *patrem suum*, versus Gulielmum de Vichend et uxorem ejus de placito terræ in Cotes.'‡ Alicia de Fundenhale ponet loco suo Robertum filium Reginaldi, *virum suum*, versus Herbertum de Helgeton de placito advocationis ecclesiæ de Duneston.'§ Is it to be supposed that the father or the husband of the plaintiff was able to address the Court in Norman-French, and to apprehend the subtleties of the Anglo-Norman law, better than the Plaintiff? But, then,

---

* Chronicle, anno 1363: cited Herbert's Inns of Court, 171.
† Published by Royal authority, 1811.
‡ Page 3. § Ibid.

it is said* that 'the practice soon grew up of appointing professional lawyers Attorneys in certain cases.' It is very difficult to fix with certainty the date at which this change took place. The best-founded conjecture appears to be that of Mr. Serjeant Manning that it took place, A.D. 1292, by virtue of the Order in Parliament of 20 Edw. I. In Normandy, the two classes of amateur and professional Attorneys appear to have existed side by side. The term ' Attorney' is applied, in the 65th Chapter of the 'Custumier,' to the person substituted by the plaintiff or defendant for himself in legal proceedings (attourné par devant la justice pour aulcun' :— ' Et si doibt estre receu en tiel estat de la querelle come c'il qu'il atournera.' This, as already observed, is the literal meaning of the word 'Attorney,' one put in the stead or 'turn' of another. The word ' Attourne' had, also, in Normandy, the meaning of ' Procureur aux causes' :—' Procureurs' were agents of the parties, who conducted causes through the forms of the Courts. ' On les appelle en Normandie, passes Attournes, ou auxquels on baille procuration qu'on appelle ad lites, desquels le pouvoir cessait en la presence de la partie qui les avait constitués.'† The Custumier calls this kind of Attorney a ' Pledour,' and devotes its 63rd chapter to him. These 'menent les querelles en Court en

* Pearce's Inns of Court, p. 16.
† See, as to these two kinds of Attorney, the Dictionnaire Analytique, s v. 'Attournes.'

demandant et en defendant.' Advocates, in certain departments of justice, performed the functions of Procureurs: this power was given them 'pour epargner des frais aux Pledours'—to save the Attorneys' fees.* It was, however, the opinion of all the doctors, that a 'personne noble' undertaking the duties of a 'Procureur aux causes,' forfeited his 'noblesse.'† The views of Mr. Serjeant Manning and of Mr. Foss clearly point to a similar union of the functions of Advocate and Attorney-*at-law* in the persons of the 'Apprenticii,' and that by virtue of the Order in Parliament of 20 Edw. I. 'Apprentices-at-law and Attorneys-at-law formerly constituted one class,' says Mr. Serjeant Manning, in the notes to the famous 'Serjeants' Case.'‡ 'There can be no doubt,' says Mr. Foss, 'that the Apprentices-of-the-law were, in fact, Attorneys for their clients, representing them in the Courts.'§ And, commenting upon the Order in Parliament of Edw. I., Mr. Foss|| observes, 'The words Attornatis et Apprenticiis are probably here used synonymously.' Elsewhere¶ Mr. Serjeant Manning expounds his views more fully:—' When a general power to appear by Attorney had in 1285 been given by

* Dictionnaire Analytique: tit. 'Avocats.'
† Terrien's Commentary on the Civil Law of Normandy, 353.
‡ Serviens ad Legem, 188.
§ Vol. iii. p. 372. || Ib. 49.
¶ Note to Doe d. Bennett *v.* Hale, 15 Q. B. 225.

Statute Westminster 2 (1 Stat. 13 Edw. I.), it was thought expedient to restrict the appointment to persons presumed to be acquainted with the Common Law. An Order was made in Parliament in 1292 (1 Rot. Parl. 84 b), intituled, De Attornatis et Apprenticiis, by which the Justices of the Common Pleas were required to appoint a certain number de quolibet comitatu, de melioribus et legalioribus et libentiùs addiscentibus, to attend the Courts. From this period Apprentices-at-Law enjoyed the double privilege of appearing as Attorneys for suitors, in all the Common Law Courts, and of acting as Advocates in those Courts, in which Serjeants did not regularly attend. Thus in the 11 Edw. III. (2 Rot. Parl. 96 b) John de Codyngton, an Apprentice *and* Attorney, was discharged by the Council from a command of the Lord Admiral to appear at Orewell, (? Irwell), armed and apparelled as a Man-at-arms.'* Mr. Macqueen takes a view of the Order in Parliament exactly the opposite to that of Mr. Serjeant Manning and Mr. Foss. ' The duties of the Attorney,' say Mr. Serjeant Manning and Mr. Foss, ' were performed by the Advocate.' ' The duties of the Advocate,' says Mr. Macqueen,† 'were performed by the Attorney.' Mr. Marshall, taking the same view as Mr. Macqueen, observes,‡ that the Order in Parliament of 20 Edw. I. affords 'good evidence,' that the Attorneys

* Note to Doe d. Bennett *v.* Hale, 15 Q. B. 225.
    † Page 8.   ‡ Page 7.

became recognised functionaries of the law towards the close of the 13th century, with a right of audience before the Justices in Itinere.' It is easy to shew the illogical character of the views put forward by Mr. Marshall and Mr. Macqueen as to the meaning of the Order in Parliament of 20 Edward I. The Order is headed ' De Attornatis et Apprenticiis,' as Sir William Follett, in arguing for the Petitioners in the Serjeant's Case,* pointed out. Mr. Marshall and Mr. Macqueen wrest these words (which were probably added by the compiler of the Parliament Roll as a kind of title to what follows,) from their position at the head of the Order, and place them in the middle of it. Mr. Marshall, in justification, I suppose, of this, cites Sir William Dugdale's reading, 'Ordinent certum numerum de Attornatis et Apprenticiis,' in a foot-note. The whole passage seems to have bothered Sir William Dugdale not a little. He construes, ' Attornatis et Apprenticiis,' which he thus takes out of its proper place, ' Attorneys *and lawyers!*' He uses that word 'lawyer,' no doubt, as sufficiently indefinite to include, 'student,' 'Pleader,' and 'Serjeant,' with all of which he identifies the ' Apprenticius!'‡ Sir William Follett thus explains the Order :§—'It was the appointment of a certain number of *persons* to act as Attornies in the different counties.' This is a very proper translation, as there is no sub-

* Manning's Report, 45.   † P. 6.
‡ Chap. 55.   § Manning, 45.

stantive after 'de melioribus et legalioribus et libentiùs addiscentibus.' Dugdale's version would make the Order the worst possible 'dog:'— 'Ordinent certum numerum de Attornatis et Apprenticiis de quolibet 'comitatu de melioribus et legalioribus et libentiùs addiscentibus.'"

"Our forefathers," interrupted Pennyless, laughing, "were not very choice in their Latinity, but I cannot think that they wrote such 'd . . . . d' stuff as this!"

"Mr. Macqueen says* that the Justices of the Common Pleas were to select 'Attorneys to practise *and pupils* to study:' and then he tells us that '140 *Attorneys* might suffice for the purpose in view.' How could '140 Attorneys' supply the place of the Attorneys *and pupils* to be chosen? Mr. Macqueen caps this extraordinary explanation by saying that *the students* are to be 'libentes addiscere.'—Why not the Attorneys? Thus Mr. Macqueen first wrests the words 'Attornatis et Apprenticiis' from their position at the head of the Order, and places them in the middle of it: then he makes the words 'septies viginti,' refer only to the Attorneys, (as well as the words 'et se de negotiis in eâdem Curiâ intromittant et alii non'); and then he makes the words 'libentes addiscere' refer to the pupils (or students) only! Whoever the appointees were to be, their total number was to be 140, and they were *all* to be

* P. 7.

'libentes addiscere.' Aye, and more than that. All the appointees were to enjoy the *same* rights and privileges. 'Et quod ipsi quos ad hoc eligerint Curiam sequantur et se de negociis in eâdem Curiâ intromittant et alii non.'—Will Mr. Marshall or Mr. Macqueen affirm that these words apply only to the Attorneys, and not to the 'pupils'? The 'pupils,' whoever they were, would have something else to do than to sit in Court, and listen to the Attorneys, for they themselves were to enjoy the same rights and privileges as the Attorneys. Mr. Marshall says* that 'it may be inferred from the language of the Order (1) That there were a considerable number of Attorneys *and students* in the habit of attending before the Justices on Circuit, and (2) that *those who* were selected, or some of them, followed the Court from place to place and had the right of appearing and arguing before it. The duties of Serjeants *and Apprentices* are more difficult to determine.' Who are 'those who'? The antecedent is 'Attorneys *and students*,' which is a free translation of 'Attornati et Apprenticii.' Mr. Marshall, however, evidently means by 'those who' the Attorneys only; for he says, that the duties of *Apprentices* are more difficult to determine.' This strained construction involves Mr. Marshall in a neglect of Lindley Murray, as the equally strained construction of Mr. Macqueen had involved him in zig-zag

* P. 6.

translations!—Mr. Marshall has, I think, mistranslated the word 'suæ.' He renders 'Curiæ suæ' '*their* Court,' and says* that 'the precept addressed to John de Metingham had reference to the Common Pleas only.† It seems to me that the sense requires that 'Curiæ suæ' should be rendered '*his*'—i. e. 'the King's — Court.' The expression, 'Curiam sequantur,' receives elucidation from Magna Charta. 'Communia Placita *non* sequantur Curiam nostram.'‡ The Common Pleas was now stationary at Westminster.§ The King's Bench and Exchequer accompanied the King in his royal progresses—'ubicunque fuerit in Angliâ.' So late as the reign of Edward III. the King's Court is spoken of ‖ as 'wandering about all over the realm.' The Order in Parliament of 20 Edw. I. was evidently designed for the convenience of suitors in the King's Bench and Exchequer. The persons selected were to follow the Court (Curiam sequantur '), and being chosen from every county ('de quolibet comitatu'), the suitors of every county would have a representative in the King's Court, wherever it

---

* Page 8.

† Although pp. 6 & 7, he considers it applicable to the Eyre, only!

‡ 9 Hen. III. cap. 11.

§ The only place that it seems to have removed to occasionally was York. 1 Rot. Parl. 143.

‖ 38 Edw. III (1364-5.) 2 Rot. Parl. 286. Manning, 180·

might be. The Order does not seem to have any reference to the Courts held by the Itinerant Justices, so that Mr. Marshall's conjectures, founded on that hypothesis, fall to the ground.

" The only hypothesis, that I can frame, as equally probable with that of Mr. Foss, is, that the selection of Attorneys-at-law may have been first made from the Apprentices libentiùs addiscentes *below* the position of Apprentices-at-bar. These would be likely to frequent that Court in which they were afterwards to practise as Serjeants, and the selection would naturally be left to the Justices of that Court. It is extremely probable that the Judges allowed students of more than seven years standing to practise as Advocates *before* 20 Edward I. It is somewhat remarkable also that in the subsidy, which led to Wat Tyler's rebellion, the lowest grade of Apprentices are classed with, and assessed at the same rate as Attorneys, viz., 6s 8d; while the Apprentices-at-bar are assessed at 20s, and the 'Grand Apprentices,'* (who are classed with Serjeants,) are assessed at 40s.

" Next to the Order in Parliament of 20 Edward I., Mr. Marshall† relies upon the Statute of Carlisle (15 Edw. II.). ' The Statute of Carlisle,' says Mr.

---

* The Grand Apprentices were probably Benchers of the Inns of Court. Wats has an amusing mistake in the Index to his edition of M. Paris. He confounds the ' Banci narratores ' mentioned by that historian with ' Benchers vel Bancatores.'—(Edition 1640, s. v. "Narratores Banci," in the

Marshall, 'directed the Barons of the Exchequer and the Justices not to admit Attorneys except in Pleas in Banc, and in places where they might be assigned. .. The object of this clause in the Statute of Carlisle was to authorise the Judges of the Exchequer and King's Bench to exercise similar powers of appointing Attorneys in specified cases' [to those exercised by the Justices of the Common Pleas under the Order of 20 Edward I.]. . . 'This ordinance is chiefly noteworthy for the evidence it furnishes of the right of Attorneys to appear before the Judges at Westminster. The possible inference that they appeared for the parties in the modern sense of the term, 'appear,' &c., 'is negatived,' &c. But the word 'appear,' does not anywhere occur in the Statute: and if it is an enabling Statute, it is singular that it is so negatively expressed. Mr. Marshall admits that it was intended to check 'the practise,' which ' had grown, of making Attorneys without reference to the immediate business of the Court.' In the time of Glanville responsales might be appointed in the Curia Regis to represent their principals in *other* Courts.* The two chief officials in the Curia Regis were the Lord Chancellor and the Chief Justiciar. To the Chief Justiciar succeeded the Lord Chief Justice of England. At the date of the Statute of Carlisle the Lord Chancellor and the Lord Chief Justice of England continued to exercise the power of admitting Attorneys which

* See B. xi. caps 1 and 2.

they had exercised as officers of the Curia Regis. The Curia Regis having now parted with many of their powers to the Exchequer, the Common Pleas and the King's Bench, the Barons and Justices, who presided in these Courts, as well as the Itinerant Justices, seem to have assumed the power of admitting Attorneys in any cause and in any place. The clerks and officers of these Courts seem to have assumed similar powers. The object of the Statute of Carlisle was to restrain the Barons and Justices from admitting Attorneys 'nisi tantum in placitis coram eis et sociis suis in locis et placeis ubi per nos assignantur:' and to put a stop to the assumptions of the clerks and officers altogether. The Statute contains an express reservation of the power of admitting Attorneys theretofore always enjoyed ('hactenus semper observata') by the Lord Chancellor and the Lord Chief Justice of England. Such are the provisions of the Statute of Carlisle. Mr. Marshall must have the power of a magician to extract from its negative provisions any argument in favour of the right of audience of Attorneys in the Superior Courts. This so-called 'Statuté of Carlisle' is not a Statute at all,* and it is addressed (unfortunately for Mr. Marshall's view that it applies exclusively to the King's Bench and Exchequer) to the Justices of the Common Pleas!

* Reeve's Hist. of Eng. Law : Vol. ii. 304.

It commences thus, 'Rex Justiciariis suis de Banco, salutem!' The restraint imposed by this writ (for such it is) was continued down to the reign of Henry V., when the Commons, in a petition to that King (already cited*) made a fruitless endeavour to get it removed.

"'The brief,' says Mr. Marshall,† 'with which Advocates were then armed, was not the lengthy document to which we are accustomed, but a short abstract of the pleadings.' Surely Mr. Marshall must be aware that the 'brief' was neither more nor less than the 'breve' or writ. All the pleadings were vivâ voce, and settled by the Judges in Court. Everything advanced was treated as matter in fieri, which might be withdrawn, and other matter substituted for it.

"Supposing a union of the functions of Attorney and Counsel to have taken place, when did the final separation occur? 'Afterwards, persons were admitted,' says Mr. Serjeant Manning, 'to practise as Attorneys, who had not taken the degree of Apprentice-at-law; and Utter Barristers were allowed to appear as Advocates in the Itinerant Courts without qualifying themselves to act as Attorneys within the order of 1292 by taking the degree of Apprentice.' Mr. Serjeant Manning does not define the date to which the word 'afterwards' points. Some light, however, is thrown upon this difficult subject by the Statute

* 3 Hen. 5 (1415). 3 Rot. Parl. 80.   † P. 8.

4 Hen. IV. c. 18 (1402) which first instituted legal examinations and a* roll of Attorneys, assigning for a reason, in the recital, that 'pleuseurs damages et meschiefs ont advenuz devaunt ces heures as diverses gentz du Roialme par le grant nombre des Attournees nient sachantz naprises de la loye, comme ils soloient estre pardevant.'† These words seem to point back to a period when Attorneys were imbued with a knowledge of legal science. 110 years had passed since the Justices of the Common Pleas were directed by Edward I. to select 140 of 'the better-informed, more lawyerlike and more addicted to study' to enjoy an exclusive right of representing suitors as Attorneys in all the Courts of Common Law ('et se de negotiis in eâdem curiâ intromittant, et alii non'). Three generations had come and gone; during the third the Apprentices may have withdrawn from 'practising Attorneyship,' and a race of 'illiterate' Attorneys may have taken their place. The short period during which Apprentices would thus have acted as Attorneys might account for the absence of any notice of their so acting in the Year-books‡ and the text writers of the period. Mr. Marshall,

* Ruffhead erroneously translates "mys en rolle," "put in *the* roll."

† This interesting Act was repealed by the Stat. 6 & 7 Vict. cap. 73, s. 1.

‡ See infra as to Mr. Horwood's mistake about Westcote: Year-book, 30 & 31 Edw. I. 151.

however, says* that 'the separation between Attorneys and Apprentices had certainly not taken place in the reign of Edward IV.'† That the separation had taken place in the reign of Henry VII.‡ is evident from the following passage in the Statute 11 Henry VII. c. 12:—'A mean to help and speed poor persons in their suits' (A.D. 1494). ' The Justices shall assign to the same poor person, or persons, *Counsel learned*, by their discretions, which shall give their counsels, taking nothing for the same. And *likewise* the Justices shall appoint *Attorney* or *Attorneys* for the same poor person or persons, and all other officers requisite and necessary to be had for the speed of the said suits, which shall do their duties without any reward for their counsels, help, and business in the same.'

" Mr. Marshall gives ' some curious details' from the 'Liber Albus.' written in the reign of Henry V.,§ but containing a digest of regulations affecting the Sheriffs' Court and Hustings Court of the City of London of earlier date. This book throughout treats the Pleaders and the Attorneys practising in these inferior Courts as distinct. *E.g.* in Book III., part 4, under the title, 'Quid ministri jurent animatim,' the following entry occurs:—'Item, the *Pleaders*, who are commonly residing in the city, shall be sworn, that they will not plead or

---

* P. 9.   † A.D. 1461—1483.
‡ A.D. 1485—1509.   § A.D. 1413—1422.

give Counsel against the usages and franchises of the City of London, but that they will maintain the same to the best of their power both within the city and without. Item : the *Attorneys* shall be sworn in the same manner and further that they will not answer as Attorney for any one, if they are not admitted and set forth in the Roll.* The right of appearing by Attorney was still considered a privilege. Thus a foreigner† impleaded in the Court of Hustings for land, which he held in the City, could appoint an Attorney to represent him in the suit: but he could not appoint an Attorney to represent him in a suit instituted *by him* against a citizen.‡

"It is noteworthy too, that about the same time ' that the Order in Parliament empowering Apprentices to act as Attorneys in the King's Court was passed, a regulation was made by the City of London,

---

* Liber Albus: Book III., part 4. p. 473.

† *i. e.* One not a citizen of the City of London.

‡ Liber Albus : B. I. pt. 1, c. 7 : B. I. pt. 2, p. 63. Mr. Marshall's inaccuracy of reference haunts him even in his references to the Liber Albus. He mixes up the 'head' (heading?) ' Coment l'Attornes et autres communes Pledours usent lour Office ' with ' B. IV. pp. 570-399 (sic !) ' The heading will be found in B. III. p. 525. The regulations he mentions as to imprisonment of Attorneys for negligence, and their maximum fee of 40 pence will be found in B. IV. p. 571-2. The date of these regulations was Edward I. (imprisonment) and Edw. III. (40 pence) ; that of the oaths of Pleaders and Attorneys was Hen. VI. ! (See Ryley, p. 644).

that in the Hustings Court and Sheriffs Court, 'No Countor shall be either Attorney or Essonier, no Attorney shall be a Countor or Essonier and no Essonier a Countor or Attorney.'*

"The suggestion that I have ventured to throw out, that if Apprentices were the first Attorneys-at-law, in the Superior Courts, the union of the two branches of the profession in the same person only lasted for about 100 years, receives some strength from the mention of Counsel and Attorney as distinct from each other in the 16th year of Richard II. (A.D. 1392) ten years before the Statute 4 Hen. IV. :—'Que nul clerc qui escrivent recordes et pleas soit Atturne, ne de Conseill:' Rolls of Parliament : Vol. III. p. 306.

"Sir John Fortescue's work, 'De Laudibus Legum Angliæ,' was written in the reign of Edward IV., A.D. 1463. Sir Walter Raleigh terms the author, 'that notable bulwark of our laws.' Sir John Fortescue mentions the Jurisperiti of his day, viz. :—Serjeants-at-law, and Apprentices-at-law.† He does not include under that title, Attorneys at-law. Indeed he does not condescend to notice them!

"Mr. Marshall argues, that, because in the Paston Letters 'matters which fall' (by which he means,

* Liber Albus, Book 4, 570. The letter 'A' shews the date of the regulation. See p. 644, of Mr. Ryley's Edition.

† 'Advocati, qui in regno Angliæ Servientes-ad-Legem appellantur, similiter et alii periti, quos Apprenticios vulgus denominat.' (c. 8.)

now fall) 'within the exclusive province of the Attorney,' were 'disposed' of by 'Counsel,' ergo, Attorneys acted then as Counsel (or, as he terms them 'Pleaders'). But the matters to which he refers, were *then* considered within the exclusive province of Counsel, and not only then, but for centuries afterwards. It is only by a series of encroachments on the Bar that Attorneys have acquired a monopoly in these matters."

"What are the matters in question?" asked Perceval.

"'Instructions for actions,' 'marriage treaties,' 'realizing securities,' 'settlements of pending suits,' 'communication with the client for deeds to be produced in evidence.'* 'Men like Yelverton and Paston,' says Mr. Marshall,† 'transacted business with which no modern Barrister would be permitted to interfere.' Ergo, I suppose Yelverton and Paston were Attorneys! There is not a tittle of evidence to be found in any text book or report for Mr. Marshall's quaint fancy that 'Pleaders,' *i.e.* Counsel, were called in the country, 'Attorneys,' and in the metropolis, 'Apprentices.'

"The expression 'Homines Consiliarii,' which Mr. Marshall thinks might include Attorneys, is expressly tied by Sir Edward Coke to Apprentices, in his Commentary on 28 Edward I. c. 11: 'Councell' (a term used in that Statute), 'is taken of advice and direction, and that is to be had of three persons.

---

* P. 12. † P. 14. ‡ 2 Inst. 563-4.

1. Of Servientes-ad-Legem; 2. Of Apprentices-atlaw, in pleading called Homines Consiliarii, et in lege periti; and these have officium ingenii. 3. Attorneys of law, that have officium laboris, in following the advice of the learned and despatching matters of course and experience.'

"Mr. Marshall's difficulties all arise from his failing to perceive that the duties of the Attorney were, even when he became an Attorney-*at-law*, very restricted indeed. So late as the reign of Henry VI. it was mentioned by the Legislature* as singular that certain Attorneys 'had no other thing to live upon, but only their gain by the practise of Attorneyship;' which seems to shew that it was not an uncommon occurrence for persons to unite the profession of Attorney with some lay calling. Mr. Shaw Lefevre has pointed out† that 'up to quite a late period of our legal history, all the more important duties were undertaken by Counsel.' .... 'The Attorney was a mere ministerial Officer conducting the suit through the forms of the Court.' This agrees with the judgment of Lord Chief Justice Campbell in the case of Doe d. Bennett, *v.* Hale.‡ 'For a long time the Attorney only sued out process and did what was necessary in the offices of the Court for bringing the cause to trial and for having execution on the judgment.' So also Mr. Pulling, in his standard work

---
* Stat. 33 Hen. VI. cap. 7.   † P. 19.
‡ 15 Q.B. 171. See p. 185.

on Attorneys :'*—' The practice of Attorneys and Solicitors at the present day usually extends over a much wider field than the terms Attorney and Solicitor import, *encroaching*, to a great degree, on the formerly *exclusive* province of Barristers.'"

" This is turning the tables on Mr. Marshall and Mr. Saunders with a vengeance," said Percival, rubbing his hands gleefully. "If the Attorneys continue to encroach upon us, what say you to an agitation for the repeal of the Statutes,† which consecrate their peculiar privileges?"

* P. 10 (3rd Edn.)
† 'There is an Act (2 Geo. II. c. 23) which gives Attorneys a monopoly in their department of practice and protects them with penalties.' Mr. Shaw Lefevre on The Discipline of the Bar, p. 22. [This Act was repealed by the Stat. 6 & 7 Vict. c. 73.] 'No encroachment by the Bar or any other class of persons on the exclusive privileges of Attorneys is possible, so long as the Attorneys' Act, 6 & 7, Vict. c. 73, remains unrepealed.'—Report of the Law Amendment Society on the Bar, the Attorney and the Client, p. 12. "No person shall act, as an Attorney or Solicitor, unless such person shall have been admitted and enrolled as an Attorney or Solicitor." 6 & 7 Vict. c. 73. s. 2.

SECTION IV.

THE YEAR-BOOKS.

"Mr. Marshall appeals to the Year-books 20 and 21 Edw. I. and 30 and 31 Edw. I;* and to these Year-books I shall chiefly confine myself. Mr. Marshall says that there are 'numerous instances' to be 'found' in these Year-books of Attorneys 'appearing and arguing before the Justices in Itinere.' He gives three references, in proof of this:—The first is to the Cornish Iter, 30 Edw. I. p. 160—(a mistake, evidently, for p. 162.) In a writ of entry brought by Richard Wysard and Catherine his wife against B, 'B's Attorney, when the inquisition was about to be taken, said, that the tenements were taken into the King's hands, wherefore, &c. Berrewik, J.— The tenements are taken into the King's hands, saving all persons' rights: and he took the inquisition, which found for Richard and Catherine.' In this case, the parties originally were Richard and Catherine, the plaintiffs, and B the defendant. 'On another day,' B being absent, possibly having made de-

* These Year-books may be consulted by the reader, who is ignorant of Norman-French, as Mr. Horwood, under the direction of the Master of the Rolls, has translated them; and the translation and the original text are placed in juxtaposition, so that the accuracy of the former may be tested by the reader acquainted with the latter.

fault,' the person who appeared in his stead, *i.e.*, his Attorney, explained that the lands were taken into the King's hands—a matter of fact merely. The meaning of the words ' wherefore &c.,' is cleared up by the report of another case in this Year-book.*
' A writ was brought against a man and his wife; the husband made default, &c.; the wife came into Court and prayed to be admitted to defend her right, and she was admitted. She said, Sir, my husband is a fugitive and all our lands are taken into the King's hands, *wherefore* we do not think that we ought to answer concerning these tenements, which are in the King's hands.—Berrewik, J.: You have been admitted to defend your right; answer in such wise as you think best.' Here a married woman was allowed to explain to the Court a similar matter of fact. If Mr. Marshall contends that Attorneys had a right of audience in the Superior Courts, he must concede that married women had the same right in civil cases. How Mr. Jacob Bright would gloat over this concession! B's Attorney, in the case cited by Mr. Marshall, wanted to get rid of the action (just as the lady did of the action at p. 152) by stating, as a matter of fact, that the tenements had been taken into the King's hands. But Mr. Justice Berrewik said that that, no doubt, was quite true, but ' all persons rights were saved,'

* P. 152.

and, therefore, the inquisition must be taken. In a case reported at p. 188, Mutford observed that the King never allows any person's right to be delayed in such a case by reason of his seisin.*
" The second case, cited by Mr. Marshall, is from 31 Edw. I., p. 338 (Mr. Marshall cites it erroneously as from 30 Edw. I.) ' Sheweth unto you William, the son of Jordan of Standish, by his Attorney, that John, the Clerk of Langeton, tortuously deforces him of the advowson of the chapel of Wygan.' The phrase, ' sheweth unto you A. B.' is a common form of opening the pleadings,† and does not mean that the person mentioned addressed the Court. It repeatedly occurs where Counsel are employed for the plaintiff; and where the words, ' by his Attorney,' follow, it is not dissimilar from the form now in use:—'A. B. by C. D., his Attorney, sues E. F., for that,' &c.; only that in the Year-books the Attorney's name is never mentioned. In the present case of Standish v. Langeton, the vivâ voce pleadings on behalf of the defendant were conducted, not by his nameless Attorney, but by Willoughby, who became Lord Chief Justice of the Court of Common Pleas in Ireland in 18 Edw. II.; in 2 Edw. III. a Justice

* See 20 & 21 Edw. I. Year-book 12, 98, 236 (in default, land seized into King's hands.)

† See this Year-book, pp. 14, 22, 40, 42, &c. In the Yearbook 20 & 21 Edw. I., p. 472, *Kynge counted thus*, ' Sheweth unto you, &c , R. de Verdoun, who is here, that the Abbot, &c.'

of the Common Pleas in England; in 4 Edw. III.
a Justice of the Court of King's Bench in England;
and in 14 Edw. III. a Justice of the Common
Pleas in England again. In the 1st year of Edw.
III., having been removed from the Chief Justice-
ship of the Common Pleas in Ireland, 'he resumed,'
says Mr. Foss (from whom these facts are taken),*
'his practice *at the English Bar*, as he is mentioned
as *an Advocate* in the Year-book of that year.'
Although the count commences, 'sheweth unto
you William, the son of Jordan of Standish, by his
Attorney,' yet Willoughby speaks of the count as
his: 'W,e now tell you that it was a chapel iu the
time of our† ancestor, as we have counted' (p. 340).

" The third case cited by Mr. Marshall is from
31 Edw. I., p. 354-8. Mr. Marshall twice refers
to this case, and both his references are erroneous.
At p. 6 he cites it as from the Cornish Iter, 30
Edw. I., p. 358; at p. 8 he cites it as from the
Stafford Iter, 21 Edw. I., p. 424. It is a case
decided in Michaelmas Term *in the Court of Com-*

* Vol. III., pp. 537-8.

† This method, on the part of Counsel, of identifying themselves with the party, whether appearing in person or by
Attorney, was common in those days (as it is, indeed, still,
where the party appears by attorney); *e.g.* Counsel for
doweresses, speak of 'our husband' (20 & 21 Edw. I. 150).
'We tell you,' says Counsel in a case reported in this Year-
book (p. 86), 'that your grandfather was seized of the homage
of our grandfather aud your father of the homage of our
father.'

mon Pleas at Westminster! Thomas de Grandcourt wished to levy a fine* to one Edmund. Several objections to levying the fine were raised by Warrlee, Counsel for Adam Bacon. He alleged that Thomas could give no estate to Edmund by the acknowledgment, as all his interest had, by virtue of a certain assignment and attornment passed to Adam, who now sought to prevent the levying of the fine to his disinheritance. The report proceeds:—

" 'Howard, J. Thomas is here by Attorney against Edmund only; say then, against whom you would aver this assignment and this attornment.

"' Warr. Against him, who is desiring to acknowledge to our disinheritance.

" 'Howard, J. He is here by Attorney against Edmund only, and not against you.

" 'Herle. We have seen cases, where, when† the Attorney could not explain the matter in dispute, the principal has been made to come—(homme ad *fet venir* le principal.') Thomas de Grandcourt was not present, having put an Attorney in his place for the purpose of levying the fine to Edmund. Howard, J. having raised the difficulty that the Attorney of Thomas de Grandcourt

---

* 'A fictitious suit in the Court of Common Pleas at Westminster.' 1 Steph. Bl. 537. (Ed. 1853).

† This necessary word is omitted by Mr. Marshall.

could not represent him as against Adam Bacon, Herle, apparently as an 'amicus Curiæ,' suggested that Thomas himself might be called to explain all about the alleged assignment and attornment, as a witness, on his own behalf. The Attorney of Thomas could not explain the matter, having been appointed for another purpose, and, therefore, knowing nothing about it. There is not a tittle of evidence in favor of the right of audience of Attorneys in the Superior Courts in the capacity of Advocates, to be gathered from this statement of Herle. As an illustration of Mr. Marshall's inaccuracy, I may mention that he cites this statement as that of 'Herle, J.' Mr. Horwood carefully points out* that 'the names of the Judges are printed in small capitals and the names of the Counsel in italics;' and the name of Herle is printed in italics in the case of Thomas de Grandcourt. The case occurred in 1302, and Herle was not made a Judge till 1320,† eighteen years after the date of this case! The mistake of Mr. Marshall is the more remarkable, because Mr. Horwood the Editor, cites the statement of Herle in his Preface,‡ but without the "J." appendant. I need scarcely point out, in dismissing this case, that the assumption by an Attorney in the Court of Common Pleas of any right of audience, would have been an infringement

---

* Y. B. 30 and 31 Edw. I. page 3.
† Foss's Judges, vol. 3, p. 440-1.
‡ Page xxviii.

of the exclusive right of audience in that Court enjoyed by the Serjeants-at-law.

"A case is mentioned at p. 300 of the Y. B. 20 and 21 Edw. I., as having occurred in the Common Bench. The question arose in it, whether, where the husband, before the Statute de Douis (13 Edw. I. st. 1), aliened a tenement, which had been granted to him and the grantor's daughter in frankmarriage, and then died, and the wife confirmed her husband's act after the Statute, their issue could recover by writ of Formedon? The person who makes a Note of the case is of opinion that they could, observing that if a fine were under these circumstances levied after the Statute, it could not hold good; à fortiori, the confirmation could not hold good, being a thing of a lower nature. The Report then proceeds:—'*The Attorney*'—(*i. e.* for the alienee, 'one Robert')—'*said*, that in this case the confirmation was good, though a fine would not have been good: and he said, that the Confirmation was effective to for ever bar the issue from an action, even though he had nothing by descent.' Here we have the Attorney for one of the parties apparently laying down Law to the Court of Common Pleas, where the Serjeants had an exclusive right of audience!

"At p. 478 of the Y. B. 30 and 31 Edward I., the following case occurs:—'In an attachment on a Prohibition the Defendants waged their law, that they did not prosecute any Plea, &c. When they came to the Bar to do their law, the Attorney (of the Plaintiff) said, As to T, we will release the law.'

"'Malore, J. Then you don't wish to sue T?

"'No.

"'Malore (? Mellor) J. Let them go quit. Adieu.'

"The forensic jargon makes the case a little unintelligible. The Plaintiff had sued out a writ of attachment against T, and his co-Defendants, for proceeding in the Ecclesistical Courts against the Plaintiff, contrary to a writ of prohibition. The Defendants 'waged their law,' *i. e.* offered to swear they did not proceed after prohibition: and on the day fixed for 'doing their law,' *i. e.* for swearing, they came, (as was usual) to the bar of the Court. Each of the Defendants would then have had to go through the ceremony of swearing that he did not proceed after prohibition, and his compurgators would next have had to swear that they believed him. While the Defendants, however, were standing at the bar, ready to go through the ceremony, which would have operated to defeat the attachment, the Plaintiff's Attorney, in the Plaintiff's absence, expressed his willingness to let one of them off. This excited Mr. Justice Malore's surprise, and he enquired if the Plaintiff's Attorney really meant it. On his assuring him that he did, the Judge let the Defendants all off, the Attorney, apparently, being ignorant of the rule that a release as to one of several persons jointly liable, is a release as to them all.—A formal ceremony like 'wager of law' required no argument of Counsel. The name of the Judge who dismissed the case seems to shew, likewise, that the 'law' was to have been 'done' in *the Court of Common Pleas :*[*] and it is conceded that the Attorneys had no right of audience in *that* Court.

"Passing on to the Year-books of 32 and 33 Edward I., we come first upon the case of a husband appearing as Attorney for his wife.[†] 'The husband came in proper person and answered as Attorney for his wife.' The expression means that he appeared as Attorney for his wife in her absence. The inquest had passed for himself and his wife, who were the Defendants in a writ of entry sur disseisin en le post: and therefore there was nothing for him to 'answer.' He came, simply, on his own behalf and on his wife's, to receive the Judgment of the Court in his and her favour.—What Court that was is evident from the report. 'The verdict was sent into *the Bench*,' *i.e.* into the Court of Common Pleas, where Attorneys, it is conceded, had no right of audience.

"The next case in this volume will be found at p. 180. 'A writ of waste was brought against a tenant for term of life; but he did not come either

---

[*] Mr. Justice Mallore was appointed a puisne Justice of this Court in 1293, and was removed in 1309:—(See Foss's Judges, vol. iii. pp. 125, 278. [†] P. 64.

by summons or by attachment, in consequence of which the distress was awarded, and was returned at the three weeks of Easter; on which day the Sheriff made return that the tenant had nothing in his bailiwick, whereby he could be distrained. Then said the Attorney of the Plaintiff that the tenant had passed away all his tenements to an abbot, who is now the tenant, &c. since the writ was purchased : and he prayed a writ to the Sheriff to enquire of waste according to the Statute, &c. Mallore, J.* You cannot have a Writ according to the Statute,† before the tenant is distrained; and if he do not come at the other day, then the writ, &c. lies; wherefore sue out a distress to distrain the tenant, into whose hands soever the tenements have come.' The similarity of this case, which occurs in the Common Pleas, to that reported in Y. B. 1 Edward III. in which an Attorney prays for a writ of execution, will strike the reader. Praying for a writ of execution, is, as an eminent reporter said to me the other day, rather office-work than Court-work: and the party or his Attorney might pray for it, it seems, in the Common Pleas, without infringing the privileges of the Serjeants.

"The case I mentioned just now, reported 1 Edward III., is more favourable to Mr. Marshall's view than any of the three that he has cited

* His name is, by mistake, printed in italics in the English translation.
† 13 Edw. I. W. 2, c. 14.

in proof of the right of audience of Attorneys in the Superior Courts.* It is, strangely enough, twice reported.† An Attorney is stated to have come to the bar of the Common Pleas, and prayed a writ of execution to the Bishop on behalf of a creditor, whose debtor was a Parson. The writ was granted, on the Attorney explaining that the creditor had been prevented from having execution by the death of Edward II., which caused an abatement of the writ of execution previously granted. Mr. Serjeant Manning sets out this case, and heads it, 'Prayer of Execution in Common Pleas by an Attorney.'‡ As, however, by Mr. Marshall's own shewing,§ the Serjeants had an exclusive right of audience in the Court of Common Pleas, an application and explanation of this sort was evidently regarded as a mere matter of form, and not in the nature of forensic pleading or argument, otherwise it would have been a usurpation of the privileges of the Serjeants by the Attorney.

"At p. 426 of Y. B. 32 and 33 Edw. I., the following case is reported:—A Writ of Cosinage was brought against Thomas the Notary of Oxford, who made default after default. Whereupon Sarah la Power his wife prayed to be received, and she put forward a writing, which said that the Chancellor and

---

* See Year-book, 1 Edw. III. fol. 17, pl. 10. S. C. Edition, 1596, fol. 14, pl. 10.
† Ib. and fol. 5, pl. 33: Edn. 1596, fol. 5a, pl. 33.
‡ P. 267. § P. 7.

the University, &c. had granted the same tenements to Thomas the Notary for the lives of Thomas the Notary and his wife and the children of their first issue. Willoughby'—(Counsel for the Plaintiff)— ' You are not named in the writ; therefore, &c.

"' Hengham, C.J.—We agreed in Parliament'— (13 Edward I. West. 2, c. 3)—'that if the wife be not named in the writ she shall not be received.

" ' Passeleigh '—(Counsel for the Defendant).— ' Then we pray that the Chancellor and the University may be received.

" ' Willoughby.—They are not here in propriâ personâ, therefore, &c.

' " Hengham, C. J.'—We agreed in Parliament' (13 Edward I. West. 2, c. 10)—'that they ought to be received by Attorney, and we have a warrant in this Court, that he who prays, &c. and their Attorney.

" ' Willoughby.—We pray oyer of that warrant.

" ' Hengham, C. J.—You shall not have oyer of our warrant.

" ' Whereupon the University was received by Attorney, who said : The tenements demanded are divisible, in which case no such writ runs; judgment.

" ' Willoughby.—You ought not to be received to abate the writ, therefore, &c.

" ' Passeleigh.—He did not die seized, ready, &c. And the other side said the contrary.'

" Hengham was at this time (1305) Lord Chief

Justice of the Common Pleas, having succeeded to that office on the death of Lord Chief Justice de Metingham, in 1301.* The case appears to have occurred during term in the Court of Common Pleas. The Act of Parliament, to which Lord Chief Justice Hengham referred was the Statute of Westminster 2, A.D. 1285, which gave suitors a power to make a general Attorney. The University put in a plea by Attorney; and Willoughby objected that the University had no right to do so. The Attorney does not attempt to argue the question; but Passeleigh, as Counsel for the Defendant, pleads in bar to the action, traversing the seisin of the relative, through whom, by Writ de Consanguinitate (Cosinage), the Plaintiff claimed.

"These cases shew in what sense the words of Mr. Horwood†—'The Attorneys took part even where Counsel were employed,' are to be understood, with reference to the Court of Common Pleas.

"The argument from analogy may fairly be used. If we find Attorneys 'taking part' in the Court of Common Pleas, where the Serjeants had an exclusive right of audience, it need not surprise us to find them 'taking part' in other Courts and on Circuit. And if the 'part' which they 'took' in the Court of Common Pleas did not carry with it the right of audience *as Advocates*, neither did it in the other Courts and on Circuit. It is

* Foss's Judges, vol. 3, p. 263.
† P. xxviii. of Preface to 30 and 31 Eliz.

not a little singular, however, that the majority of cases in which Attorneys in these three volumes are represented as 'taking part' are cases in the Court of Common Pleas! Throughout the three volumes I can only find the following cases in other Courts and on Circuit where the Attorney '*took part.*'—The case on the Cornish Iter 30 Edw. I. p. 162, mentioned by Mr. Marshall and already discussed;"* the case of Mortymer *v.* Mortymer, 20 and 21 Edward I., p. 188, and the case of Tovyn *v.* William, 30 and 31 Edward I. p. 146. The case of Mortymer *v.* Mortymer, 20 and 21 Edward I., page 188, is as follows:—

"'Roger Mortymer brought a Writ of Detinue of Charter against Dame Maud de Mortymer; who came by Attorney, and said, Sir, on the day and in the year, in which they say that the Charter was bailed to Dame Mortymer, Roger le Mortymer her husband, was alive. Judgment, if she be bound to answer. If you adjudge that she ought, she will answer willingly.' This is Maud's plea in bar of the action—that she was a feme covert at the time the Charter was bailed to her and could not, therefore, bind herself. The plea is put in by her Attorney, instead of by herself, though so completely is the Attorney substituted for her that it is she, who is spoken of as coming and putting in the plea. She 'came by her Attorney and said.' As

* The case 31 Edw. I. p. 338 does not go for anything, as the expression, "Sheweth unto you," is a mere common form.

soon as the plea had been formally put in, Roger's Counsel replies to it. ' Huntingdon :—Sir, our plaint is of the tortious detinue of a Charter which the lady now at this time detains from us: judgment if she ought not now to answer as to her tort. The plea is then supported—by whom? By the Attorney of Maud? No: but by her Counsel, Hugh de Lowther, the 'King's Serjeant.' Spigornel follows on the same side: and Howard replies to him on behalf of Roger. The functions of the Advocate are discharged by Lowther and Spigornel for the Defendant, and by Huntingdon and Howard for the Plaintiff. The Attorney of Maud appears upon the scene solely as her substitute in the action.*

" The case of Tovyn *v.* William is as follows :— ' Sheweth unto you R. Tovyn, by his Attorney, who is here, that William, who is there, tortiously does not do suit to his mill of B, as he ought and used to do; and tortiously for this, that the said William used to grind at the mill all his wheat, and the corn and malt baked and brewed at his house paying therefor the twentieth vessel, until five years ago the said William withdrew his suit tortiously and to the damage,' &c. Willoughby pleaded in bar of the action, as Counsel for William, the Defendant, 'I never did suit, and I owe you no suit ready, &c. Therefore to the country,'—(*i.e.*, an

* Y. B. 20 and 21 Edw. I. 188.

issue of fact was arrived at, to be tried by a Jury.) The case would, regularly, end here ; but the reporter adds :—' A tenant came and admitted the suit; and inasmuch as he, at first, denied the suit, but afterwards admitted it, it was adjudged that he should do the suit, and that he should be fined. R.'s,' (*i.e.*, R. Tovyn's) ' Attorney said, Sir, forgive him the fine, for he is poor. Berrewik, J. You have said well for him. Sheriff, take pledges of him for the fine.'*

The Attorney of the Plaintiff did nothing more than a merciful Plaintiff might do; *i.e.*, asked the Judge to deal leniently with the Defendant. The count ran in the common form.

" It does not strike me that in any of these cases on Circuit or in the King's Bench or Exchequer, the Attorney claimed or exercised any right, which he did not equally enjoy in the Common Pleas.

" In order to enlarge the domain of that creature of his own fancy, the Attorney-advocate, Mr. Marshall confines the Serjeants as much as possible to the Court of Common Pleas (the Bench.) ' There are' but ' two instances,' says Mr. Marshall,† ' in the Year-books of 21 Edw. I. of Serjeants appearing in Itinere, but in each case they represented the Crown in matters in which the rights of the Crown were affected.' It seems as if Mr. Marshall had

* Y. B. 30 and 31 Edw. I. 146-9.
† P. 7, note.

looked out 'Serjeants' in the Index to the Year-books, 20 and 21 Edw. I., and finding 'Serjeant (the King's,) pp. 68, 422,' and no other reference, concluded that these were the only instances of Serjeants appearing on Circuit. At p. 188, however, Sir Ralph de Toune, we are told, came into Court, '*and he ratified all that his Serjeants had said.*' In the report of the case Howard appears as Counsel for Sir Ralph. Lowther appears on the other side, with Spigurnel. The two references given in the Index relate to one and the same person, Hugh de Lowther, who is styled 'The King's Serjeant,' a phrase equivalent to ' qui sequitur pro rege,' given to him, p. 164. His name does not occur in Dugdale's list of Serjeants; but this, I admit, is no pı ɔof that he was not a Serjeant. I may observe, however, that at p. 56 of the Year-book that we are considering, he is mentioned as appearing 'on behalf of the King'—('pur le Roy')—without the title of 'Serjeant.'* Mr. Marshall is in error in supposing that he only appeared on circuit on behalf of the Crown and in cases where the rights of the Crown were affected. In the very next case to that reported at p. 68,† he will be found acting as Counsel for Edmund le Mortimer, a private individual. There are, indeed, few names that occur so frequently on Circuit, as that of Hugh de Lowther; and, except in the two cases cited by Mr. Marshall, and half a dozen

* So also pp. 76, 112, 158, 160, 164, (qui sequitur pro domino Rege), and 418.   † P. 74.

others, he appeared as Counsel for private individuals. He was an ancestor, I may add, of the Earls of Lonsdale, and became a Justice Itinerant in 1307. Mr. Foss* says of him, that he 'practised as an Advocate, and acquired sufficient celebrity in 19 Edward I. to be employed by the King.' Mr. Serjeant Wynne, in his work on the 'Antiquity and Dignity of the Degree of Serjeant-at-law,'† points out the difficulty that there is in deciding whether the Counsel mentioned in the Year-books were Serjeants or not.' 'The Year-books,' he observes, 'are very indistinct, not mentioning whether the Counsel, whose names they preserve, were Serjeants or not.' This, he thinks, 'makes it fruitless to wade through the Year-books in quest of names, which give no information, and which themselves want explanation, being, most of them, expressed in those reports by the first syllable (such as Cant.' Belk.')' The presumption, however, is, that, where the suit was brought in the Court of Common Pleas (which can generally be ascertained in the cases occurring during term by the names of the Judges), *all* the Counsel mentioned in connection with it were Serjeants.

"Although it may be somewhat difficult to distinguish the Counsel, who were Serjeants, from the other Counsel, especially on Circuit, yet there is no difficulty in distinguishing the Counsel, as a body,

* Vol. III. p. 276. † P. 130.

from the Attorneys. The Attorneys are spoken of simply as 'A's Attorney,' 'B's Attorney,' 'C's Attorney,' 'A. B. venit per Attornatum,' &c.; the names of the Attorneys are not given in the report.* The names of the Counsel, on the other hand, are generally given; and can, frequently, be identified with those of Judges at a subsequent period. Take, *e.g.* the case reported in the Yearbooks 20 & 21 Edw. I., p. 268 (which I select at haphazard). The case occurred in the Salop Iter. The Counsel engaged in it were Howard for the Plaintiff, and Spigurnel and Lowther for the Defendant. Howard, as we have seen, is spoken of, on another circuit, this year, as a Serjeant. He became an Itinerant Justice in 1293—the year following that in which these Circuits were held†— 'having attained,' says Mr. Foss,‡ 'sufficient eminence in his profession, to be selected' for that office. Spigurnel became an Itinerant Justice in 1302.§ Lowther, as we have seen, is mentioned as the 'King's Serjeant,' and became an Itinerant Justice in 1307. Mr. Marshall's contention really amounts to this:—that Howard and Spigurnel were both Attorneys! 'The Attorneys would be the ordinary practitioners.' || If we pass from the

* Mr. Horwood gives some names of Attorneys from the Roll of the Cornish Iter, 30 Edw. I. (p. xxix.) but the names are omitted in the Reports.
† Foss's Judges, Vol. III. pp. 107 and 265.
‡ Ib. 266. § Ib. 155. || Page 7.

Year-books 20 & 21 Edw. I. to the Year-books 30 & 31 Edw. I., we find persons appearing on circuit as Counsel, who afterwards became Judges; *e.g.* Mutford, Itinerant Justice, 1307, and Justice of the Common Pleas, 1316;* Westcote, Itinerant Justice, 1310;† Middleton, Itinerant Justice, 1305.‡ Were these eminent men all Attorneys?

" Mr. Reeves, the learned author of the History of English Law, whom Mr. Marshall cites, traces the history of Attorneys, and also gives us specimens of the vivâ voce pleadings preserved in the Year-books; but he never applies the term 'Attorney,' to the persons conducting these pleadings. He styles the persons conducting them either 'Advocates,' or 'Counsel.' 'The Advocate for the plaintiff stated his case; then the Advocate for the defendant put in his plea.' § 'Herle, one of the Counsel for the defendant, demanded judgment of the writ.' ||

" Mr. Horwood, whom Mr. Marshall cites, distinguishes between the Counsel and Attorneys in the Prefaces to the Year-books, which he edited. The persons who conducted the vivâ voce pleadings are termed by him either Advocates,¶ Pleaders,**

---

* Foss's Judges, Vol. iii. pp. 134, 280, 467.
† Ib. p. 313.   ‡ Ib. 132, 279.
§ Vol. II. p. 267.
|| Ib. p. 345, (citing Maynard, 4 Edw. II.)
¶ 32 and 33 Edw. I. Preface passim.
** 30 and 31 Edw. I. Preface, pp. xxiv, xxv, and xxx.

or Counsel.* 'The plaintiff and defendant,' he says, 'appear, as it were, personally before the reader. The Counsel narrates the circumstances of the case; according to the instructions that he received from the plaintiff, and his opponent answers in the version of the defendant.'† Whenever Mr. Horwood mentions the Attorney, which he does frequently,‡ he speaks of him as the 'Attorney' simply, and not as an 'Advocate,' 'Pleader,' or 'Counsel.' There is only one apparent exception. In his Preface to the Year-books, 30 and 31 Edw. I. p. xxviii. Mr. Horwood says, 'That the Attorneys did during the trial refer matters to the discretion of their principals appears from p. 151.' Turning to p. 151, we find the following passage in the Report :—' Westcote, Veez le cy en present: seyt en descrescion de nos mestres.' Mr. Horwood translates this (rather freely, I think) :—' Here he is present; let him be disposed of by our clients.' No mention is made in this case of any Attorney appearing for any of the parties. Even if mention had been made of an Attorney appearing for any of the parties, the Attorney's name would have been omitted (as in the case immediately previous,

* 20 and 21 Edw. I. Preface, p. xviii ; 30 and 31 Edw. I. Preface, pp. xii, xxi, xxviii, xxxi, xliv, xlvi, xlvii, and lii ; 32 and 33 Edw. I. Preface, pp. x, xxv, xxvii, xxx, xxxii, and xxxv.

† 30 and 31 Edw. I. Preface, p. xii.

‡ 30 and 31 Edw. I. Preface, pp. xxviii, xxix, and xxxii; 32 and 33 Edw. I. Preface, pp. xxxii, xxxv, xxxvi, and xl.

that of Tovyn v. William, already cited.) Mr. Horwood was, no doubt, misled by the expression, 'nos mestres,' used by Westcote, which is usually employed to denote the principal of an Attorney. The Report says, ' It was answered by Westcote.' If Westcote had appeared as Attorney, the Report would have said, 'It was answered by R.'s Attorney.' Westcote appeared as Counsel, and not as Attorney, for Robert. That Wesctote was an Advocate, and not an Attorney is also evident from the frequent occurrence of his name among the Counsel who went this Circuit (the Cornish Iter), and from the fact that he became Itinerant Justice in 1310.* 'He was an Advocate,' says Mr. Foss, 'in the Courts.'†

" 'It is clear,' says Mr. Marshall, 'that parties were allowed to appear in person before the Judges in Eyre.'‡ No doubt it is. I will go further, and affirm that, in the vast majority of cases, not

* Foss's Judges, Vol. III. p. 313.
† Ibid. And see List of Counsel, p. 208. Is it not possible that, in this passage of the Year-books, " nos mestres" may mean the Judges presiding at the trial? Robert, the defendant, for whom Westcote was Counsel, alleged that he was merely tenant by the courtesy, and prayed aid of John, the reversioner. John came into Court, and Westcote then alleged that John was not of age. The other side affirmed that he was of age, and wanted to have that issue tried by the country; but Westcote preferred leaving it to the Judges. The Judges inspected the alleged Infant, and adjudged him to be of full age.
‡ P. 6, (note).

merely on the Eyre, but in Banc, the parties appeared in person. Let me illustrate this by a few figures. Out of the 373 cases reported in the Year-books of the 32nd and 33rd Edw. I. one or more of the parties appeared by Attorney in 27 only. In the Year-books 30 and 31 Edw. I. out of the 335 cases reported, one or more of the parties appeared by Attorney in only 9. In the Year-books 20 and 21 Edw. I. out of the 261 cases reported, Attorneys are mentioned as appearing for one or other of the parties only in 6!*

"What becomes, then, of Mr. Marshall's statement (page 7), that 'the Attorneys were the ordinary practitioners on circuit?' The Year-books 20 and 21 Edward I. are taken up almost entirely with the report of cases on Circuit, and it is 'the earliest report of cases on Circuit:' yet there are only six instances of parties appearing by Attorney in the entire volume! Who, then, were the Advocates in the 200 cases on Circuit in which Attorneys

* For convenience of reference, I append here a list of all the instances in which one or other of the parties is stated to have appeared by Attorney, in the Year-books of Edw. I. published under the direction of the Master of the Rolls: 20 and 21 Edw. I. pp. 106, 186, 188, 204, 302, 484. 30 and 31 Edw. I. pp. 16, 114, 146, 162, 338, 350, 478, 482, 549. 32 and 33 Edw. I. pp. 42, 48, 54, 64, 68, 70, 144, 180, 248, 426, 428, 434, 446, 448, 497, 498, 501 (twice), 502, 507, 508, 509, 510, 511 (twice), 525, 529. Dicta about Attorneys will be found, 20 and 21 Edw. I. pp. 202, 244; 30 and 31 Edw. I. 260, 358; 32 and 33 Edw. I. pp. 86, 186.

did not appear? did the party 'speak by Attorney, although he did not appear by Attorney? " It may be, as Mr. Horwood says,* that on the Eyre the parties might elect to *plead* in person; yet a perusal of the Year-books of the reign of Edward I. will shew that when the parties appeared in person, as well as when they appeared by Attorney, they were *assisted by Counsel*, both on the Eyre and in Banc, in the great majority of cases. 'Defaute de Serjeantie,' and not election to plead in person was probably the cause of the mishap, alluded to by Mr. Horwood.† In the case of Richard Talker *v*. B.‡ the Defendant ought, apparently, to have pleaded in bar judgment recovered in a previous suit, which operated as a merger of the original cause of action: instead of which he traversed the Plaintiff's allegations, which the Jury found to be true, and was obliged to pay 18*s* 4*d* by way of damages. This drew from Mr. Justice Berrewik the observation, 'Defaute de bon Serjant fet B. perdre sez deniers.' Mr. Horwood concludes that the Defendant had no Counsel, having 'elected to plead in person.' 'Defaute de Serjeantie,' is, however, a standing complaint of the Commons in the times of the Edwards. Thus in the 38th year of Edward III. (1364) the Commons complained that the suitors were 'thrown back, defeated and de-

---

* Preface to Year-books, 30 and 31 Edward I. p. xxviii.
† Ibid. ‡ Y.B. 30 Edw. I. p. 172.

stroyed,' for 'want of wise Counsel, whereof they can find none, by reason of the uncertainty of the place.' In the case of Blagreve v. Belne, 6 Edward I.,* after long pleadings, the Plaintiff's case suddenly collapsed, 'quia non habuit narratorem.' At a critical moment the Defendant in Talker v. B. may have failed for want of Counsel to advise him. (The absence of Counsel when your case is called on is an evil not entirely unknown to suitors at the present day!) The grievance 'defaute de Serjeantie' is stated by Mr. Serjeant Manning† to have induced King Edward I. to authorize the Judges to allow Apprentices to practise as Advocates.

"'Such a distinction,' says Mr. Marshall,‡ 'as that between being allowed to appear and allowed to speak is quite foreign to the spirit in which justice was then administered.' Mr. Marshall, however, cites,§ apparently with approbation, the observation of Mr. Horwood,‖ that 'in the Bench a litigant would not probably have been allowed to dispense with the services of a Serjeant.' 'In the Bench,' therefore, the parties could not elect to 'plead in person.' Yet in all the cases reported in the Year-books 20 and 21 Edw. I. as having occurred in the Bench, the parties (with one soli-

* 1 Rot. Parl. 4 a. See 2 Rot. Parl. 140 a. b.
† Note to Doe d. Bennett v. Hale, 15 Q.B. 225.
‡ P. 9.   § P. 7 (note).
‖ Preface to the Year-books 30 and 31 Edward I. p. xxviii.

tary exception, already referred to) *appeared* in
person.—This alone is sufficient to disprove Mr.
Marshall's assertion, that there was no distinction
between 'appearing' and 'speaking.' But, as
already stated, a perusal of the Year-books of the
reign of Edw. I. will shew that, in the great
majority of cases, whether the parties appeared in
person or by Attorney, Counsel were employed.
When an argument arose, it was the Counsel on
either side who conducted it, both on Circuit and
in Banc. Only skilled Pleaders could have kept
up the rapid fire of pleas in abatement, pleas in
bar, demurrers, replies, rejoinders, surrejoinders,
rebutters, and surrebutters. The absence of the
names of Counsel, occasionally, is not conclusive
evidence that, in the cases in which no Counsel are
mentioned, no Counsel were engaged. In many
of them a mere note of the point debated is given
by the reporter, accompanied sometimes by the
initials of the names of the parties, sometimes not
even by these initials. In some of them, the
names, no doubt, of the parties occur in the arguments, where we would expect to find the names
of Counsel: but here the use of the analogical
mode of reasoning may not be out of place. The
very first case inserted in the Year-book 20 Edw.
I., under the title 'Pleas in the Common Bench,'—
('Placita de Banco')—seems to contradict the
opinion expressed by Mr. Horwood, and echoed
by Mr. Marshall, that 'a suitor wonld not be

allowed to dispense with the services of a Serjeant in the Bench.' It is a case of replevin. The Defendant, Thomas Bardolf, avowed the taking to be good; inasmuch as it had been presented at his Court Leet that John de Redvers, the Plaintiff, was resident within the precinct of the Leet; and that he was in a decennary, and was amerced for making default, and distrained: 'and so we avow the taking for the amercement.'

"'John. Sir, we ought not to be in a decennary; for the reason that I am a clerk, studying at the schools.

"'Thomas. He cannot say that, for he is our reseant, and all our reseants ought rightfully to come to our Leet; but he made default for which he was amerced. So we pray judgment, if our avowry be not sufficiently good.'

"'John. And we pray judgment, inasmuch as we are a Clerk, studying at the schools. See here the letter of the Bishop and of the Chancellor of the University of Cambridge, which testifies this.—And we pray judgment, &c.'

"The Lord Chief Justice of the Common Pleas then delivers the following judgment of the Court:—'Inasmuch as the person is by his Clerkship (sa Clergye) so privileged that he ought not to do suit, and suit to a Leet ought not to be demanded, by reason of reseance, but by reason of the lay condition of the person, and you have distrained him against the law, it is therefore adjudged that the amercement be annulled, and the beasts be given up in the same condition in which he held them, and that he do recover his damages to be taxed by the Court, and that you be in mercy.' This is the entire case* as reported in the Yearbook, and certainly it is as strong an instance of pleading (*i. e.* conducting the viva voce pleadings) in person, as any that will be found in the reports of cases on Circuit. If, therefore, the names, 'John' and 'Thomas' stand for (say) 'Lowther and Howard' Serjeants-at-law,' in the reports of cases in the Common Pleas, we must be careful of concluding that the names (say) of 'William' and 'Richard,' at p. 32 of the same Year-book, in a case reported in the Hereford Iter mean 'William' and 'Richard,' and cannot by any possibility stand for (say) 'Lowther and Howard, Serjeants-at-law,' Counsel for William and Richard, respectively. The argument from analogy should at least be allowed its due weight.

"Mr. Marshall† fixes the reign of Edward III, (A.D. 1327—1377), as the date at which the Apprentices began to act as Advocates in the Superior Courts, or, as he naïvely phrases it, 'began to be commonly employed in the ordinary business of an Attorney,' *i. e.*, 'appearing and pleading in Court.' Mr. Marshall says that the word 'Apprenticius'

---

* See a similar case 20 and 21 Edw. I. p. 352.
† P. 9.

is the common one for 'Pleader' throughout the Year-books of this reign."*
"Alas! for the Attorneys!" exclaimed Percival.
"Sir William Dugdale," continued Stephen, "supplies Mr. Marshall with two references to the Year-books of the reign of Edward III. in proof of this statement, which are, no doubt, in point. Sir William adds a third reference, which Mr. Marshall does not cite. It is from a later reign,

* The references that Mr. Marshall gives are these:—' Y. B. 1 Edward III. Reg. 29, f. 47 b. 29, Edward III.' This is rather unintelligible; and it involves wading through the Year-book, 1 Edw. III. for the first reference. One is rather stumped by the mysterious 'Reg.' at the commencement of the second reference. The first reference, in extenso, is, 1 Edward III. f. 16, l. 24, Edition 1679; 1 Edward III. f. 13a, l. 52, Edition 1596. The second reference is, 29 Edward III. f. 47, l. 22, Edition 1679; 29 Edward III. f. 47a, l. 29, Edition 1596. How the first reference is given so briefly, and how the 'Reg.' came to be prefixed to the second reference is evident on a perusal of Dugdale and Herbert. In a note at p. 171 of Herbert's "Inns of Court," the second reference is thus given:—' Reg. 29, f. 47b.' Herbert took his reference from Dugdale's Origines, p. 143, prefixing ('Reg.' for ' anno regni') to it. Dugdale gives the first reference '1 Edw. III.' without more, and the second reference, '29 Edw. III. fol. 47 b.' Mr. Marshall's two references are taken from Dugdale, with the addition of Herbert's 'Reg.' to the second reference. Both Dugdale and Herbert are in error in putting ' 47 b,' for 47 a.' Mr. Marshall repeats the error.

Can it be that Mr. Marshall copied the two references, without verifying them?

that of Henry VI; and it seems, at first blush, to be a precedent for a right of audience on the part of Apprentices in the Court of Common Pleas. The point is cleared up by Sir William Follett, in his argument for the Serjeants,* where he shews that the Apprentice was sent by the Court of Exchequer to ask the opinion of the Court of Common Pleas on a case pending in the Exchequer. The Judges of the Common Pleas consulted 'the Serjeants at the bar,' and then sent the reply of their Court to the Exchequer; which, as appears from the report of the very next case,† decided in accordance with the opinion so communicated.

"A few words more as to 'appearance,' and I have done. It is quite evident from the language of the Year-books and the form of recording the appearance on the roll, that the party was supposed to be present in the person of his Attorney. 'A. B., per Attornatum suum, *venit et dicit*.' 'Sir Philip came by Attorney.' 'The woman *came* by Attorney and *prayed* to be received.' It is equally evident that in the cases in which the party appeared by Attorney, the party himself was absent, and the Attorney himself was present, bodily, in Court. On the other hand, where the party ap-

---

* Reported, Manning's Serv. ad Leg. 49.

† D'Arcy *v.* the Abbot of Rowham, H. 2 H. 6, fo. 5, pl. 1. The supposed case is reported, M. 2 H. 6, fo. 5, pl. 3.

peared in person, he himself was present, bodily, in Court. Thus, in the first of the six cases, in which one or other of the parties appeared by Attorney, in Year-books 20 & 21 Edw. I. (p. 106), it is reported that B. (the Defendant) 'came and appeared in person,' ' and C.' (the Defendant's wife) ' by Attorney.' ' On another day came.C., the wife of B., and said,' &c. In 30 & 31 Edw. I, p. 482, where the co-plaintiffs, in a writ of account, had separate interests, the Attorneys, appointed to represent them as against the Defendant, could not represent them as against each other: 'and because they *were not present* in person ('en propre persone'), and had not an Attorney, except against A.' (the Defendant), 'the Attorneys were told that their principals (lour meistres) were *to be personally* (en propre persone) *in Court* at the Quinzain of Easter.' In the first case in the 32 & 33 Edw. I. in which the plaintiff appeared by Attorney, the report proceeds :*—'A.' (the plaintiff), who came by Attorney, sued out the per quæ servitia against B.; and prayed attornment. Herte (defendant's Counsel): 'If B. were willing to attorn to A., on condition that he agreed to warrant and acquit, the Attorney could not do this, so we think that he ought to come in person' (qu'il covent *quil veyngne meisme en propre persone*). In another case in this volume† (replevin for a cow), Mr. Justice Howard asked,

* P. 42. † P. 54.

'Is A. (plaintiff) here by Attorney or in proper person? Tilton (Counsel for defendant): By Attorney. Howard, J. Cause him to be here next Monday in proper person. On that day he came in proper person.' Again:* 'A man and his wife brought a writ of entry sur disseisin en le post. On the day when the verdict' (which was in their favour) 'was sent into the Bench, the husband came in proper person, and answered as *Attorney for his wife:* and it was adjudged that execution should be stayed for a fortnight in order that he might bring his wife (feyt venir sa feme—literally, *cause her to come.*') These instances shew conclusively that the Attorney appeared in the absence of the party, and that it was only when the party appeared in person, that the party was, bodily, present in Court. We are now speaking of a state of things which existed 600 years ago. What possible analogy can there be between this system, and the one pursued at the present day? Nowadays, if the party appears in person, it means that he conducts his own case, performing the duties of party, Attorney, and Counsel.† If the party appears by Attorney, it means that he appears in propriâ personâ, in Court all the same; but he comes, flanked by two sets of agents, one of whom

---

* P. 64.

† The case of Doe d. Bennett *v.* Hale, 15 Q.B. 171, shews, however, that he may, if he pleases, instruct Counsel.

is called an Attorney, and the other a Barrister. The legal agent, called an Attorney, is employed by the party; the legal agent, called a Barrister, is employed by the legal agent, called an Attorney. The two legal agents appear in person, in the sense of being present in Court during the trial. The duties of the legal agent called an Attorney are, previous to the trial, to see the party and his witnesses, to advise the former, and extract the raw material of the evidence from the latter, to satisfy all the legal formalities, and on the evening, or possibly the morning of the trial, thrust a huge, but well-digested mass of closely-written paper into the hands of the other legal agent, called a Barrister, who knows nothing either of the party or of the witnesses, but who is expected by his patron, the Attorney, to assimilate the well-digested mass of closely-written paper in the course of the evening, or morning, as the case may be, and (as they say at Oxford) 'spit it out' in open Court at the trial!

"I cannot help thinking that a good deal of the confusion of thought exhibited by writers on the legal system of the time of Edward I., arises from want of due attention to the change that, in the course of six centuries, has taken place with respect to 'appearance.'

"Whether the right, which at a subsequent period to that of Edward I., the suitor undoubtedly exercised, of pleading in person, when he appeared in person, in Courts other than the Common Pleas, could be transferred to the Attorney, when the suitor appeared by Attorney, or could not, is, indeed, to my mind, wholly immaterial. If the Attorney had a right of audience in the times of the Plantagenets, or of the Princes of York and Lancaster (which I don't admit),* he enjoyed it solely because the party would or might have addressed the Court, or exercised the same right of audience, if he had been present in Court. Any privilege of addressing the Court or right of audience that the Attorney may have enjoyed depended on his character of *substitute* for the party. The party, though absent, was considered to have 'come and spoken' by the mouth of his Attorney, deriving, from the appointment, the same advantages as if he were present. As soon as the Attorney lost his character of substitute, he lost with it, any claim, that he may have had, to address the Court.

"Under the existing system, the party, by appointing an Attorney, sacrifices his right of audience. If the party shuts his own mouth by appointing an Attorney, à fortiori he shuts the mouth of his Attorney, who has no claim to be heard, except as

---

* It is remarkable that in the case of Paston *v.* Genney, A.D. 1471, Bryan, C. J. observes, 'nul doit pleder icy per auter forsque Serjant, mes *un apprentice et chescun auter en son matter demesne* sera resceu de pleder *aillors.*' T. 11 Edw. IV. f. 3 pl. 4.

the substitute for the party. The Counsel now, as formerly, argues on behalf both of parties and Attorneys: but whereas he formerly argued for the party, when the party appeared in person, and for the Attorney, when the party appeared by Attorney, the Counsel now does not argue for the party, when the party appears in person; and, when the party appears by Attorney, the Counsel argues for both party and Attorney."

" And now," cried Percival, " I think I can sum up. There is no conclusive evidence that the Attorney had a right of audience in the Superior Courts. If he had any such right, it was solely by virtue of his character of substitute for the party, in the party's absence. The change in the condition of the Attorney from an Attorney layman to an Attorney-del-ley, did not give him a right of audience in the Superior Courts, at least not quâ Attorney, if he did not enjoy that right before. On the hypothesis that a temporary amalgamation of the two branches of the profession, in the person of the Apprentice-attorney, took place, the Attorney had a right of audience in the Superior Courts, while the temporary amalgamation lasted, but only quâ Apprentice, not quâ Attorney ; it ceased, when the final separation (if any) of the two branches of the profession took place. The Attorney's character of substitute for the party, the only ground on which, quâ Attorney, he could ever have enjoyed a right of audience in the Superior

Courts, has long since become obsolete, the party always being present in propriâ personâ at the trial. Argal, the Attorney's claim to a right of audience in the Superior Courts is dismissed—and with costs."

(HERE ENDETH Y^E "SKETCH.")

§ 5. THE OFFICE OF JUDGE PROMOTED BY THE ATTORNEYS AGAINST THE INNS OF COURT.

A few days after the discussion of Messieurs Rich and Readymoney on the right of audience of Attorneys in the Superior Courts, Mr. Readymoney, while "interviewing," as usual, the senior partner, suddenly exclaimed, " By the way, we took only one point the other day, touching the ' Wrongs of Attorneys '—the Right of Audience in the Superior Courts. You mentioned, I think, that there are other things from which we are rigidly shut out, but to which, if there be any virtue in historical precedent, our constitutional right is clear."

" Well, there's the right of membership in the Inns of Court," said Mr. Rich:—" Whatever mistiness and obscurity there may be about our right of audience in the Superior Courts, there is none whatever about our right of membership in the Inns of Court. It rests upon the most solemn sanctions."

" Let's discuss that point this morning," said Readymoney. " Business is business, I know: but still we can give half-an-hour to this interesting subject."

Mr. Rich was nothing loth to display his antiquarian lore to his junior partner, and was about to open the subject, when Mr. Readymoney exclaimed,

" I ought to tell you that I've been looking into a great authority on the history of the Legal Profession, Mr. Serjeant Manning,"—

" Great authority!" interrupted Mr. Rich, contemptuously; " Why don't you know that he stole his black letter illustrations from the chambers of Mr. Serjeant Wilde, for whose use Griffiths had compiled them."

" ' Who's Griffiths?' " enquired Mr. Readymoney, flippantly.

Mr. Rich looked reproachfully at his junior partner, but, taking his question *en serieux*, replied :—

" A translator of ancient Records, and Master."

" Never mind," said Mr. Readymoney, " the Serjeant's authorities, whether he consulted them himself, or took them at second-hand, are unimpeachable. Mr. Macqueen, too, in that Lecture of his that you cited, terms Mr. Serjeant Manning's Report of ' The Serjeant's Case,' ' Serjeant Manning's *most learned* Report.' There is a conclusion that Mr. Serjeant Manning draws, which has a direct bearing on the question before us. His authorities, he says, prove that 'Apprentices-at-law and Attorneys-at-law formerly constituted one class.' The case which he cites in proof of it is taken from the

11th year of Edward III. Now Mr. Marshall admits,* as I understand, that Apprentices at that period 'began to be commonly employed in the ordinary business of Attorneys—*i.e.* appearing and pleading in Court.'"

"Certainly," said Mr. Rich. "Prior to that reign Attorneys were the Junior Bar, the Serjeants the Senior. In the reign of Edward III. the Apprentices, or pupils, began to act as Attorneys and Advocates."

"After all," said Mr. Readymoney, "it is not a matter of much importance, with respect to the claims of the Attorneys at the present day upon the Inns of Court, whether in the days of the Plantagenets, when the foundations of the Inns of Court were laid, the Attorneys acted as Advocates, or the Apprentices as Advocates and Attorneys. One thing is clear, that the Inns of Court were designed to be of benefit to the entire Legal Profession."

"Undoubtedly," said Mr. Rich. "If the views of Mr. Marshall, Mr. Macqueen, and Sir William Dugdale be correct, then the Inns of Court owe their origin to the necessity of educating a race of Attorney-advocates. If the views of Mr. Serjeant Manning and Mr. Foss be correct, then the Inns of Court owe their origin to the necessity of providing a legal education for the

* P. 9.

Apprentice-attorney, as Mr. Serjeant Manning calls him, or Barrister-attorney, as he would now be called. Mr. Clode's statement to the Royal Commission on the Inns of Court and Chancery,* in 1854, would fit in with either theory :—' The selection of a body of persons qualified to act as Attorneys in the Courts mainly contributed to the establishment of the Inns of Court and Chancery, and, accordingly, to† both class‡ of Inns *the Attorneys had for centuries the right of membership.*' Mr. Macqueen states§ that ' as matter of right, it would appear that the Attorneys did not properly belong to the Inns of Court.' ' for,' he says, ' I find some entries stating that they were admitted ex gratiâ.' I have never seen any of these entries, and I take leave to set over against them, if they do exist, the express authority of all the Courts of Common Law at Westminster. In Michaelmas Term, 1704, all the Courts of Common Law at Westminster made a Rule, to which I shall presently have occasion to refer, and in the preamble they stated, that 'the ancient custom and usage' was that Attorneys should be 'admitted into the Inns of Court or Chancery,' 'by which they might be resorted to, and the business of law better managed, to the greater ease of the Queen's' (Anne's) 'subjects, the neglect whereof is to the

---

* Printed in the Appendix to the Commissioners' Report, p. 295.   † ? In.   ‡ ? Classes.   § P. 15.

great detriment and decay of the Societies of the Law.'* Nothing could well be more authoritative than this ; and it fully bears out Mr. Marshall's statement† that 'all the existing Inns of Court and Chancery were founded for the common benefit of the Legal Profession ;' and not for one branch of it—Barristers—only. 'The absolute exclusion of seven-eighths of the Profession at the present day from these Inns, by whatever else recommended, cannot be defended on the plea of the true, ancient, and laudable government thereof.'‡ Mr. Macqueén alludes§ to the existence of several orders for the exclusion of Attorneys from the Inns of Court. These I *have* seen.

" The reign of Philip and Mary is hardly the period of English History to which a Lawyer would resort for Constitutional precedent. It is to this gloomy period that we must naturally have recourse for the unconstitutional exclusion of Attorneys from the educational advantages of the Inns of Court.

" The first authoritative exclusion of Attorneys from the Inns of Court is contained in the Order

---

* See Paper prepared by Mr. Clode, Appendix to Report of the Royal Commission, 1854.

† P. 23.

‡ See F. Whitmarsh, Q. C. Treasurer of Gray's Inn, Royal Commission, 1854, p. 77, (Q. 590).

§ P. 15.

affecting all of these Inns, dated 22 June, 1557—
3 and 4 Philip and Mary :—*

"'That none Attorney shall be *admitted* into any of the Houses. And that *from henceforth* this condition shall be implied, that if he, that shall be admitted, practise any Attorneyship, that then, ipso facto, to be dismissed, and to have liberty to repair to the Inn of Chancery, whence he came.'"

" The education of the framers of this crabbed clause appears to have been neglected," exclaimed Mr. Readymoney, laughing.

"Mr. Thorndike," continued Mr. Rich, "the late Principal of Staple's Inn, now Registrar of the Southampton County Court, in reply to the questions of the Royal Commissioners of 1854, stated† it to be his opinion, that it was in the time of Philip and Mary that the Inns of Chancery were deprived of the privilege that they anciently enjoyed, of qualifying Students for being called to the Bar.

"The bad precedent set by Queen Mary was, I am sorry to say, followed by her sister, Queen Elizabeth. In 1574, we find among the 'Orders for the government of the Inns of Court, established by the commandment of the Queen's Majesty,' the following harsh edict, worthy of the worst days of the arbitrary Tudors :—

"If any hereafter admitted in Court practise as

* Dugdale's "Origines," 311 : " Orders to be kept in all the Inns of Court."

† Appendix to Report, 261.

Attorneys or Solicitors, they shall be dismissed and expelled out of their Houses thereupon.'*

"That similar edicts should have been issued by the Stuarts will not surprise you. *C'la va sans dire.* The language of James I. is so coarse that I hardly like to repeat it:—'For that there ought always to be preserved a difference between a Counsellor-at-Law, which is the principal person next unto Serjeants and Judges in administration of justice, and Attorneys, and Solicitors, which are but ministerial persons and of an inferior nature; therefore it is ordered, That from henceforth no common Attorney or Solicitor shall be admitted of any of the four Houses of Court.'†

"The language of James I. was copied, almost word for word, by his successsor, Charles I. 'For that there ought always to be observed a difference between Utter Barristers, Readers in Court, and Apprentices-at-law, which are the principal persons next unto Serjeants and Judges in administration of justice, and Attorneys and Solicitors, which are but ministerial persons of an inferior nature, therefore it is ordered that from henceforth no common Attorney or Solicitor shall hereafter be admitted of any of the four Houses of Court.'‡

An order of Charles II., which bears date the

---

* Dugdale's "Origines," 312.
† Dugdale's "Origines," 317 (7 November, 12 James I.).
‡ Ib. 320 (15 April 6 Car. I.)

18th June, in the 16th year of his reign,* is couched in precisely similar terms, except that it styles Attorneys and Solicitors ' *immaterial* persons!'

" What is the logical conclusion to be drawn from these reiterated edicts of the Tudors and Stuarts ? That Attorneys were only admitted to membership *ex gratiâ* ? Nay, but that they had established, in the course of centuries of possession, so firm a foothold that it was impossible even for the Bacons, Burleighs, and Walsinghams† of Elizabeth, of glorious memory, to turn them out. The Judges, too, of Westminster Hall upheld the social status of the Attorneys. By a rule‡ of the Court of King's Bench, made in Hilary Term, 1632, it was provided as follows:—

" 'None hereafter shall be admitted to be an Attorney of this Court unless he have served a clerk or Attorney of this Court by the space of six years, at the least, or such as for their *education* and study of the law shall be approved by the Justices of this Court to be of good sufficiency, and every of them admitted of the Inns of Court, or Chancery.'

" In Michaelmas Term, 1654, the following Rule of Court was made:—

" 'That all Officers and Attorneys of the Court

* Dugdale's " Origines," 322 (18 June, 16 Car. II).

† The Order of 1574 was signed by these illustrious statesmen.

‡ See these Rules in the Appendix to the Report of the Royal Commision, 1854, p. 286.

be admitted of some Inns of Court or Chancery by the beginning of Hilary Term next, and in the same term wherein they are admitted Officers or Attorneys, and be in Commons one week in every term.'

"In Trinity Term, 1677, and, again, in Michaelmas Term, 1684, the Court of Common Pleas ordered that the Attorneys of that Court should be members of some Inn of Court or Chancery.

"In the reign of Queen Anne—(Michaelmas Term, 1704),—the last Rule upon this subject was made by *all* the Courts of Common Law, which ordered, that, 'all Attorneys, not already admitted into one of the Inns of Court or Chancery, should procure themselves to be admitted, and that for the future no person should be sworn an Attorney, or admitted, *unless first admitted of one of such Inns, and bring a certificate from the treasurer* or principal *of the Inn, testifying such his admission.'**

"We must pass from the times of the Stuarts to the reign of George III. for the next effort to exclude Attorneys.

" The progress of the hostile movement appears to have been gradual. Attorneys were not all at once put on precisely the same footing as the ordinary Student, and compelled to abandon all practice, and study gastronomy solely for *three* years.

* Paper handed in by Mr. Maugham, Secretary and Solicitor to the Incorporated Law Society, on his examination by the Select Committee of 1846. Parl. papers, Vol. 416, p. 167.

In 1762, a conference took place between eight Benchers, two selected from each Inn of Court, when the following resolution was come to:— 'That no Attorney or Solicitor be *called to the Bar* till they (sic) have actually discontinued the practice of their former profession *two years*.'*

" In 1828, in direct opposition to the Rules of the Judges, the four Inns of Court reverted to the unconstitutional precedent of Philip and Mary, and resolved that every person applying to be *admitted* into Commons to keep his terms, should sign a Memorandum to the effect that he is not on the Roll of Attorneys.

" 'It *only* makes a difference to an Attorney,' said Mr. Wyatt, Treasurer of the Inner Temple, to the Common Law Commissioners of 1834,† 'of twelve months before he is called.'

" Thus a whole year of enforced idleness was added to the restriction imposed in 1762.—This three years probation of a gentleman, who has been for five years an articled clerk, has passed three examinations, one of them extremely severe, and has practiced for years as a lawyer, having had charge, perhaps, of cases involving thousands of pounds, is the second grievance of which Attorneys and Solicitors complain.‡

* Appendix to the 6th Report of the Common Law Commissioners, 1834, p. 57.

† Appendix to the 6th Report of the Common Law Commissioners of 1834, p. 70.

‡ The Benchers of the Middle Temple resolved, on the 5th of

" Mr. J. G. Langham, Junior, Attorney-at-law, of Uckfield, called attention to this grievance, in a Letter, which appeared recently in *The Law Journal*.* He writes :—'I have heard that this is a rule of modern date, and that it was first established when Mr. Wilde, who was a Solicitor, went to the Bar, and, by his rapid success, became Chief Justice of the Common Pleas, and afterwards Lord Chancellor. Be that as it may, it is a very unjust rule, and such as does not obtain in any other profession. In the Army, the Navy, the Church or the Medical profession, every one is entitled to his successive steps upon due proof of qualification, without being debarred from the active practice of his profession for any intervening period, however limited. The establishment of a Law University seems a fitting occasion for the removal of this in-

May, 1825, " that no *recipiatur* for entering into Commons shall hereafter be granted to any person, whether owner of Chambers or not, whose name stands on the Roll of Attorneys or Solicitors." On the 8th Feb. 1828, the Benchers of the Inner Temple resolved, "that no *recipiatur* for entering into Commons be granted to any person, whose name stands on the Roll of Attorneys or Solicitors or who is articled to any Attorney or Solicitor." On the 21st Feb. 1828, the Benchers of Lincolns' Inn resolved, "that no person be admitted of this Society, whose name stands on the Roll of Attorneys or Solicitors or who is articled to an Attorney or Solicitor." 6th Report of the Common Law Commissioners, 1834, pp. 50, 60, 63. (There are Attorneys members of Gray's Inn.)

* Law Journal, Feb. 23, 1872.

justice, so as to allow any Solicitor to pass on to the Bar at any time upon undergoing successfully the proper examination which may be required for that branch of the Profession, taking his name off the Roll of Attorneys immediately on his admission to the Bar.' The view presented by Mr. Langham of the relations of the two branches of the Profession is somewhat novel, but the grievance and the remedy are clearly stated. Mr. Jevons has ably stated this grievance.* 'An Attorney, however clear his head, however great his powers of advocacy, is unable to give them full scope without abandoning all the progress he has made in life, and giving up, perhaps, his whole livelihood, to commence a new career at the Bar on the same terms as a raw youth fresh from college or school.' There are Attorneys and Solicitors, who feel the hardship of the Examination preliminary to admission to an Inn of Court, keenly. One of them wrote to the *Law Journal* some months ago. To him 'the study of the law had become a kind of second nature,' but he found that he must pass an examination in Cicero and Sallust, as if he were a raw schoolboy, before being admitted to the three years course of dining for the Bar! The mature age of fifty is not favourable to the resumption of long-neglected studies of the classics: and so this preliminary discipline formed an insuperable obstacle to the

* P. 7.

realization of his wishes.* The Bar is regarded by many Attorneys and Solicitors as a step in the social scale, a passport to good society ; and yet, however large may be their fortunes, Cicero and Sallust stop the way, and prevent their attaining a very laudable object of ambition.

" The effect on, the other hand, of the restriction upon poor men versed in classic lore was well stated by Mr. George Gregory, the eminent Attorney and Solicitor, in the course of the debate on Lord Selborne's motion last Session. I am reading from the Times of March 2nd, 1872 :—' He would commend to the attention of the Bar a practical grievance of which the other branch of the Legal Profession had to complain. An Attorney desirous of becoming a Barrister could not be called to the Bar until he had ceased to practise as an Attorney for three years. Such a condition, except in the case of a man of realized property, was obviously tantamount to starvation.' Mr. Gladstone cheered this statement. I heard him do it."

"And well he might," observed Mr. Readymoney.

" There are many men, of small means, fitted to shine at the Bar, and who have, from accident, or, at the desire of relatives or friends, been admitted as Attorneys and Solicitors. They cannot get on. They have an utter distaste for the dry

* See his letter in the Law Journal of January 5th, 1872, signed, ' A. B. C.'

routine of an Attorney's office. They have mistaken their vocation. These arbitrary edicts of the Inns of Court offer an insuperable obstacle to the transfer of these misplaced men to that branch of the Profession, in which their natural gifts would enable them to succeed. I may add, that I have here a very apposite passage from the Report, that, twenty years ago, the Special Committee of the Law Amendment Society on the Relation between the Bar, the Attorney, and the Client, presented.*
'Your Committee consider the existing rule upon this subject unnecessarily harsh, as, without any corresponding benefit, its obvious effect is to deprive every Attorney, who wishes to become a Barrister, of three years of professional life. Such a rule does not exist, in the case of officers of the Army or Navy, who are desirous of being called to the Bar, and there seems to be no good reason why it should prevail in the case of Attorneys. Indeed, the connection between the qualifications and the course of study required for the two Professions is so close, that every facility should be given for transition from the one to the other, and for the application of talent to that department for which it seems best adapted. Your Committee, therefore, recommend that an Attorney, desirous of being called to the Bar, should, if in other respects a fit person, be admissible into an Inn of

---

* Pp. 20, 21.

Court, for such purpose, without previously removing his name from the Rolls: that he should be permitted to keep his terms without discontinuing his practice; but that his name should be removed from the Rolls before his call to the Bar.' "

"'Bravo, the Special Committee of the Law Amendment Society;" cried Mr. Readymoney, with *empressement*.

" And the recommendation," said Mr. Rich, " is all the more to their credit, because they say* that ' they have not in their deliberations had the assistance of any of those members of the Society whose position as Attorneys would have rendered their cooperation most valuable.'

" ' An Attorney-advocate,' in commenting, in the *Law Times*† on a remark of the Editor,‡ that " to Solicitors aspiring to the Bar every facility should be given," but that 'the Bar is an excessively jealous and exclusive body, and to introduce a Reform would be a work of much difficulty,' uses this vehement language, ' Acts of Parliament have dealt with greater and more serious matter (sic) than the power at present wielded by the Benchers. . . . . Is it too much to hope that the Attorneys and Solicitors of England may take up the question with the earnestness and the gravity that it merits ?

* P. 10.
† May 4th, 1872 : L. T. (Journal) Vol. 53, p. 18.
‡ April 27th, 1872: L. T. (Journal) Vol. 52, p. 471.

If they will do this, they may be assured the remedy is swift and sure, and that the crying injustice of the three years probation before they can be called to the Bar will be speedily and for ever abolished.' 'Studens' writing to the same paper* suggests that 'Students who have been articled and passed the final examination of the Incorporated Law Society (whether actually admitted Attorney or not) should be eligible to be called to the Bar after one year—instead of three —at one of the Inns of Court, provided they pass the same examination as other [Bar] Students.' To return, however, to the question of the right of Attorneys to Membership in the Inns of Court."

" The simplest method of dealing with that question would be, for the Judges to enforce the Rules laid down by the Courts at Westminster in 1632, 1654, 1677, 1684, and 1704," suggested Mr. Readymoney.

"I quite concur in that view," said Mr. Rich. " The allusion in the Rules to the Inns of Chancery would, of course, have to be omitted, as those Inns are now private property, unaffected by any known trusts. They have long since ceased, as Mr. Thorndike points out,† to be part of the legal ὀλιγαρχία. I may observe, in conclusion, that the Royal Commissioners of 1834 have made recom-

* Law Times, March 23rd, 1872, (Vol. 52, p. 396).
† Appendix to Report of the Royal Commission, 1854, p. 261.

mendations,* which, if carried out, would enable the Judges to completely overrule any objections which the Benchers of the Inns may entertain to the admission of Attorneys and Solicitors into membership."

* 6th Report of the Common Law Commissioners, 1834, pp. 8, 9.

§ 6. HOW TO GET FROM THE TEMPLE TO CHANCERY LANE.

"Do you know, Starvington," said Pennyless, one day, "I've half a mind to give up the Bar, and to become an Attorney!"

"Have you any particular reason for the change?"

"I fancy," said Percival, "I've mistaken my vocation: I want to make money: and I'm quite certain, from what you tell me, that I've no chance of making it at the Bar. In the first place, I've no Attorney connection—in the second place"—

"You needn't give any more reasons," said Starvington. "Your first is unanswerable."

"Besides, if I were an Attorney, I could give you plenty of briefs, old friend," said Percival.

"Very kind of you to say so," replied Starvington. "But are you aware of what you must go through in order to become an Attorney?"

"Get disbarred, I suppose," said Pennyless, "and then admitted and enrolled. The honours, which I obtained at the final examination for my Call to the Bar will convince the Incorporated Law Society, I hope, of my fitness for the other branch of the Profession."

"Not a bit of it," said Stephen, laughing. "Your honours won't advance you one hair's breadth, in your flight 'over the border.' Not merely the River Tweed, but the Rocky Mountains, intervene!"

"How so?" enquired the Honourable Percival.

"As thus," replied Stephen, smiling, "The Legislature of your country in its wisdom—"

"Come, come," said Percival, "none of that, if you love me!"

"Well, in its sublime indifference to our interests, then, passed an Act intituled the 23 and 24 of the Queen, chapter 127, which provided—(I've got a copy of the Act here)—that 'every person, who has been called to the degree of Utter Barrister in England, and who, before becoming such Barrister, has been bound by contract in writing to serve as a clerk for the term of five years, or who, after ceasing to be a Barrister, has been bound by contract in writing to serve as a clerk for three years to a practising Attorney or Solicitor:'"—

"Serve as a clerk for three years to a practising Attorney or Solicitor, after ceasing to be a Barrister!" exclaimed Percival indignantly. "What a degradation! And yet the men who framed this precious enactment could prate, no doubt, as glibly as any *parvenu* placeman about the honour and dignity of the Bar! But I beg pardon for interrupting you."

" 'Or who, after ceasing to be a Barrister," repeated Stephen, "has been bound by a contract in writing to serve as a Clerk for three years to a practising Attorney or Solicitor, and has, in either of the said cases, continued in service for the term of three years, and, during the whole of such three years, served in such manner, as is required in the case of persons who have taken degrees in the Universities, and, having been examined and sworn after the expiration of such term of three years (the examination and swearing taking place, in the first-mentioned case, after the person has ceased to be a Barrister,) may be admitted and enrolled as an Attorney or Solicitor: Provided always, that in the case of any such person as aforesaid, who has been bound for five years, it shall be necessary for such term to be determined with consent, as in the case of persons having taken degrees, who may have been bound for five years before the passing of this Act.'"

"The policy, I take it, of this enactment," said Percival, "is to put the Barrister-at-law on precisely the same footing as the Bachelor of Arts with respect to his initiation into the 'so-called lower walks of the Profession,' as Mr. Jevons calls them."

"Precisely."

"'Such a getting' *down* 'stairs, I never did see!'" cried Mr. Pennyless.

'The Committee of the Law Amendment Society, while recommending that 'every facility should be given for transition from one' branch of the Legal Profession 'to the other,' and that Attorneys and Solicitors should, therefore, be admitted to and 'allowed to keep their terms' at the Inns of Court, 'without previously removing their names from the Rolls,' were so struck by the 'manifest incongruity' of 'the two conditions of Barrister and Attorney's Clerk,' that they 'did not suggest' that Barristers should be allowed to serve their articles without being previously disbarred. It never seems to have struck them that it is preposterous for the Legislature to put a Barrister-at-law on the same footing as a Bachelor of Arts, with respect to admission and enrolment as an Attorney and Solicitor."

" Now that the student *must* pass an Examination before his call to the Bar, this enactment cannot stand," said the Honourable Percival. " At the time that it was passed (1860), there was no guarantee that a student called to the Bar knew anything of Law, and this may be some excuse for the Legislature passing it. But, why oblige the Barrister, who wishes to become an Attorney and Solicitor, to go through this degrading ceremony of serving under Articles of Clerkship? The student of the Inns of Court becomes the *pupil* of the Conveyancer or Special Pleader, not his *Clerk*. Why should not (say) a year's experience *in statu pupillari* with an Attorney and Solicitor be deemed sufficient qualification for a Barrister, who ha kept his terms at an Inn of Court, has passed a compulsory examination, and wishes to be enrolled as an Attorney and Solicitor ?"

" Why not, indeed ?" replied Starvington.

" Especially if the suggestion of a correspondent of the *Law Times* be carried out, and it is made a *sine qua non* that a student should pass a year in a Barrister's, Special Pleader's, or Conveyancer's Chambers, before becoming a Barrister himself."

" And an excellent suggestion, no doubt. With regard to the rule laid down by the Benchers, that an Attorney must be struck off the Rolls, before applying for admission to an Inn of Court, and must eat his way to the Bar, like an ordinary Student, I confess I see no reason for altering it. A Barrister seeking to become an Attorney has nothing to gain by his previous connection with the Bar. An Attorney seeking to become a Barrister has everything to gain from his previous connection with the other branch of the Profession.

" The following question was put, in 1854, to Mr. J. G. Phillimore, Q.C.:*—' At present one of the best methods of ensuring success at the Bar is for an Attorney's Clerk to go from an Attorney's Office to an Inn of Court, and be called to the Bar ?' And one of Mr. Phillimore's answers was,† 'I

---

* Royal Commission, 1854, Question, 1516.
† Question, 1519.

think it is a great evil that a man from having been an Attorney's Clerk, should come to the Bar and have chances such as other people have not.'

" Mr. Phillimore might have cited the names of many eminent Judges, who have owed their rapid rise at the Bar to their early connection with an Attorney's office. The first Lord Truro was an Attorney for twelve years previous to his call to the Bar.* Mr. Baron Garrow 'at fifteen was articled to a respectable Attorney in Milk Street, Cheapside.' ' In that gentleman's office,' says Mr. Foss, naïvely, 'he acquired a practical knowledge of his Profession.'† No doubt; and what was of more importance to him, a practical knowledge of his future patrons. Mr. Baron Wood was articled to an Attorney, in early life. Instead of becoming an Attorney himself, he entered the Middle Temple, and 'soon got into full practice as a Special Pleader.'‡ Mr. Baron Hullock was articled in early life to an Attorney.§ Mr. Justice Holroyd was articled, in early life, to an Attorney.|| Lord Gifford, Lord Chief Justice of the Common Pleas, is a brilliant instance of the advantage of beginning life as an articled clerk. 'He served the whole of his time,'

* " He became an Attorney in 1805 : and in 1817 he was called to the Bar, and speedily rose to be a leading Advocate." Encyclopædia Brit. s. v. " Wilde."
† Foss's Judges, Vol. IX. p. 87.
‡ Ibid. p. 53.   § Ibid. p. 28.
|| Ibid. p. 25.

says Mr. Foss.* 'At the termination of his clerkship he entered the Middle Temple.' His father was a grocer and linendraper in Exeter; so the young man, on his call to the Bar, not unnaturally 'joined the Western Circuit, and the Exeter and Devon Sessions.' Amongst the causes of his 'soon acquiring an extensive business,' Mr. Foss, enumerates 'his local connection.' He had been only nine years at the Bar, when he was appointed Solicitor-General, knighted, and elected a Bencher of his Inn. Two years after he became Attorney-General. He had only been Attorney-General about four years, when he was raised (at the age of forty-five) to the Bench as Lord Chief Justice of the Common Pleas, and to the Peerage as Lord Gifford. His career caps that of Lord Truro so well, that I will not attempt to 'paint the lily or gild refined gold,' by narrating that of another Lord Chief Justice of the Common Pleas, Lord Wynford, who is said† to have commenced his career as an articled Clerk. The three years study of gastronomy at the Inns of Court is the only barrier that we have against the inroads of these free lances. I am afraid it is little better, after all, than the traditional pitchfork, employed to stop the advancing tide; but we can't afford to pull down any of the bulwarks of our branch of the Legal Profession."

* Foss's Judges, Vol. IX. pp. 18-21.
† Law and Lawyers, Vol. I. p. 29.

"Not at least, without compensation," said Pennyless.

"The illustrations," resumed Starvington, "that I have given you, of the rapid rise at the Bar of men, who commenced their career in an Attorney's office, are all taken from a single volume of Mr. Foss, and do not go back beyond the commencement, in 1820, of the list of Judges of the reign of George the Fourth. The hardships, on the other hand, which a Barrister, who wishes to become an Attorney, has to undergo, are well illustrated by the case of *In re Bateman*. A similar case could not arise now, because three years service under articles before becoming a Barrister are now sufficient to entitle a person duly disbarred to be examined by the Law Society. But the case illustrates the absurdity of requiring from a Barrister any service at all under articles of clerkship. Mr. Bateman, the unfortunate hero of this Cause Celèbre,* was articled in September, 1826, to Mr. Hughes, Attorney-at-law. He served under these articles for three years. The articles were then determined by mutual consent. In October, 1829, Mr. Bateman entered as an undergraduate, at Christ's College, Cambridge. In 1831, he was admitted, as a student, into the Inner Temple. In January, 1833, he took his B.A. degree at the University of Cambridge. He then entered the chambers of a Conveyancer, with

---

* Reported, 2 D. and L. 725, 6 Q. B. 853: 9 Jur. 29: 14 L. J. (Q. B.) 89.

whom he studied for more than three years.
May, 1835, he was called to the Bar; and practise
as a Conveyancing Counsel from 1836 to the clo
of 1842. He then wholly ceased to practise at tl
Bar. On January 22nd, 1843, he entered in
fresh articles with Mr. Brabant, Attorney-at-la
for a period of five years, with a proviso, that if,
any time previously to the expiration of that ten
he should, by virtue of his service with Mr. Hughe
and his new service, be entitled to be admitted
an Attorney, he should be at liberty to put an er
to his articles. On the 17th January, 1845, M
Bateman was disbarred, on his own petition, by tl
Hon. Society of the Middle Temple. During h
second service under articles he was not 'engag(
in any other practice, profession, or business wha
soever.' Mr. Knowles moved the Court of Queer
Bench, in Hilary Term, 1845 (immediately aft(
Mr. Bateman had been disbarred, it would seen
for a rule to direct the Examiners of Attorneys
examine Mr. Bateman, with a view to his beir
admitted an Attorney, they entertaining doubts
to his admissibility. The affidavits in support
the motion set out the above facts, and also state
that Mr. Bateman's omission to apply sooner to l
disbarred, ' arose from inadvertence, and from h
not being aware that such a course would be coi
sidered necessary in order to a valid service und
his' second 'articles.' The Solicitor Gener

shewed cause in the first instance, and used the curious argument that 'it would give the party an unfair professional advantage to allow him to qualify' for one branch of the Profession while belonging to the other. (But why 'unfair,' if others could do the same?) Mr. Knowles argued that the simple fact of Mr. Bateman having inadvertently allowed his name to remain on the books of the Middle Temple, after discontinuing practice at the Bar, ought not to render his service with Mr. Brabant invalid. There was no statutory enactment, nor any Rule of Court preventing service under articles from being a good service, because the party had not been previously disbarred. Mr. Bateman's pursuits had been eminently calculated to qualify him for the duties of an Attorney. The Court (composed of very distinguished Judges— Lord Denman, C. J., Patteson, J., and Coleridge, J.) refused to grant a Rule, and based their refusal solely on the ground of 'unfair and improper advantage,' and the danger of 'malversation;' admitting, at the same time, that Mr. Bateman laboured under no statutable disqualification, and that no imputation rested upon his personal behaviour!

"Their Lordships seem to have been in happy ignorance of the numerous ways and means by which Barristers bring themselves into contact with the other branch of the Profession!

"Any student of the Inns of Court, and, as far as

I know, any Barrister, is at perfect liberty to enter an Attorney's office, and study under him *as a pupil*, and very properly so. It is the best method of acquiring a practical knowledge of the forms of procedure in the Superior Courts. By the Statute law of the realm* an articled clerk may serve part of his time in a Barrister's Chambers. We have seen the ways and means by which the local Barrister may get into the 'good graces' of Attorney's clerks. I know a clever young London Barrister rapidly rising into practice, who laid the foundation of his fortunes at the Bar, broad and sure, by 'coaching' articled clerks for the Examinations of the Incorporated Law Society. People might sneer at him as 'only an Attorney-grinder;' but how easy it was for him to stipulate that his pupils should give him briefs, if successful in their examinations!

"All these methods of coming in contact with Attorneys being open to the Bar, (besides relationship and marriage, which we may, perhaps, one day consider,) how 'fearfully and wonderfully made' must be the judicial conscience which winks at all these things, and yet solemnly excludes a deserving man, who has abandoned practice at the Bar, from the other branch of the Profession, because, forsooth, he inadvertently allowed his name to remain on the books of the Middle Temple,

* 6 and 7 Vict. Cap. 73 : s. 6.

while serving his time under articles with an Attorney ! 'Unfair and improper advantages !' 'Malversation !' O my dear Pennyless ! it is the bane of our noble Profession, this straining at gnats and swallowing of camels ! this cleansing of the outside of the cup and platter ! this technical morality !

"Mr. Gregory, the Member for Sussex, has complained, I believe, of the hardships of the rule laid down by the Benchers of the Inns of Court, that an Attorney must abandon all practice, in other words must 'starve'—for three years, before he can be called to the Bar and earn a livelihood at it. What does he think, I wonder, of the statutory restraint upon men, who are starving at the Bar, and are condemned, by the Legislature, to wait for three years before they can be admitted and earn a livelihood as Attorneys ? That eminent Attorney, Mr. Jevons, observes,* 'There is almost no position for an unsuccessful Advocate to fall back upon.' And he then points out that 'if it were possible for a learned stuff gownsman, who from deficient health, or other of the varied causes of imperfect success at the Bar, has failed in that career, to fall back upon the practice of the other branch of the Profession, many an unsuccessful life might have ended in prosperity and honour.' 'Failing to win advancement in the narrow walk of advocacy, those

* P. 9.

men at the Bar who have mistaken their vocation, might find their legitimate and successful development in the less ambitious, but more varied practice of the Attorney."*

* Saunders on the Leg. Prof., p. 29.

§ 7. CLIENT JILTING. A SUITOR'S GRIEVANCE.

" Well, O'Dougherty, and how did you get on in the Exchequer, to-day?"
" See here now! As bad luck would have it, the Counsellor that Mr. Smith, me Attorney, had engaged to defind me, didn't turn up at the thrial, at all, at all. He sint a spalpeen, that they called his 'divil,' to represent him: and faix, this divil was for all the wurrld like wee Johnny Russell at the Furrin' Office: he meddled and muddled till he couldn't tell his horns from his tail! The ould boy, that was to defind me, was sittin' all the while next door at the Common Plays—*on*commonly *on*playsed he was, I asshure ye, when I gave him a poke in the ribs, and I says, ses I, ' Ould chap! arn't ye comin' to defind me?' He looked blue murther at me, and wid that up came Mr. Smith, bedad, and lugged me off to the Exchequer. There were two cliver chaps agin' me, and, bad scran to them, but they snuffed out the spalpeen that definded me in a jiffey: and the jury found a vardict for the Plaintiff—£100. I'm quite kilt wid it, entoirely."

" And no wonder," said Mr. Brown (Mr. Brown

was a warehouseman in the City). "I was once done in the same way myself and lost £1,000 by it. I took to investigating the subject in spare hours, as a kind of relief to my mind. I have here a few notes that I made upon it. Would you care to hear something about it?"

"Be the powers, I'd like to wring that ould chap's neck—figuratively, ye know, if ye'll only shew me the way to do it."

"The rule at the Parisian Bar is that the Advocate should not accept too many briefs: and if he is hindered from attending the trial, he ought *previously* to inform the client of it, and give him a voice in the selection of another Advocate, as well as offer, at least, to return the fee that he himself has received.* It's rather curious that this rule of the Parisian Bar is similar to one laid down by the Court of Common Pleas, as long ago as the reign of King James I. The Court not only laid down the rule, but gave the means of enforcing it. 'If any Serjeant or Counsellor-at-law shall take any fee to be of Counsel with any, and to be with him at any time certain for any cause and shall

---

* " Il n'acceptera point un trop grand nombre d'affaires." Régle 15 : Mollot, Vol. I. p. 32.

" Est-il malade ou empêché? il pourra se faire suppleer par un confrère, *lorsque le client averti ne s'y oppose pas;* et dans ce cas même je pense *qu'il dont offrir de restituer* à ce dernier *les honoraires* quil en a receu." Régle 90. Ib. p. 106.

not attend the same cause accordingly, that then, upon complaint made or information thereof given to the Judges of that Court, where the cause shall be depending, or any of them, the Judges,* by their discretion, shall *give order for the repayment and satisfaction thereof to the client.*' The Royal Commissioners on the Procedure at Common Law (Mr. Serjeant Stephen, and Messieurs Bosanquet, Patteson, Alderson, and Parke, who became subsequently distinguished Judges) expressed† their approval of the principle of this rule in their First Report:—'We think it very desirable,' they said, 'that the principle of this rule should be honourably observed.'"

"Thin, by jaybers, I'll have th' ould chap up before the Judges, and see if I don't shake him till the guineas come jumpin' into me hand out of his breeches pocket! What's the year iv King James the First that ye're citin'?"

"The 14th year of King James I.—Hilary Term."

"I'm off to Mr. Smith, me Attorney. Thank ye kindly, Mr. Brown. Ye're a well-informed gintleman, an' no misthake!"

O'Dougherty ran, or, rather, flew to his Attorney's office, and was gratified to find him within. Ushered into the presence, "And now, Mr. Smith,"

---

* Not the Benchers of his Inn, "quod nota," as the old law-writers say.

† 1st Report (1829) pp. 26 and 27.

said O'Dougherty, "ye remimber that ould chap that sould us this morning'. It's the Counsellor ye engaged to defind me, I mane," he added, seeing that Mr. Smith looked puzzled, "I've jist found out the way to be evin' wid him. If ye'll look at the first Report iv—what's their name at all, at all—O, yis, the Common Law Commissioners, ye'll see the rimidy I have agin' him."

Mr. Smith had the volume on his shelves, and taking it down, read as follows:—

"'We are of opinion that no gentleman at the Bar ought to accept a brief in any cause upon which he has not good reason to be assured that he will be able personally to attend.'"*

Mr. Smith nodded his head approvingly.

"'The distraction occasioned by the engagements of Counsel in several Courts is prejudicial in several ways.'†

"But what is the remedy?" asked Mr. Smith.

"No action for negligence will lie against Counsel for malfeasance or nonfeasance. That was decided by Lord Kenyon in the case of Fell v. Brown,‡ as long ago as 1791. Mr. Fell brought an action against Mr. Brown, a Barrister, for 'unskilfully and negligently settling and signing a bill,' filed by the Plaintiff in the Court of Chancery. The bill had been referred by the Lord

---

* Report, p. 26. † Ibid. pp. 25, 26.
‡ Peake's Reports : 131, [96.]

Chancellor to the Master, for scandal and impertinence, and the Plaintiff had been obliged to pay the costs of the reference. Lord Kenyon was clearly of opinion that the action could not be supported. He believed this action was the first, and he hoped it would be the last of the kind. So the Plaintiff was nonsuited without one witness being examined! The case of Turner *v.* Phillips.* decided by the same Judge in the year 1792, is precisely on all fours with your case. In that case Mr. Garrow held the brief for the Plaintiff on behalf of Mr. Phillips, the Defendant. The marginal note is to this effect:—' No action lies to recover back a fee given to a Barrister to argue a cause which he did not attend.' These are old cases, decided in England. But I'll give you, Mr. O'Dougherty, a new case, fresh from your own country, Mulligan *v.* M'Donagh, Q. C.† argued in the Irish Court of Exchequer. The marginal note is:—' An action against a Barrister, for negligence or non-attendance on a trial, is not maintainable.' Mr. Heron, the present member for Tipperary, of Counsel, with Mr. Whiteside, now Lord Chief Justice of Ireland, for the Defendant, Mr. McDonagh, cited the cases of Fell *v.* Brown and Turner *v.* Phillips, as conclusive.† Lord Chief Baron Pigot and the full Court of Exchequer, allowed Mr. Heron's demurrer to the declaration.

* Peake's Reports, 166, [122].
† 2 Law Times Reports, (N. S.) 136 : 5 Ir. Jur. (N. S.) 101.

M

'Such an action,' said the Irish Lord Chie: Baron, 'cannot be maintained. As the points raised have been abundantly ruled, we have only to follow the decisions already made upon the subject.' So, I ask you again, what is your remedy Mr. O'Dougherty?"

O'Dougherty seized the volume containing the First Report of the Commissioners, and pointed to the rule of Hilary Term, 14 James I. (1616) Mr. Smith read the Rule, (a smile overspreading his countenance as he proceeded). He also read the note of the Commissioners:—"We think it very desirable that the principle of this Rule should be honorably observed."

"'Honorably observed!' Fiddle-de-dee," exclaimed Mr. Smith. "You might just as well, my dear sir, expect the Benchers to 'honorably observe' the Rules—(all of them more recent than this)—requiring that the members of my branch of the Profession shall be admitted to the Inns of Court! The sword, my dear sir, with which you seek to frighten the very eminent Counsel, who violated his engagement this morning, is as rusty as the 'penalties of præmunire,' with which Lord Westbury facetiously threatened the 'most potent, grave and reverend signors' who condemned the 'Essays and Reviews!'" And Mr. Smith laughed heartily at the simplicity of his client. Then, in a confidential undertone, he added,

"Take my advice, and say no more about the matter."

O'Dougherty returned, crestfallen, to Mr. Brown, in whose sympathizing audience he said, as may be supposed, a great deal more about the matter. When he had done, Mr. Brown, (who was a methodical man,) took out his pencil and entered upon the margin of his note-book:—

"Rule of Court obsolete: Public without remedy for this grievance."

§ 8. ETIQUETTE FOR GENTLEMEN.

"I constantly read in the Legal Press of the 'Etiquette of the Profession.' What does it mean, Starvington?" said Pennyless, one day, after Hall, as he and Stephen sat together in Stephen's Chambers.

"It means," replied Stephen, "a kind of Indian jungle. The knowing ones can wriggle through it in safety, by crooked courses. It is pretty sure to trip up the straightforward man: and the knowing ones will come round him, and kick him when he is down, to shew their zeal for the honour and dignity of the Profession!"

"Where am I to find the Rules of Etiquette?" asked Percival. "I've never seen them, not even in Blackstone."

"Nobody has ever seen them," said Stephen "They have never been defined. They rest *in gremio legis.*"

"How, then, can we be expected to obey them?" enquired Percival.

"By instinct, I suppose," said Stephen.

"Would they, then, suggest themselves spontaneously to an unsophisticated child of nature?" asked Percival, laughing, "to Galatea, for example, Pygmalion's statue-bride?"

"By no means," replied Stephen, smiling. "They are most of them artificial and arbitrary; and some of the most rigid are mere modern innovations, destitute alike of any foundation in Constitutional precedent or common sense."

"Let's take one at a time," said Pennyless.

(I.) INSTRUCTION OF COUNSEL BY ATTORNEY.

"Perhaps the most remarkable," said Stephen, "is the Rule that it is dishonourable for a Barrister to accept instructions in civil causes from any one but an Attorney. This preposterous rule of etiquette, which renders the superior branch of the Profession in reality the inferior,—which makes the Bar utterly impervious to public opinion, so long as they can please their patrons, the Attorneys,—which fosters nepotism among the Attorneys of the grossest kind,—which leads to repeated failures of justice from the total want of personal knowledge, on the part of Counsel, of the witnesses they have to rely upon till they see them for the first time in the witness box"—

"Hold, Stephen Starvington," exclaimed Percival, "you are getting excited."

"And well I may," replied Stephen, somewhat fiercely: "It is this miserable rule of etiquette that has blighted my prospects at the Bar. And

what is its origin? I believe we have ourselves
blame for it. The Special Committee of the Socie
for Promoting the Amendment of the Law hit,
think, upon the truth, when it reported,* th
the rule 'arose from a fastidiousness and ove
refinement of feeling, which induced the Bar
seclude themselves from the Public, in the mistake
idea of consulting their own ease and dignity.'"

"That is very neatly expressed," observed Pe
cival. "The circumvallation of Attorneys, was r
doubt, invented, in order to keep the Bar a cas
apart from the people."

"The rule is barely a hundred years old," r
sumed Starvington. "The Report of the Commi
tee points out† that 'even during the last centur
it was not fully established.' 'It is quite of la
years,' observes Mr. Shaw Lefevre,‡ 'that Attorney
and Solicitors have become the dispensers of a
business that comes to the Bar.' Mr. Pulling, i
his learned work, on Attorneys,§ affirms the
during the last century, the practice was graduall
introduced of Barristers *requiring* the interventio
of Attorney and Solicitors, in cases which cam
professionally before them, either as Advocate
Counsel, or Draftsmen, and such is the practic
now generally followed, though the legal right c
Barristers to dispense with such intervention is un

* Page. 12. † Page 8. ‡ Page 19.
§ Pulling, on the Law of Attorneys, p. 12.

questionable.' It certainly was a strange way of enhancing the dignity of the Bar to make it entirely dependent on the patronage of Attorneys.

"The grand old Roman ideal of a Counsellor as something more than a mere Advocate—as a Jurisconsult, with whom every citizen is entitled to advise personally, has been blotted out by our short-sighted glorification of caste. No longer can we cite, as applicable to ourselves, the glorious saying of Cicero, which Waterhous applied* to the Counsel of his day—' Quid aliud est jurisconsulti domus, nisi oraculum civitatis?' The briefless Barrister without Attorney connection sits, like Edgar Allan Poë, in his lonely dungeon, the sides of which seem to close in upon him on every quarter, forcing him nearer and nearer to the fatal brink.

"Let us now, however, recur to the search for precedents. I have a copious series of extracts here in my note-book from which I will refresh my memory. 'He is called a Countor, whom *one* appoints to speak and count for *oneself* in Court.'† It is evident, therefore, that, in Normandy, the Plaintiff and Defendant each selected his own Counsel. And not only was the happy suitor clothed with the power

---

* " Fortescutus Illustratus," p. 137 (margin).

† Grand Coustumier, cap. 64, ' De Conteurs.' The learned editor of the Year-books has missed the exact meaning of this passage. In his Preface to the Year-books 32 and 33 Edw. I. (1864), he translates ' que aulcun establit,' ' who is appointed,' and ' pour soi,' ' for him.'

*

of appointing his own Counsel, but also with th power of dismissing him, and appointing another i his stead. ' When he likes, he can change him an appoint another.' ('Quand il vouldra, il le pourr changer, et establir ung aultre.') And this is th system that was introduced into England at th Norman Conquest. The Commentator on the Cus tom of Normandy speaks of the Conteurs 'unde the reign of the Norman Kings' of England a 'vindicating the rights of the *parties, whose* confi dence they had acquired.' And, indeed, it woul(have been difficult for the Advocate in those day. to have relied for success on the patronage o Attorneys, because Attorneys were only employe(in exceptional cases ; whereas Counsel migh always be employed. Let me remind you of th(celebrated note of Serjeant Manning :*—' Befor(the Statute 13 Edw. I. c. 10, Plaintiffs and Defend ants were bound to appear in person, unless author ised by the King's writ of dedimus potestatem d(Attornato faciendo to substitute an Attorney Once before the Court, they (*i.e.* Plaintiffs anc Defendants) were at liberty to avail themselves o the services of a Countor, who might stand bj them, advise with, and speak for them.'

" 'Serjeants Countors,' says Lord Campbell, Lor(Chief Justice of England,† ' there is every reasoi

* Note to Doe d. Bennett *v.* Hale, 15 Q.B. 225.

† Judgment in the case of Doe d. Bennett *v.* Hale, 15 Q.B 171.

to believe, long continued to communicate directly with the parties. Chaucer speaks, in the Prologue to the Canterbury Tales,* of—

'A Sergeaunt of the lawe, ware and wise,
'That often had yben at the Parvise.'

'The Parvise is well-known to have been a sort of Exchange at St. Paul's, where all ranks met to do business, and the Serjeants-at-law, like Roman patrons, gave advice to all who came to consult them. Afterwards each Serjeant-at-law had a pillar in the Cathedral assigned to him, where he stood and conversed with his clients.' According to Mr. Reeves, the learned author of the History of the English Law,† the Apprentices had pillars at St. Paul's, as well as the Serjeants:—'It is said,' he observes, 'that the Serjeants and *Apprentices*, each at his pillar, used to hear his client's case, and take notes thereof upon his knee.' During the period that Apprentices practised as Attorneys (that is, probably, for about a hundred years—from the latter end of the 13th to the latter end of the 14th century), 'the Apprentice-attorney,' as Serjeant Manning points out,‡ 'would have no one to instruct but himself.' When the Apprentice ceased to practise as an Attorney, he merely abandoned the performance of the ministerial duties incident to conducting suits through the forms of the Courts, retaining the privilege or

* Tyrwhitt's Edition, 1830: Vol. I. 13.
† P. 360, Vol. II, Edition, 1787.
‡ Note to Doe d. Bennet *v.* Hale, 15 Q. B. 225.

duty (at Rome it was both) of advising clients personally, and taking instructions from them. Mr. Marshall himself has pointed out,* that in the Paston Letters, written during the 15th century,† 'and which abound throughout in allusions to litigation,' 'in the cases where advice is sought, Counsel only are referred to.' ‡

My Lord Coke observes § that 'the son may of his own money and in his own name give fees to his father's *Counsel* or Attorney, without any expectation of repayment, and so may the father to his son's *Counsel.*'

"Whatever change may have taken place in the relations of Attorneys and Barristers, that Barristers continued to receive instructions from the Public, is evident from the language of the writers of a subsequent period. The standard text-book on the 'Law of Attorneys' is the learned treatise of Mr. Pulling to which I have already referred: and what does it say? 'It seems clear from the insight into the habits and manners of our forefathers afforded by biographers and dramatists, that the practice formerly prevailed of Barristers being ordinarily resorted to in the first instance for counsel and general legal assistance.'|| Take, for example, the 17th century. Lord Campbell,¶ in his life of Lord Chief Justice Hale, who flourished

* P. 11. † A.D. 1433-1485.
‡ P. 12. § 2 Inst. 564.
|| Pulling on "the Law of Attorneys," p. 12.
¶ "Lives of the Chief Justices," Vol. I. pp. 585-6.

in the time of the Stuarts, observes, 'He did n[o]
take the profits that he might have had by h[is]
practice, for, in common cases, when those w[ho]
came to ask his counsel gave him a piece, he use[d]
to give back the half, and to make ten shillings h[is]
fee in ordinary matters that did not require muc[h]
time or study.' Lord Campbell appends th[is]
note to the passage:—'At this time the clie[nt]
consulted the Barrister in person and paid t[he]
honorarium without the intervention of Attorne[y]
Mr. North, afterwards Lord Keeper Guilford, w[as]
the first King's Counsel, tempore Car. II. 'O[ne]
thing,' writes his biographer,* Roger North, 'w[as]
principally his care; which was, to take good i[n]
structions in his Chamber. He examined careful[ly]
the issue, as the pleadings derived it; and perus[ed]
all the deeds, if it were a title, and not seldo[m]
examined the witnesses, if it were a fact; by th[is]
he was enabled to make a judgment of the caus[e]
and to advise his client as to going on or no[t]
'Nor can I say,' observes his biographer,† 'ho[w]
many families of nobility and others, having on[ce]
made use of his advice, made him afterwards a[n]
biter of all their concerns.' The extensive natu[re]
of the duties which then devolved upon Couns[el]
as well as the ready resort of clients to that 'li[eu]
sacré—le Cabinet de l'avocat,'‡ are well illustrat[ed]

---

* Life of Lord Keeper Guilford, p. 46. † P 55.
‡ Mollot, Vol. I. 63.

by a case in which North was engaged—Cuts v. Pickering. I have it here. If you like, I'll read it."

" Do."

"' Sir John Cuts, of Childerfly in Cambridgeshire, had an aunt, one Mrs. Weld, who married Mr. Pickering, and, by his will, gave her an estate called Drayton, value £300 per annum, for 99 years, *if she should so long live.* Mr. Pickering, desiring not to hang upon the thread of his wife's life for such an estate, but to have it for the term absolute, thought fit to erase from the will the words in reference to her life. He had opportunity to do it, for he was made executor, and, accordingly, had the will in his keeping, which, in his good time, was proved and lodged in the Prerogative office. The relations, that were the heirs and devisees of the capital estate, and, among other things, of this (subject to Mrs. Pickering's life,) were minors, and their affairs were managed by their mother. North's first acquaintance with the family went no further than Sir John Cuts, and this Mr. Pickering and his wife. He (Pickering) was a subtle fellow, money hunter, and very avaricious. He was not without suspicion that some suits might be stirred against him by the Cutses upon this will, and much dreaded a discovery of this erasure; and for a whole term, almost every day, called upon his cousin North (there was some relation, but remote, between him and Pickering's wife). He never had the civility to offer a fee, or

to ask North to be of Counsel with him in general,
or particular, or on any account whatever. I remember, one night, North came out from his study
in a great pet, wishing heartily that his' (Pickering's) 'adversaries would come and retain him:—
and the next day Mrs. Cuts came, with much apology for her presumption, in tendering a retainer
in her cause against Mr. Pickering, fearing he
might be under engagements to him. He told her
'No,' and took her fee, and wrote her down in his
Book of Retainers; so she went away, satisfied.—
And well she might, for that minute's work saved
the estate. Pickering, that dogged this gentlewoman to see where she went, perceived her
go up to and return from his cousin North's
Chamber, and then he concluded she was in earnest, and up he goes, and offers his retaining fee.
'No,' North told him, 'he was already retained on
the other side,' and shewed him his book. 'His'
(Pickering's) 'discourse upon the matter signified
nothing; he must have patience, and provide himself elsewhere. He might repent his neglect, but
it was too late. After this Mrs. Cuts came to
North in very great concern, saying she had very
credible information that there was a foul erasure
in Sir John Cuts's will, that in consequence lost
Drayton, after Mrs. Pickering's death, from her
(Mrs. Cuts's) children. North immediately took
coach and went to Doctors' Commons, to view the
original Will. There he found the erasure most

evident, and not done so carefully, but that by the bottoms and tops of the long letters and the distances that determined the intermediate ones, the words, 'if she shall so long live,' might be read. —Thereupon he took a paper, and made facsimile of the marks and distances of those small specks, as were not scraped out.—Then he called the officers, and shewed them the erasures and the marks, with the resemblance he had made of them, and charged them all to take care that none should see the will, but in the presence of an officer; for there would be a suit at law to be determined by a view of that erasure. The matter being fixed, the lady went into Chancery, and having filed a Bill for a Discovery, Pickering answers fully, and denies the erasure; and at the hearing a trial was directed to be had, to find if this erasure was since the publication and by whom. The cause came to be tried at the King's Bench Bar, before the Lord Chief Justice Hales, and the rest of the Justices of that Bench; and North managed in chief for the Cutses. .... The Jury found Pickering author of the erasure since the will published.' "*

" Why, there's no mention," exclaimed Percival, "of an Attorney in the case from beginning to end!"

" As for the evidence to be deduced from the dramatists, let me refer you to the golden age of

* Life of Lord Keeper Guilford, pp. 58, 59, 60.

Queen Anne. Study the scenes between Widow Blackacre and her various Counsel, in Wycherley's 'Plain Dealer,'* and between Mrs. Sealand and her Counsel, Mr. Serjeant Target, and Mr. Counsellor Bramble, in the ' Conscious Lovers' of Sir Richard Steele.

"If you wish for evidence from the poets, read Pope's ' Imitation of Horace,' dedicated to Mr. Fortescue, a well-known Barrister.†

"Lord Commissioner Whitelock, in addressing the new Serjeants, 18 Nov. 1648,‡ said:—" For your duty to particular clients you may consider that .... some clients are of mean capacity; you must take the more pains to instruct yourself to understand their business. Some are of quick capacity and confidence, yet you must not trust to their information. ˙Some are peaceable; *detain them not, but send them home* the sooner. Some are contentious; *advise them* to reconcilement with their adversary. Amongst your clients and all others endeavour to gain and preserve that estimation and respect which is due to your degree and to a just, honest, and discreet person.'

" Even within the 19th century, instances have

* Act III. Scene 1.
† ' Tim'rous by Nature, of the rich in awe,
 ' *I come to Counsel* learned in the law,
 ' You'll give me as a friend both sage and free,
 ' Advice, and, *as you used*, without a fee.'
‡ Whitelock's Memorials, 352.

occurred 'in which Counsel of great eminence and high honour have thought that, from peculiar circumstances, they were justified sometimes with, sometimes without, a fee, in holding a brief delivered to them by the party, no Attorney being employed.' In illustration of this, the great name of Lord Brougham, who accepted briefs, without fee, from the party, is mentioned. Mr. Baron Richardson and Lord Abinger, when at the Bar, gave professional advice, and accepted fees without the intervention of an Attorney. In application for a Hab. Corp. Counsel have taken briefs from the wife of the party.*

" The decision in the case of Doe d. Bennett v. Hale† no little disconcerted the sticklers for this rule of etiquette. The marginal note is as follows:—' There is no Rule of Law requiring that Counsel appearing in Court for a party, who pleads in person, should be instructed by an Attorney. Therefore, where a Judge' (Patteson, J.) ' at Nisi Prius had ruled that Counsel appearing for such party and not instructed by an Attorney, could not cross-examine, or address the jury, the Court granted a New Trial.' Lord Campbell, C.J. in delivering judgment, said (inter alia):—' In this case we are called upon to consider whether in the

* See Lord Campbell, and Newton arg., in Doe d. Bennett v. Hale, 15 Q.B. 171, and Report of Committee of Law Amendment Society, 9.
† 15 Q.B. 171.

Superior Courts there be a Rule of Law, which prevents a Defendant in a civil suit, who has appeared to the process in person, from having in the stages of the suit, in which Counsel, if regularly instructed by an Attorney might assist him, the assistance of a Counsel instructed by himself without an Attorney. There certainly has been *an understanding* in the Profession, that a Barrister ought not to accept a brief in a civil suit, except from an Attorney; but we are of opinion there is no Rule of Law, by which it can be enforced.' After referring to Constitutional precedents, his Lordship added, ' I revert to the practice of former ages only for the purpose of shewing that the onus here does not lie upon the defendants.'

" This decision is all the more valuable, because the judgment is thickly strewn with obiter dicta, on the part of the venerable Judge, strongly in favour of the existing etiquette, against the binding force of which he was compelled to decide. It evidently caused him some pain to admit that the system, under which, by Attorney favour, he had himself thriven, was totally destitute of any legal foundation.

" It is laid down by Mr. Justice Lush in his great work on ' Practice,'* that ' If the plaintiff appears at the trial in person, he must examine the witnesses, as well as address the jury, and it seems he will not

* Vol. I. p. 236, n(n).

be permitted, in civil cases, to have the aid of Counsel merely to argue legal objections. Moscati *v.* Lawson, 7 C. and P. 32' (1835). With great submission—(as we say in Court)—I think that the case hardly bears out Mr. Justice Lush's dictum. The case clearly shews that if the plaintiff in a civil case appears in person he *can* instruct Counsel; but the Counsel, whom he instructs, must conduct the entire case. The plaintiff cannot have Counsel to argue points of law and conduct *the rest* of the case himself. ' I think,' said Mr. Baron Alderson, ' that Counsel ought either to appear as such, *altogether*, or not at all.' The marginal note to Shuttleworth *v.* Nicholson,* cited by Mr. Justice Lush, is quite wrong, and confounds appearing in person with arguing the case in person.

"Mr. Shaw Lefevre observes :†— ' It has been feared by some that if it were proper for Counsel to advise his clients without the intervention of an Attorney, and for the latter to be called in when litigation commenced, it would lead to the Counsel naming the Attorney, instead of the Attorney naming the Counsel. This is so, to some extent, in France, where the Advocates invariably see their lay clients, and where the local Bar in the provinces derive much of their emoluments by giving advice to their neighbours without the intervention of an

* 1 Moo. and Rob. 254. The case clearly shews that in a civil case a party appearing in person may instruct Counsel.
† P. 21.

Avoué. It does not appear that any evil consequences follow, or that the Bar is at all lowered in the estimation of the public, or in any of its qualities, as compared with our own.' In France, let me observe, the Avocats always come to the front, when the dynastic rulers, one after another, run away from their thrones. In the English Parliament, on the contrary, 'it is notorious,' says Mr. Jevons,* 'that Barristers don't succeed.' Thé Parisian Bar is the only institution in the capital of France that has not, at some time or other, been swept away or levelled down. It has its roots in the Capitularies of Charlemagne, which enjoin that none should be admitted into the profession of Advocate except 'hommes doux, pacifique, craignant Dieu, aimant la justice et la verité.'†

" A reference to Mollot's Rules of the Legal Profession will throw some light on the Parisian system of Chamber-practice. 'Clients,' he says, 'must come to seek the Advocate in his Chambers:'‡ ' It is there always that conferences should take place'§—not between (mark you) the Barrister and Attorney, but between the Barrister and the layman, who needs the advice. Thus the Parisian Bar has preserved the grand old Roman ideal, which we have, if we follow etiquette, irreparably

---
* P. 14.
† Titre Premier des Capitulaires, p. 10, § 9.
‡ Rule 58.   § Rule 80.

lost. 'In France,' observes Mr. Jevons,* 'the Avocat frequently employs or recommends the Avoué (Attorney): from the English system it arises that the Attorney is the employer of the Advocate.' Which, I would ask, is the most 'honorable and dignified' position for the Bar?

"In his History of the French Bar,† Mr. Jones observes:—'The French Advocate, unlike the English Barrister, in this respect, always sees his clients personally, without the intervention of an Attorney, whether in civil or criminal matters; nor has any need to be instructed by an Attorney in any cause whatever.' A learned North German practitioner, Dr. Pavenstadt, of Bremen, writes to Mr. Saunders,‡ 'We consider it of the first importance that the client should always communicate directly with the Advocate.'

"General Thomas, in his evidence before the Royal Commission of 1854, thus enumerated the advantages which accrue in the United States from the direct contact of the Advocate with his client:—

"'Q. 1056. The Attorney here does all the practical part, and the Counsel only opens his mouth in Court?' 'We think that the intercourse of the client with the Counsellor has a very beneficial influence upon society. If a client comes

---

* Pp. 10, 11.
† History of the French Bar, by Robert Jones, 1855, p. 198, n(1).   ‡ P. 22.

with a bad cause, or one in which he is guilty himself, and if the Counsellor is a man of station and character, which most Counsellors occupy or possess, a direct personal influence upon the client would be exercised, that is beneficial in correcting his morals, if they be bad, and in preventing his bringing into litigation a matter, which has not a plausible and fair appearance of justice.'

"'Q. 1058. Do you mean to say that in New York it is the province of the Counsel to ascertain the facts from the party?'—' It depends altogether upon the nature of the case. If it is a case of great magnitude (I am not speaking now of Criminal Law, but questions of property,) the Counsel always has an interview with the client himself; he wishes to understand distinctly the grounds of the action.

"'Q. 1059. That is after the materials of the case, the facts, have been previously laid before him in the Brief, is it not?'—' No, it is in the outset. That is a privilege which the client claims, of seeing the Counsel, and conferring with him, whether he is to go to law, or not.'

" There are some sensible remarks in the Report of the Special Committee of the Society for the Amendment of the Law* in support of this view of the morality of the question. ' Those who think that the present practice is favourable to the

* P. 11.

morality of the Bar, rely on the argument, that if fraudulent claims or defences are to be set up, witnesses tampered with, or any other species of malpractice resorted to, it is now necessary to find both an Attorney and Barrister, who are jointly ready to lend themselves to such chicanery; whereas, under the supposed alteration' (of the rule of etiquette) 'either one or the other will alone be sufficient. Unfortunately, this check is of little practical force. *Unscrupulous practitioners are endowed with an instinct, which enables them readily to recognize each other;* and we fear that no dishonest scheme devised by a member of either branch of the Profession has ever miscarried from his inability to find a coadjutor equally unprincipled. Nay, the compulsory employment in all cases of two legal agents has a tendency to encourage such practices, by offering to them a sure prospect of impunity. It is easy for two men, without detection, and without absolute loss of character, to do things that one dare not attempt. In the last resort, each may throw the blame on the other.'* Every one familiar with the composition of the two branches

---

* It is not a little curious, that, a few pages further on, the Committee should have flatly contradicted this sensible line of argument: "Your Committee are clearly of opinion that the Bar should be preserved as a separate profession *on account of the wholesome check which Barristers and Attorneys must reciprocally afford to the conduct and charges of each other.*" p. 20.

of the Legal Profession, especially in our large towns, will recognize the truth of these remarks. The Barristers and Attorneys, who will condescend to do 'dirty work,' are unpleasantly notorious in every populous centre. They could scarcely exist without each other. They flourish on the same garbage.

"Mistakes frequently occur through the imperfect nature of the instructions laid before Counsel. I have known of instances where amended cases had to be laid before Counsel. Facts communicated to the Attorney are held back from Counsel. 'Counsel is often obliged to assume alternative states of fact in order to give any opinion at all.'* Facts, sifted through the brain of an Attorney's clerk, are often presented to Counsel in a distorted form. Cases go to trial, which 'a single question put by Counsel' to the client would have exploded.

"'As long as Authors relied' upon a few noble or wealthy 'patrons, they were a servile and dependent class:' but since they have had 'the Public' for patrons, 'they have risen in self-respect' † and in social status.

"The best kind of Free Trade in law, would, you may depend upon it, be to give the Public the option of going to the Barrister's Chambers or the Attorney's office for legal advice.

* Ibid. p. 16. † Ibid. p. 11.

"Place a person wanting legal advice (*e.g.*) in the centre of Pump Court, Temple. Within a few yards of him are clear-headed men, who would be only too glad to give him the best advice for a guinea or two. Why can't he walk up the first staircase and knock at the door of a Barrister? Because the etiquette of the Profession says 'No. You must go (*e.g.*) into Lincoln's Inn Fields, and consult a Solicitor.' He goes into Lincoln's Inn Fields and consults a Solicitor. The Solicitor lays a case before (*e.g.*) one of the Counsel, who have chambers in Pump Court. Counsel advises on the case, and receives one or two guineas from the Attorney, who charges the client at least double the amount."

"Does the same Rule of Etiquette apply to Conveyancing?" asked Percival.

"Yes. 'It is not customary,' observes Mr. Pulling,* 'for Barristers, practising as Conveyancers, to give their services, except through the intervention of Solicitors.' 'Conveyancing,' this learned author points out, was 'formerly the exclusive province of Barristers.' A curious illustration of this is afforded by an old case cited in Rolle's Abridgment.† It is laid down in this case that it is slanderous to say of a Barrister, 'He is no lawyer, he cannot make a lease;' but it is not

---

* "Law of Attorneys," 481.
† Banks *v.* Allen, 1 Roll. Abr. 54, l. 47.

slanderous to say of an Attorney, 'He made false writings,' because it is not the business of an Attorney to make writings.* The form of the ordinary covenant for further assurance stipulated for 'such assurances, as *Counsel* learned in the law shall advise or require.' The rule of etiquette, which requires the client to go to a Solicitor's office, instead of a Barrister's chambers, to give instructions and seek advice on the preparation of wills, deeds, and other legal documents, is of comparatively recent' origin.† It consecrates one of the numerous 'encroachments' (that is Mr. Pulling's phrase) of the other branch of the Profession on ours. The practice of others than Counsel drawing conveyances, is 'very severely reprobated in a work of great authority.' Mr. Shepherd, in the Preface to his celebrated 'Touchstone of Common Assurances,' describes it as 'an evil fit for the consideration of Parliament.' That the rule of etiquette is not a hundred years old appears from the language of Lord Mansfield, A.D. 1778, in the case of Willet *v.* Chambers:—'The business of conveyancing, in the very nature of it, as carried on in the country is this :— Where there is an Attorney *or Counsel* of credit, they receive money to place out upon securities, and persons who want to borrow, as well as those who want to lend apply to them for that purpose. Their profit

---

* Winch's Rep. 40.   † Pulling, 10.

arises from having the money in their hands, before it is laid out upon the intended securities, and from their fees and bill of charges upon the conveyances they draw.'* Compare with this the functions of Counsel in the reign of Henry VI. The Paston Letters shew that it was the 'exclusive province of Counsel' in those days, to take 'instructions for actions' to prepare 'marriage treaties,' to 'realize securities,' and so forth, — 'matters,' says Mr. Marshall,† 'which' (now) 'fall within the exclusive province of the Attorney.' In 1778, the Attorney competed with Counsel for conveyancing practice. Now the rule of etiquette prevails, that Clients can only communicate with conveyancing Counsel through a third party—a conveyancing Solicitor.— And what is the result? Why, that a small number of conveyancing Counsel are worked off the face of the earth, while numbers of others, as able and willing to work, are left idle for want of Solicitor-connection.—Another result is, that the expense of legal documents is enormously enhanced. ' Suppose a person wants to take a house. The Attorney, if he is a reasonable man, will prepare the lease for sixteen guineas, but that lease a Barrister has probably drawn, who thought himself handsomely paid with two.' The fourteen guineas being the toll paid for access to legal skill,

* 2 Cowper's Reports, 816.
† Page 12.

is the tax levied upon the Public for the maintenance of the etiquette of the Bar.'*

"Conveyancing Counsel, too, in the provinces, are fast dying out. In town the Conveyancing Solicitor generally instructs conveyancing Counsel to prepare the needful documents. In the provinces however, where the Solicitors have more time upon their hands, these documents are prepared, in nine cases out of ten, by the Solicitors' *Clerks*—hear it, O shade of Shepherd!"

"I see plainly," said Percival, "that our 'occupation,' like Othello's, will soon be 'gone!'"

(II.) TOUTING.

"There is no one thing," continued Stephen, "so emphatically condemned by the etiquette of the Legal Profession as ' Touting.' "

"And rightly so," said Percival.

"I quite agree with you," replied Stephen Starvington.—" The Rules of the Parisian Bar are very stringent, also, on this subject:†—" Il est indigne du caractère de l'Avocat de solliciter une clientèle: il faut qu'elle vienne le trouver dans son

* See letter of Mr. Coryton, late Recorder of Rangoon, these cited in the "Post" of 14th January, 1873, and "Times," Article there cited.

† Régles de la Profession d'Avocat, par M. Mollot, Regle 58 (Vol. I. p. 74).

Cabinet.'—And again,* "Il n'est pas digne que l'Avocat aille visiter ses clients, quelque élévée que soit leur position sociale, à moins qu'ils ne soient ses amis, que leur grande age ou leur état de santé ne les empêche de se rendre dans son Cabinet: c'est tonjours là qu'il doit conferer de l'affaire.'"

"But who are these 'clients,' of whom these rules of etiquette speak? Are they Attorneys— 'Avoués,' as the French call them?"

"Certainly not," replied Stephen. "The language of the rules themselves would suffice to shew that *the general public*, and not the Attorneys are spoken of. And this is further evident from the following passage, which I take from the same author:—

"'Sa maison' (he is speaking of the Advocate's Chambers) 'n'est pas pour lui un lieu de repos, ni un asile contre les plaideurs' (suitors). 'Elle est ouverte à tous ceux qui viennent l'accabler de leurs questions et de leurs doutes.'†

"Here, on the other hand, the client seldom dreams of visiting the Advocate's chambers, but goes to the Attorney's office, and the Attorney lays the case before Counsel.

"We have already seen,‡ that in France, if a person wants an opinion upon his case, he does not go to a legal Agent, called an Attorney (or Avoué), who

---

* P. 99. Regle 80.   † P. 20.
‡ See also Mr. Jevons' paper, p. 10.

lays a case for opinion before another legal agent, called a Barrister (or Avocat), selected by the Attorney, but he himself goes direct to the Chambers of the Barrister, whom he selects, and he consults this Barrister, without the intervention of an Attorney. If the Barrister advises him to go to law, the suitor then, but not till then, calls in an Attorney, to take the necessary formal proceedings to bring the case to trial."

"It is precisely similar to the former practice in this country," exclaimed Percival, eagerly. "Why not revert to our former practice? If any Frenchman may visit the Chambers of a Parisian Advocate for the purpose of consulting him, and your visitor's name must here appear upon the Roll of Attorneys, it follows that the possible 'clientèle' in Paris is 36,000,000, while in London it is only 11,000! How much greater, therefore, the chances are in Paris of a visit from a client! The rule of etiquette, therefore, that the client must seek the Advocate and not the Advocate the client, which, I agree with Mr. Shaw Lefevre,* is 'one that should be observed by all men of right feeling, whatever the etiquette may be,' does not operate in France, as it does in England, harshly to Advocates, who have no Attorney connection. And what is the result of the present practice in England? Why, that three thousand Barristers are not

* P. 22.

visited at all, while a few leading Counsel are consigned, like Edward James, to an early grave, by overwork.

"This run upon a small number of Barristers and almost total neglect of the rest arises from the notion deeply embedded in the Attorney-mind, that unless a *particular* Barrister of their acquaintance represents their client the case is pretty sure to be lost. The Public can form no conception of the hold that this superstition has upon the Attorney-mind. The superstition is not confined to the Country Practitioner, it affects the mind of the London Attorney, also.

"Before proceeding to speak of direct touting I would like to say a few words on indirect touting. Some of the Barristers, who condemn direct touting for business the most emphatically, are precisely the men who have risen to fame by touting indirectly. We may divide them into three classes:—

"The 'consanguinei'; the 'affines'; and the less fastidious of the 'locals.' With the last-named class we have already dealt.

"First, then, the 'consanguinei.' If you look down the list of Counsel, you will be struck with the identity of many of the names with the names that appear, a little further on, in the list of Attorneys and Solicitors. Fathers, brothers, uncles, nephews, cousins, scatter themselves in loving profusion over the two lists. Like the red rose and the briar, which grew from the respective bosoms of Lady Nancy Bell and Lord Lovell, the 'consanguinei' of these two lists grow up together and 'twine themselves into a true lovyer's knot.' Poor devils, like you and me, Pennyless, can only gaze with awe and reverence at a respectable distance on this affecting interchange of sympathy.

"The system has been graphically described by Mr. C. J. Saunders, Attorney-at-law, in his Essay on the 'Amalgamation of the two branches of the Legal Profession.'* (Please to hobserve the two 'a-twinin' of theirselves into a 'true lovyer's knot'):—' As, with the improved education and position of the Attorney, it has now become of common and increasing occurrence for *one of his sons to go to the Bar*, and another to succeed to his father's practice, the partial distribution of the patronage of the Attorneys is yearly pressing more hardly upon those who are left behind in the professional race.' ' The bondage of dependence on the patronage of Attorneys must be felt at times acutely by such of the junior Bar as, conscious of ability to work and attain distinction, but destitute of Attorney connections, see the golden shower of fortune descending upon the heads of men perhaps less able than themselves, but who are so fortunate as to have that advantage.'"

* P. 28.

"A well written and caustic criticism," said Percival, approvingly.

"It is easy to illustrate 'the common and increasing occurrence,' referred to by Mr. Saunders, from the lives even of eminent Judges. Lord Chief Justice Tindal, for example, was the son of an Attorney, and the brother of an Attorney. His Attorney-brother was a man of 'great provincial fame.'* This is a case precisely in point. A more recent case and one equally in point occurs to me. The father of that distinguished Judge, Lord Penzance, was in partnership with Lord Truro, before the last-named Law-lord was called to the Bar.† The elder brother of Lord Penzance is the head of an eminent firm of Solicitors in the City.‡ Mr. Baron Platt was, I may add, 'the son of an eminent Solicitor of London, who lived,' says Mr. Foss,§ 'to be the father of the Profession,' and the Baron was, very naturally, 'destined for the Bar from his birth.' Mr. Baron Hughes, who died last year, was 'the son of a Dublin Solicitor.'"‖

"And now for the 'affines,'" said Percival.

"Ah, marriage," said Stephen, "is the philo-

---

* Foss's Judges, Vol. IX. p. 282.
† Foss's Judges, Vol. IX. p. 303.
‡ Law Journal: Legal News: vol. vi. p. 93 (1871).
§ Foss's Judges, vol. ix. p. 244.
‖ Law Times (Journal) July 27th, 1872. Vol. liii. p. 229.

sopher's stone—the talisman, that opens the gates of that secret cave—an Attorney's or Solicitor's heart. When a Barrister once gets this well into his head, it becomes the one absorbing idea of his life. I know of a great firm of Attorneys which supports—(how like the poorhouse it sounds!) no less than three Barristers, that have married into it. 'Marriage is honourable in all,' and marriage with a Solicitor's daughter is highly honourable in a young Barrister, who wants to 'form a connection.'

"The rule of etiquette as to touting and the way to evade it by marrying are clearly pointed out in a clever article (which I cut out of *the Globe*)* on ' Briefless Barristers :'—' The Barrister does not go to the Solicitor, and the Solicitor will not come to him. He must sit alone in his chambers, and, if needs be, endure the consuming fire of suppressed genius, but he must make no more sign than the Spartan boy did, when he held the fox under his garment. He will be ostracised, if he ask a Solicitor for a job, *and his own pride will never allow him.* He would recoil from the thought of touting for a brief, or advertising himself. . . . There is nothing for poor Briefless to do but to sit alone in his chambers and put up with it. . . . Let us hope that, some day, he will *fall into luck's way and marry a Solicitor's daughter.* Then,

* 18 January, 1872.

when the business of the firm flows in upon him,' &c., &c., &c."

"Poor dear, ingenuous, youth," exclaimed Pennyless, mockingly. "I wonder which is the most straightforward and honest—the Barrister who pockets his 'pride,' and 'asks a Solicitor for a job,' or the Barrister who sneaks up to the Solicitor's daughter, and gets her to 'ask papa' for him?"

"The former, decidedly," said Stephen,—"but women are such capital touters!

"Mr. Shaw Lefevre alludes to the consanguinei and affines. 'An early introduction,' he says,* 'to easy business, and familiarity with its forms, are almost indispensable to secure success at the Bar, and the opportunities which give rise to these advantages rest mainly with the Attorneys, and not with the Public; and it is neither unnatural, nor can it be said to be unjust on their part, if these opportunities are given in the first place to relations or connections of their own, whom they know, in preference to strangers, whom they do not know. There are not a few great firms of Attorneys in the present day who have of themselves sufficient business to support a Barrister with work, and it sometimes happens in such cases that a close connection exists between the firm and the Barrister, having its origin in family ties, which has all the appearance and some of the effect of a partnership, the reality

* P. 20.

of which would be opposed to the principle on which the Bar rests, and contrary to every rule of etiquette in the Profession; so true is the old saying, Naturam expellas furcâ, tamen usque recurrit.'

" The first kind of direct tout that I shall introduce to your notice is a very low fellow, indeed. ' One of the most honorable members of the Criminal (sic) Bar,' introduces us* to the Old Bailey Tout, who is a species *per se*, redolent of the greasy abominations of that historic retreat:—' Hanging about the purlieus of the Courts are a number of persons, some of whom, it is believed, have themselves stood in the dock, who, for a small payment, are allowed by some obscure Solicitor to use his name. To one of these irresponsible individuals, usually characterized by the name of touts, the constable introduces the prosecutor. A bargain is concluded, and the tout undertakes to conduct the case for the costs allowed out of the County Rates. He then puts the name of his invisible principal on the back of the bill of indictment and obtains and pays 10s for a copy of the depositions, which he makes into a brief for Counsel. For these professional services the County allows the tout one guinea in respect of each indictment, and out of each guinea the grateful gentleman pays the constable 5s for the introduc-

---

* See his letter in the Law Times, Sept. 9, 1871, Vol. li. p. 343.

tion, and besides this he has to stand treat at intervals for his thirsty patron. It will at once be seen, that the tout would never make it pay, unless there were some other means of compensation.' What that compensation is, we can better consider, when we come to the question of 'Fees.'

'In the discussion, which arose in the autumn of 1871, in reference to these proceedings, the *Law Times** deliberately made the 'following charges against a limited number of Barristers:—

" '1. Touting and underbidding.

" '2. Unblushing business intercourse with unqualified Practitioners.

" '3. Engaging in speculative business, and signing for fees before they are paid.

" '4. Taking smaller fees than those signed for, and giving the Attorney or his clerk, the benefit of the rebate.'

" The second charge was not confined to Criminal, but extended as well to Civil Courts in the Metropolis. The third charge and the fourth were confined to the Criminal Courts of the Metropolis.

" The Old Bailey tout sometimes appears in the more exalted rank of an Attorney's clerk. The 'Malpractices' at the Old Bailey, which came before the Public in the autumn of 1871, related exclusively, I think, to Attorneys and Attorneys'

---

* Sept. 23rd, 1871, (Vol. li. p. 370).

clerks. Barristers were not implicated in these transactions. The disreputable clerk of the disreputable Attorney takes the Prosecutor to a public-house adjoining the Old Bailey, and tells him that he will probably be put upon his oath as to whether he had paid the clerk any money, and, in order that he may be able to swear that he has, the clerk introduces him to a confederate, who places a guinea in his hand, saying, 'Now put the guinea into the clerk's hand.' The Prosecutor having obeyed, the clerk says, 'Now you can swear that you have paid me a guinea!' The Prosecutor may regard this proceeding with suspicion, and fear that he will, after all, be made responsible. Upon that the following document is drawn up and handed to him.

"'Regina (!) v. T.—Oct. 18th, 1871.—I hereby indemnify you against any further costs in this matter upon the payment of one guinea to me, irrespective of the amount allowed me by the County.

'For C. D.' (the Attorney)
'A. B. (the Attorney's clerk).

'*Received* £1 1.'

" The object of this piece of juggling is to defeat two rules laid down by the Clerk of Arraigns, that no allowances shall be made to the prosecuting Attorney, if there be any understanding that the prosecutor is not to be personally liable, and unless the Attorney has been retained by the Prosecutor.

Mr. Commissioner Kerr ordered in one case that the Clerk of Arraigns should not recognize any costs whatever in the name of the Attorney or his clerk, till further orders from the Court. He gave directions that a copy of the shorthand writer's notes should be sent to the Law Society. He also suggested that a 'short Bill' should be presented to Parliament for the appointment of a Public Prosecutor for the Central Criminal Court.*

" That suggestion was carried out last Session," said Percival.

" Yes," replied Stephen, "but the Bill was for the *compulsory* appointment of Public Prosecutors all over England. Such a Bill is not wanted, for the provinces. In Lancashire, for example, Public Prosecutors, to all intents and purposes, already exist. The Magistrates' Clerks get up the cases admirably. In some of the Boroughs the Town Councils have the power of appointing quasi-Public Prosecutors under private Acts. In others, the Town Clerk is the nominal Public Prosecutor, and employs a skilful Attorney to prosecute, as is the case at Liverpool, or an experienced gentleman from his own office, as is the case in Manchester. To remove the present quasi-Public Prosecutors would seriously damage

---

* See, as to these proceedings, the Law Journal, Legal News, Vol. vi. pp. 748, 749, 750, 807. Also 740, 744.

the public service. In the Central Criminal Court District, a Public Prosecutor will, on the other hand, be eminently useful, and I quite concur in the suggestion of Mr. Commissioner Kerr."

"If I recollect aright," said Percival, "the Public Prosecutors' Bill of last Session was smothered under the Amendments of the Government."

"It was. But the proposal of the Government to make the Bill permissive everywhere, except in the Central Criminal Court District, will meet with general approval and ensure the passing of the Bill next Session. There are, however, many objectionable features in the Bill, as amended by the Government. One, I believe, is the bribe held out to County Magistrates and other local authorities to appoint Public Prosecutors under the Bill, by enlarging their powers of dipping their hands into the ratepayers' pockets, in case they appoint them. There can be little doubt that, wherever the Bill is adopted, a good deal of jobbing will take place in making appointments. The Bill is too centralizing, also, in its tendencies."

"The cases to which you have referred," said Percival, "as illustrations of direct touting, were cases of downright dishonesty and cheating. There are, however, I suppose, cases of direct touting, which, however reprehensible, do not involve downright dishonesty and cheating."

"Yes, there are the two cases of stranger-Attorneys button-holing unwilling clients at the Police Courts, and of Attorneys advertising for business in the Press."

" Pray, give us some specimens," said Percival, laughing, "of the button-holing and advertising Attorneys!"

" If your son happens to get into 'a leettle trouble,' or your wife happens to take out a warrant against you for an assault, it is not at all pleasant to be accosted in the waiting room of a Police Court by an Attorney, who asks you, without a word of introduction, 'What's your game?' or, 'Give me an I. O. U. on your goods and chattels to defend you!' and then, after you have politely declined his services, to have your name and address put down in his pocket-book, and to be told by him next day, 'I've made out my brief and shall expect something for what I've done!' Yet this is stated to have occurred to Messieurs A—— and H——, at the Lambeth Police Court, last Spring.* The Attorney told H——, to reassure him, 'I'll draw you through this, as I defended the baby-farming case at Brixton!' If he meant that he defended Margaret Waters, I'm afraid the prospect was far from cheering! Mr. Ellison, the presiding magistrate, said that 'a disgraceful system of touting, utterly derogatory to the character of the Profession, had

* Law Times (Journal), May 25th, 1872, (Vol. liii. p. 65), and June 1st, 1872 (Vol. liii. p. 87).

been carried on in and around the Court;' expressed his own and Mr. Chance's (his colleague's) 'abhorrence of such dirty and disreputable practices:' and then, what then? he used the terrible threat of—reporting the case to the Law Society!

" A good illustration of the powerful influence of 'ye manners and customs of ye age' over professional men of unblemished character, will be collected from the following correspondence which I cut from the *Law Times*:*

'The enclosed advertisement is the latest sample I have seen of advertising for business. I leave it for your readers to judge whether it is professional or not. I wonder whether the advertiser has really been admitted a Solicitor, and where he received his training.

F—— W——,† of Betley, Solicitor, begs to announce that on Monday, the 29th inst., he will open an Office in Mill Street, Crewe, at the house of Mrs. F——, where he will attend personally every day (except Saturday), from 10 a.m. till 4 p.m., for the purpose of meeting and advising with clients, who may also consult him at his residence in Betley every evening after 6 o'clock.

A COUNTRY SOLICITOR.

" 'My attention has been called to a letter in the *Law Times* from a Country Solicitor, reflecting on

* May 11, 1872 (Vol. liii. p. 36). May 25, 1872, (Vol. liii. pp. 71, 72).

† The initials are purposely substituted for the full name.

an advertisement which was lately issued by Mr.
F—— W—— of Betley. With the advertisement
itself I have nothing to do, but this I feel bound
to say, that, if Mr. W—— could have supposed it
would bear the interpretation, which I am bound
to say I think may not unfairly be put upon it, he
would have been the last person in the Profession
to have adopted it. The anonymous individual,
who signs himself A Country Solicitor, asks where
Mr. W—— had his training. Mr. W—— had his
training in my office, and if the many articled
clerks, whom I have had the good fortune and
misfortune to introduce into the Profession, had
conducted themselves as honorably as my excellent friend and former pupil, Mr. F—— W——,
I should have much less cause for regret than I
now have. R—— H——.'

" In the same number of the *Law Times* as the
letter of R—— H——, appeared the following
letter from F—— W—— himself:—

" 'In reference to the letter contained in your
journal of the 11th inst., from A Country Solicitor,
I think it due to myself to explain that, when I
sent off the advertisement therein referred to, *it
did not occur to me that it would be deemed unprofessional.* It was chiefly meant as a notice to my
country clients of my intended change, in order
that they might know where to find me, and thus
be spared a useless journey to my residence. I
am told by those in whose judgment I can confide

that my advertisement is open to the construction which I am quite sure the Country Solicitor is only too glad to put upon it, and I, therefore, at once apologise for its insertion.

F—— W——.'

"This young Solicitor evidently inserted the advertisement in the innocence of his heart, thinking no ill to any one, and I have no doubt he is a much nicer fellow than the Country Solicitor, who held him up to the scorn of his professional brethren.

"I confess that the distinction between advertising for clients and advertising for pupils has always seemed to me a 'very thin' one.

'Law Examinations.—A gentleman at the Bar (Bachelor of Laws in Honours) prepares, in Chambers or through the Post, for the Incorporated Law Society, the Bar, and London LL.B. Terms moderate. Address, LL.B. care of' (here follow the name and address of a firm of Law Booksellers).

'Law Examinations. A Solicitor of ability and experience'—(modest, isn't it?)—'reads with gentlemen for the Intermediate and Final Examinations, at their own homes. Fees very moderate. Address, A.B.' (here follows the address).*

"Surely this is 'touting for business!' The concealment of the names is an indication that 'LL.B.' and 'A. B.' felt they were committing a breach of etiquette. F— W— boldly printed his name; and, therefore, I am disposed to believe that 'it did not occur to him that his advertisement' to his clients of his change of place of business, 'would be deemed unprofessional,' and he immediately apolo-

* Law Times (Journal), May 4th, 1872, vol. liii. p. 20.

gized when he was 'told by those in whose judgment he could confide,' that his advertisement *was* deemed unprofessional.

" When shall we have a similar apology from the Barristers and Solicitors who tout for pupils in the Legal Press ?

" The Solicitor referred to in the following advertisement evidently felt, like 'LL. B.' and ' A. B.' that he was guilty of a breach of etiquette in advertising for business; else, why conceal his name? ' Law—Conveyancing—A Solicitor engaged during the day, but whose evenings are at disposal (*sic*), is desirous to undertake the investigation of titles to Freehold, Copyhold, and Leasehold property, the preparation of conveyances, assignments, leases, mortgages, and all other documents connected with conveyancing, on moderate terms. Address C. P.' (Here follows the address).*

" A correspondent of the *Law Times* seems to regard touting for business in the newspapers as merely '*infra dig*' on the part of a Solicitor.† Another correspondent points out‡ 'that signboards have now been adopted by members of the Profession, and that upon the end of a house facing a public thoroughfare in the neighbourhood of the Elephant and Castle appears a huge board, nailed

* Law Times (Journal), Sept. 7th 1872, (Vol. 53, p. 345, and see letter of " Vigilans," p. 406.
† Ibid. Sept. 9th, 1871, (vol. li. p. 354).
‡ Ibid: Sept. 16th, 1871, (vol. li. p. 366).

half way up the blank wall, 6 feet long and 3 feet broad, with M——, Solicitor, painted black with flaming red capital letters.'

" It is not surprising that in a commercial age like this, when everybody is supposed to be at liberty to push his way in the world, as best he can, provided he does not violate any of the precepts of the moral law of God, or enactments of the positive law of the land, the practice of touting for business should have assumed considerable dimensions in the Legal Profession. There is nothing either morally or legally wrong in touting for business in the Legal Profession, if unaccompanied by circumstances of fraud or dishonesty, any more than in honest touting for business in the wine trade. It is, no doubt, a very glaring breach of etiquette for an Attorney to copy the manners and customs of such low fellows, as the heads of schools and colleges, clergymen, estate-agents and surgeon-dentists: he must not ' follow a multitude to do evil.' That no moral stigma attaches in the United States, at all events, to a professional man, even an Attorney, for advertising must have been abundantly evident to the visitors at last year's International Exhibition who cast their eyes over the United States' Journals, which covered the walls of the newspaper corridor in that wonderful building. Advertisements by 'Attorneys-at-law,' aye, and by ' Counsellors-at-law,' announcing their whereabouts and the professional business which they were ready to perform for the Public, appeared in the first column of almost every broadsheet. Don't suppose, my dear Pennyless, that I am advocating the introduction of the American Legal system into this country; I dislike it extremely; but I do detest the hypocrisy of those who make such a fuss about open and direct touting in an honest way of business, as if it were a crime, while they themselves are touting for business by indirect and underhand methods every day of their lives, Sunday not excepted!"

(III.) A. B. (BARRISTER) AND COMPANY.

"'Partnerships,' you say, (or, rather, Mr. Lefevre says), between the Barrister and the Attorney are 'opposed to every rule of etiquette.' Are partnerships between Barrister and Barrister sanctioned by etiquette?"

"Certainly not: they are equally opposed to it. Nevertheless, for all practical purposes, they exist. You have heard of printers' devils: there are Barristers' devils also. One Barrister devils for another Barrister. The devil is a kind of junior partner:* by no means a 'sleeping' partner: he

* The *Echo* has the following:—" Practically Barristers do go into partnership with each other now. For what is meant by devilling for a man? Is it not in reality going into partnership with him ?'— Echo, Jan. 16, 1873.

has to work late and early. At the Chancery Bar the devil frequently receives half the fees.* The Attorney General's devil is well paid. Other devils are, I fear, but 'poor devils,' after all. The only share of the profits that they receive are crumbs that fall from their master's table—stray briefs from the Attorneys, who are killing their chiefs with kindness, fall to their lot: and this is deemed an ample reward. When the chief partner is made a Judge or dies, a fair share of his business survives to his humble junior.

" A more lucrative kind of partnership, in præsenti, is that which is formed between two or more local juniors rising into practice, who take it in turns to watch each other's briefs, and so, practically, ' divide the field ' between them. I don't, of course, mean to suggest that they, literally, hand over to a common fund, divisible per capita, the fees that they, severally, receive; but by forming a kind of trades union, they contrive to keep the leading business of the Court circulating amongst themselves, to the exclusion of outsiders, or non-unionists. The local Attorney will be sure to find some one of the pair, or trio, 'standing to attention,' at his approach.

" Contrary to the French rule of etiquette, which vests a discretion in the Advocate,† ' Counsel is

* Lefevre, p. 28.
† Mollot, Rules 61, 68, 89, Vol. i. pp. 79, 88, 105. (Mr. Lefevre has, by inadvertence, (p. 29,) cited Rule 38 for Rule 68).

bound to take a brief, when offered him,' unless he is engaged on the other side. (Cases, in which Counsel have taken fees from *both* sides, are, let us hope, rare, although not altogether unknown). Suppose, however, two briefs are entrusted to a Barrister in *two different towns*, *e.g.* Manchester and Oldham, where Courts are *sitting at the same time*, if the Barrister does not wish to get a tremendous 'wigging,' he will hand back *one* of the briefs to the Attorney who entrusted him with it, and advise him to instruct other Counsel. It will not do for the Barrister to ask other Counsel to hold it for him—that would be a kind of partnership, and is strictly forbidden, even though the arrangement may be that the Barrister, who is instructed, should receive all the fees. The Attorney must have the opportunity of selecting another Advocate, and even if the Barrister, whom he originally instructed, recommend a substitute, the Attorney is not bound to accept this substitute. He may have selected the Barrister, whom he originally instructed, for some special qualities, which the substitute does not possess: and it is considered unjust to compel the Attorney to accept an untried Advocate, merely on the ipse dixit of a friend. If, however, the Attorney consents to accept the substitute, the name of the Barrister originally instructed must be removed from the brief, and the name of the substitute must be inserted instead. This qualification of the rule, that 'a Barrister is bound to accept a brief, when offered to him,' is, evidently, intended for the benefit of suitors, and is, also, beneficial to the less known members of the local bar: while, on the other hand, it has a tendency to weaken monopoly, by compelling the busier Counsel *to elect* between the two Courts sitting in different towns at the same time. Barristers, who are rising into practice, don't like the rule; but this, I think, is an argument in its favour, as it shows that it *distributes* Attorney-patronage, and gives suitors and untried Advocates a chance of knowing each other.

" The Rule, that ' a Barrister is bound to accept a brief, when offered to him,' is acted upon at the Common Law Bar, without qualification, within the limits of the Metropolis, within the limits of Manchester, of Liverpool, and of each provincial town. It frequently arises that the same Barrister is instructed by half a dozen *different* Attorneys to appear in half a dozen *different* Courts of the Metropolis *at the same time*. Several Courts sit simultaneously even in Manchester and Liverpool: how much more so in the Metropolis! It is purely a matter of accident *when* the different cases will come on; the Attorneys know nothing of the Barrister's engagements; and the Barristers think that there is always *a chance* of the different causes coming on in different Courts at different times. The result, however, is, that the Attorneys gamble for Counsel, so to speak. There is a chance of the Counsel, who has been instructed, coming up trumps, but it is only a chance. It is like engaging Mr. Sims Reeves to sing at a concert. He has as often a cold, as not. If Mr. Sims Reeves doesn't appear, however, after having been paid for, the manager knows that no other enterprising lessee is reaping the benefit of his beautiful voice, having engaged him for the same evening, and paid a higher price. How disappointed the audience would be, if the manager came in front of the curtain, and announced that Mr. Sims Reeves was singing elsewhere, and that Mr. Vance or Mr. Sam Hall would occupy his place! Risu solvuntur tabulæ. The chairs and tables would be broken up, amid the jeers of the audience!—To the leading Counsel of Westminster Hall, may we not say,

"'Mutato nomine, de te
'Fabula narratur?'"

"The principle of partnerships is resorted to. Some satellite of the great man always presents himself to the mortified Attorney, who has paid 'over the nail' for refined gold, and gets only 'sounding brass' instead. No part of the fees is, in this case, handed over to the substituted Counsel. The name of the Barrister originally instructed continues to adorn the Brief. The substituted Counsel is, in fact, his devil.

"A milder form of grievance is the absence of the Senior Counsel when the case is called on, the ,entire burthen and heat of the day falling upon the Junior. The absence of the Senior Counsel is, generally, attributable to the causes I have already mentioned."

"Why not apply to these grievances the remedy that naturally suggests itself?" asked Percival. "I mean the rule of etiquette, which prevents the Barrister, under certain circumstances, from holding two Briefs in two different Courts at the same time?—I can't see that the fact of the two Courts being in the same town makes any difference. Do you think that the audience would be better pleased, if the manager consoled them for Sims Reeves' absence, by informing them that he was singing, not at Brighton or Birmingham, but at the establishment over the way, or next door? I think it would intensify their anger. And a Barrister has more excuse for taking Briefs at Oldham and Manchester simultaneously, than in the Court of Exchequer and Court of Common Pleas, next door to each other, at Westminster Hall."

"I think there is a good deal of force in what you say, Pennyless," said Starvington. "Something of the kind has, I believe, been adopted at the Chancery Bar, where, Mr. Shaw Lefevre observes,* 'most of the leading Counsel confine themselves to particular Courts.' The old monopoly of the Serjeants in the Court of Common Pleas, had this advantage, that it secured to

* Pp. 27-8.

Suitors, or rather, I should say, to Attorneys the services of the Serjeant that they preferred."*

(IV.) CASTE-IRON.

" There are some curious rules with respect to going Circuit," said Starvington. " London Barristers must not, on any account, enter an assize town on the day prior to Commission Day, lest they should happen to meet an Attorney, who had not yet selected his Counsel, and thus obtain what is called 'an unfair and improper advantage.' This Rule was invented, I suppose, before local Bars were established. The local must, evidently, have an advantage over the London Barrister, if this Rule be now enforced. You can't compel the local to leave home, just before the Assizes commence. And even if you did, he'd take care to 'catch his Attorney' before leaving!

" The local Barrister has, of course, his Chambers to fall back upon. Not so the London Barrister, who joins Circuit. He must either put up at an Hotel, or take lodgings. Most London Barristers prefer to take lodgings, as being quieter. But some of them put up at Hotels. This, I believe, is contrary to the rules of etiquette. The rule on this point has, however, been narrowed down to this, that a Barrister on Circuit must not,

* See the Report of the Common Law Commissioners, 1829. p. 22.

on any account, enter the coffee-room of an Hotel. The reason is obvious; it would givé him 'an unfair and improper advantage,' as he might chance to stumble over an Attorney! And yet it is not an uncommon thing for the local to lunch, dine and sup with Attorneys, and offer them hospitality in return—of course not when the Assizes are on—O no!—that would be a violation of etiquette."

"These Rules must have been framed by the Priest-Serjeants of the middle ages!" said Percival. "I suppose de Bussey had a hand in framing them. They disclose cases of conscience, worthy of the manipulation of a Dens or a Liguori!"

"I fancy they are of much more recent origin," said Stephen, smiling: "they are all logical deductions from the first Rule that we considered, the instruction of Counsel by Attorney. The exquisite prudery that distinguishes them is a product of modern civilization.

"It was at one time, I believe, laid down as a rule of etiquette that the Barrister on Circuit must ride or post it from one assize-town to another. Those were the days of coaching, and just think what opportunities he might have had of meeting and chatting with Attorneys on the roof, in the rumble, on the box, in the coupé of a coach! The railway has abolished this rule of etiquette. But another rule has arisen in its stead. The Barrister on Circuit must travel first-class. This new rule has been framed, I fancy, more with a view to supporting 'the honour and dignity of the Profession,' than for the purpose of 'cutting' Attorneys. Prosperous Attorneys, with an unlimited command of patronage, (the 'trusty and well-beloved' Commissioners, Messieurs Bateson and Lowndes, for example,) are more likely to select first, than second or third, class carriages, and are certainly much better able to pay for them, than nine out of ten of the Barristers, who go Circuit."

(V.) PRECEDENCE.

" Mr. Lefevre mentions,* as a Rule of Etiquette, that 'It is against the etiquette for a Barrister to hold a brief as junior to one who was called before him.' I presume the word 'before' is a misprint for 'after.' The rule that a Barrister under the rank of Queen's Counsel and Serjeant takes precedence according to the date of his call operates very unfavourably to the older members of the 'Junior' Bar, who have been distanced in the race by younger competitors. There are many of these older men, who would gladly hold a brief with a younger man, on the condition of being 'led' by him. The Attorney wishes the younger man to do the leading business, and he would willingly give a second brief to the older, but less distinguished Advocate. This, however, is impossible. The rule of eti-

* P. 32.

quette sternly follows the maxim, 'Seniores priores.' So and so 'leads' so and so, is the well-known phrase which indicates that the former was called to the Bar before the latter. A relaxation of this rigid rule would be advantageous to many 'Juniors.'"

(VI.) FEES.

" Counsel's fees are in the nature of a honorarium and are not recoverable by legal process. I cannot cite a more weighty authority, in proof of this, than the author of the 'Commentaries on the Law of England.' 'It is established with us,' says Sir William Blackstone,* 'that a Counsel can maintain no action for his fees, which are given, not as locatio vel conductio, but as quiddam honorarium, not as a salary or hire, but as a mere gratuity, which a Counsellor cannot demand without doing wrong to his reputation.'

" There can be little doubt that Mr. Kennedy, that able, but too-confiding Advocate, 'did wrong to his reputation,' by suing Mrs. Patience Broun on her promise to pay him £20,000 for his brilliant, and successful advocacy, which secured her an estate worth £60,000; but we ought to be grateful to him for obtaining from the lips of Lord Chief Justice Erle, a final and solemn ratification of the opinion of Mr. Justice Blackstone.† 'We con-

* Vol. iii. p. 28.
† Kennedy *v.* Broun : 13 C. B. (N. S.) 677 : 32 L. J. (C·

sider,' said Lord Chief Justice Erle, delivering the judgment of the Court of Common Pleas, 'that a promise by a client to pay money to a Counsel for his advocacy, whether made before, or during, or after litigation, has no binding effect ; and furthermore, that the relation of Counsel and client renders the parties mutually incapable of making any contract of hiring and service, concerning advocacy in litigation.' Words could hardly be more sweeping and comprehensive than these : and it is difficult not to feel, in perusing them, after the masterly argument of Mr. Kennedy, that the Court distinctly overruled the older authorities which he cited, and which were in favour of his claim. That the annuities and fees formerly given to Counsel, ' pro consilio impenso et impendendo,' were given solely for ' advice in the management of property and general affairs,' and not, also, for ' advocacy in litigation ' is an asumption unsupported by a tittle of proof. The very first case cited by Mr. Kennedy* annihilates this assumption: — 'In Brownlow's Entries, published in 1654, p. 172, there is a precedent of a declaration in debt by a Counsel stating that the Defendant had retained him to be of Counsel *in any action in which he should sue or be sued* capiendo salario 6s 8d a year, claming five years arrears.' It is futile to try to distinguish such a

P.) 137 : 11 W. R. 284 : 7 L. T. (N. S.) 626 : 9 Jur. (N. S.) 119.

* 13 C. B. (N. S), p. 701.

case as this from Mr. Kennedy's own case on the ground of *express* contract. Lord Chief Justice Erle himself shewed the absurdity of saying that a Barrister can recover his fees from his Client on an express, but not an implied contract. 'If there is incapacity, words and implication are alike nullities: no contract can result.'*

"As recently as the 30th Elizabeth it was laid down by Mr. Justice Wrey, in the King's Bench,† that 'if one cometh to a Serjeant-at-law, to have his counsel, and the Serjeant doth advise him, and afterwards the Client in consideration of such Counsel promiseth to pay him £20, *an action lieth for it.*' This was a case of express promise, and we find no trace of the rule that the Counsel and Client were incapacitated from contracting. Macauley, Q. C. and Field, arguendo Kennedy *v.* Broun‡ said that this case was 'clearly not law,' but they didn't shew any strong ground for their opinion. The Court of Chancery, indeed, on several occasions, in the 17th century, refused to sanction the recovery of fees by Counsel in that Court. In the 5th year of Charles I. in the case of Moor *v.* Row,§ 'the Plaintiff,

* 13 C. B. (N. S.) pp. 732-3. Egan *v.* Kensington Guardians, 3 G. and D. 204, and 3 Q. B. 935 (n), cited in Fisher's Digest, has nothing to do with the right of Counsel to sue *quâ* Counsel.
† Marsh *v.* Rainsford, 2 Leon. 111.
‡ 13 C. B. (N. S.) 725.
§ 1 Reports in Chancery, 21.

being a Counsellor-at-law, brought his bill for fees due to him from the Defendant, being a Solicitor, who was to account with him at the end of every term. The Defendant demurred. The Court allowed the Demurrer nisi causa. Demurrer affirmed and the Bill dismissed.'

"A Demurrer was also allowed in the 25th year of Car. II. to a Bill demanding £200 'for advice and pains in several causes, in which the Defendant was concerned';* the demurrer shewing for cause that 'if the Defendant should answer the Bill it would draw him under a penal law (?), it being against the course of all Courts of Justice for any Counsellor-at-law to make *such* a contract as was suggested for his fees in a gross sum to be paid upon the event of any cause.' These two cases are cited by the late Lord Redesdale in his celebrated Treatise on Pleading,† as authorities for the rule that a Defendant may demur to a bill 'if the claim of the Plaintiff is of a matter in itself unlawfnl, as of money promised to a Counsellor-at-law, for advice and pains in carrying on a suit.'

"A curious case is mentioned by Viner, in his 'Abridgment,' of 'one Mr. Dean, a Barrister-at-law, who made a Bill as a Solicitor: a motion was made to tax it, which was granted; but the Court

* Penrice *v.* Parker, Reports temp. Finch, 75.

† P. 183, 5th Ed. (1847). In the reference to Moor *v.* Row, the page is given wrongly, as it is in Viner's Abr. tit. "Counsellor," A. 11.

said, that if he insisted upon having his Bill paid, they would hereafter *treat him as a Solicitor!* Mr. Justice Powys said, that, so it was ruled in Chancery by my Lord Chancellor Harcourt in the case of one Mr. Alston. If gentlemen would not take fees after the usual manner, they ought not to recover them'—(doesn't say, could not)—' by any action-at-law.'*

" It would thus seem that the rule that Counsel cannot sue for his fees is a creation of the Court of Chancery, and first made its appearance about 150 years ago† in a Court of Common Law, which eventually adopted it in defiance of the older authorities. This case in Viner is cited with a great flourish of trumpets by Counsel for Mrs. Patience Broun, arguendo,‡—the concluding words being italicised in Mr. Scott's Report. The oldest Common Law case cited by these gentlemen in support of their view is Morris *v.* Hunt, A.D. 1819,§ which is interesting, on account of the reason that it gives for the rule:—' The suggestion is, that by law no man is liable to pay for Counsel at all. That seems to me to arise entirely from a mistake in point of law. It is never expected, it has never been the practice, and in many instances it would be wrong, that Counsel should be gratuitously giving up their

* Viner's Abr. tit. " Counsellor :" A. 22.
† The case occurred in 12 Anne.
‡ 13 C. B. (N. S.) 722, 723.
§ 1 Chitty's Rep. 544, 550, 551.

time and talents without receiving any recompence or reward. It is the recompence and reward which induce men of considerable ability and certainly of great integrity and with every qualification, which is necessary to adorn the Bar, to exert their talents. It is the emolument in the first instance, to a certain degree, that induces them to bear the difficulties of their profession and to wear away their health, which a long attendance at the Bar naturally produces; and it is of advantage to the public that they should receive those emoluments, which produce integrity and independence, and I know of nothing more likely to destroy that independence and integrity than to deprive them of the honorable reward of their labours: But it is *said* that Counsel can maintain no action for their fees. Why ? Because it is understood that their emoluments are not to depend upon the event of the cause, but that their compensation is to be equally the same whether the event be successful or unsuccessful. *They are to be paid beforehand*, because they are not to be left to the chance whether they shall ultimately get their fees or not, and it is for the purpose of promoting the honour and integrity of the Bar, that it is expected all their fees shall be paid at the time when their briefs are delivered. That is the reason why they are not permitted to maintain an action. It is their duty to take care, if they have fees, that they have them *beforehand*, and therefore the law will not allow them any remedy if they disregard their duty in that respect.' This was the language of Mr. Justice Bayley. The language of Mr. Justice Best was much more vehement:—'Was it ever understood by any man that gentlemen who are put to the most enormous expense in rendering themselves competent to appear in a Court of Justice, are to act for nothing? No man is so ignorant or so stupid as to suppose that this can be the case. The argument now used, that a Counsel cannot recover his fees at law is answered by the usage which has for a great length of time prevailed, of allowing the fees of Counsel on the taxation of costs. This stands upon as ancient a usage and as sound a principle as any other doctrine of the law of England.' In this case fees were allowed for three Counsel on taxation of costs. It was a case of difficulty in which the Plaintiff obtained a verdict. Defendant had argued that it was contrary to law to require a Defendant to pay the fees paid to Plaintiff's Counsel, such fees not being recoverable by the Counsel in a Court of Justice.

"After the decision in Kennedy v. Broun it would be as futile for a Barrister to bring an action for his fees against his client, as for Mr. P. A. Taylor to sue the ratepayers of Leicester for his wages as a Member of Parliament. The older authorities are as clearly in favor of the one as of the other;* the modern authorities are as clearly against both.

* See Hallam's Middle Ages, Vol. iii. p. 114.

"The rule, no doubt, which is a rule of law, as well as of etiquette, that Counsel cannot sue his client for his fees, sometimes works considerable injury to Counsel. It is made use of by a low class of Attorneys to get Counsel to allow a rebate. Having no legal demand for the fee, Counsel have been known to be thankful to receive part. Low Attorneys will often keep Counsel out of their fees for years. A Barrister told me the other day that £1,000 worth of fees were due to him by Attorneys! In these cases there can be little doubt that the Attorneys got the fees for Counsel from the clients and never paid them over. Fees are nominally paid at the time the brief is delivered; but in nine cases out of ten* they are not actually paid till after the case has been heard. Counsel can, I believe, prevent the Attorneys from pocketing the fees, by refusing to endorse a receipt for them upon the brief until the fees are actually paid. No *honest* Barrister will sign for fees that he has never received. If he does, and it is discovered, he ought to be disbarred."

"I quite agree with you," said Percival; "the most scrupulous honesty is necessary in such delicate matters. You spoke, some time ago, about dishonest transactions at the Old Bailey. What is the 'compensation' which the unprofessional tout receives?"

* Lefevre, p. 25.

" The compensation which the unprofessional tout at the Old Bailey receives arises from a rebate on the fees which he pays the prosecuting Counsel. 'One of the most honourable members of the Criminal Bar' says, that 'Barristers, unfortunately, are found sufficiently regardless of the honour of their Profession to lend themselves' to the conspiracy of the touts, 'by accepting briefs and signing for fees which they' never 'receive. At the close of the case the tout receives the brief' back 'from the Barrister, with the fee signed for, and with this voucher obtains the money'—for the (apparent) costs of the prosecution—'from the treasury of the Court, the proportion received by the Counsel being a matter of arrangement between him and the tout, the tout, it may well be conceived, taking the lion's share.'*

" I am afraid that the *Law Times* has only too much ground for the charge that it brings against certain members of the Bar† of taking smaller fees than those signed for, and giving the Attorney or his clerk the benefit of the rebate, and that the charge is applicable to civil as well as criminal business.

" I was told the other day, by a Barrister of great experience, that a learned Serjeant once appealed to him for sympathy because he had only

* Law Times: Sept. 9th, 1871, vol. li. p. 343.
† Sept. 23rd, 1871, vol. li. 370.

received two guineas out of the eight for which he had just signed, and, becoming communicative, the learned Serjeant stated further that the Attorney had recently half-a-dozen cases at Guildhall, and, not getting from him a single brief, he went to the Attorney and said, 'I see your name down for half-a-dozen causes, and you haven't given me a brief in one of them,' and that thereupon the Attorney smiled and said, 'My dear fellow, A. B.' (mentioning a then well-known Queen's Counsel) 'has got the whole six briefs—*he is working out a judgment I have against him!*" *

" ' O tempora! O Moses!' " exclaimed Percival.

"The *Law Times* speaks of arrangements between the Managing Clerks of Attorneys and certain members of the Bar—a kind of partnership, in fact, for the purpose of dividing the spoil; and the experienced Barrister to whom I just now referred, assures me that it is a fact that such arrangements are made. 'It is rumoured,' says the *Law Times*,† 'that more than one flourishing member of the Bar owes his rise to the kind aid of these useful individuals.' The *Law Times* 'disclaims any intention of casting the slightest reflection upon managing clerks, as a class,' and I need

---

* "Making a secret agreement with an Attorney to work off a debt," is among the breaches of etiquette mentioned by Mr. Lefevre, (p. 15), and he calls it "Dishonest."

† Sept. 23rd, 1871, vol. li. p. 870.

scarcely say, my dear Percival, that I, too, disclaim any such intention. The devotion to the interests of their employers shown by managing clerks, as a class, is beyond all praise. If the suggestions, thrown out by several of them in the Legal Press,* that a Society for the protection of their interests, as a class, should be formed, were carried out, such a Society would be only second in importance to the powerful organizations of the Attorneys and Solicitors."

" Have Counsels' clerks any legal demand for their fees?" asked Percival. "Our clerk-boy, for example?"

"No. Fees to Counsels' clerks are mere gratuities, for which they have no legal demand.† Mr. Lefevre‡ doesn't seem quite to like the rule laid down by Lord Chief Justice Erle in Kennedy v. Broun. But I confess I entirely approve of it. It protects, in the highest and truest sense, the honour and dignity of the Bar, and Lord Chief Justice Erle seems to me to have risen as grandly to the occasion as Lord Chief Baron Pollock did, when he laid down the broad principle, that a Barrister, acting bonâ fide, is not liable to an action at the suit of his client 'for any mistake, or indiscretion, or error of judgment, of *any sort*.'§ This

---

* See 'Law Times,' 10th and 24th Feb., 1872; Nov. 11th, 1871. (Vol. 52, pp. 31, 278, 318.)

† Cotton, ex parte, 9 Beav. 107, 10 Jur. 84.

‡ See *e. g.* pp. 25, 26.

§ Swinfen *v.* Lord Chelmsford, 5 H. and N. 890, 924.

decision of the late Chief Baron was equally contrary to the older authorities, which make a Barrister responsible to his client in an action on the case for indiscretion. If we wish to maintain an immunity from suits for 'negligence,' or 'deceit,' we must also maintain our incapacity to sue for our fees. Swinfen *v.* Lord Chelmsford,* and Kennedy *v.* Broun, reversing the older authorities, have established two great principles, alike conducive to the dignity and independence of the English Advocate, which must stand or fall together."

"What is the rule of the Parisian Bar with respect to Counsels' fees?" enquired Pennyless.

"The rule of the Parisian Bar," replied Starvington, "as to the right of Counsel to recover fees is thus stated by M. Mollot:*—'Il n'est pas douteux que, selon le droit actuel, l'action en payement d'honoraires serait permise à l'Avocat, et, qu'en fait, quelques Barreaux l'autorisent ou la tolèrent; mais il est certain qu'à Paris, nous avons consacré la règle immuable de notre ancien Barreau, d'après laquelle toute demande judiciaire en payement d'honoraires est interdite à l'Avocat, sous peine de radiation du tableau.... Si vous admettez l'action en payement d'honoraires, vous altérez profondément,

---

* The Committee of the Law Amendment Society (p. 22) advise that Counsel should be made liable to an action at the suit of his client, thus restoring the authority of the older cases.

† Regles de la Profession d'Avocat, No. 96.

vous anéantissez les fonctions de l'Avocat; vous les transformez en un mandat salarié ou en un louage d'ouvrage.'

" The rule of the Parisian Bar as to the liability of Counsel to an action at the suit of his client, is thus stated by M. Mollot:*—

"' Le ministère de l'Avocat étant independant, étant étranger au contrat de mandat, et à celui de louage d'ouvrage, il suit de ce double principe qu'il ne répond pas plus de ses conseils que le magistrat de ses sentences, qu'il n'est passible ni d'un désaveu ni d'une action en dommages-intérêts.' S'ils se trompent l'un et l'autre, *la présomption est toujours en faveur de leur bonne foi*. Pour l'Avocat, c'était un ancien usage que le droit actuel a consacré.' It thus appears that, in point of law, a Parisian Advocate may sue his client for his fees. In point of etiquette he may not, and will be disbarred if he does. In point both of law and of etiquette the Parisian Advocate is not liable to an action for damages at the suit of his client."

"What is the American rule as to fees?" enquired Percival."

" The American usage and law on the subject of fees was thus stated by General (!) Thomas to the Royal Commission of 1854 on the Inns of Court and Chancery :—

"'·In the case of a gentleman who confines him-

---

* Mollot, Regle, 92.

self solely to the duty of an Advocate, his fee would be arranged by the Attorney or Advocate conducting the cause?' 'No, he would send in a charge in his own name, or that of the firm, and probably there are fewer of those bills disputed than any others in the world.'

"'*Is it recoverable by law?*' ' Yes. He sends in a bill for arguing the cause in Court of Appeal, 500 dollars, or whatever the charge may be.'

"' Is it a quantum valeat?' ' If it were resisted, it would be left, of course, to the Court, and to the opinion of lawyers of some standing whether it was too great a fee or not.'

"' Would not the Court refer it?' ' Yes.'

"' It could be sued for before a jury, could it not?' ' Yes.'

"' Does that fee go to the partnership, or to the Advocate alone?' ' To the partnership.'

"' The bill is sent in as a partnership bill?' ' Yes. The bill is sent in as a partnership bill for arguing cause, so and so, and the name of the firm.'

"' In ordinary causes it does not depend upon success?' ' No.' "*

" What is the rule in Germany as to fees?" asked Percival.

" Mr. Adolphus Bach gave the following evidence on this subject:—

---

* Minutes of Evidence, taken before the Commission on the Inns of Court and Chancery, (1854), Questions, 1074, 1075, 1076, 1077, 1078, 1079, 1080, 1081, and 1085.

"'Is the remuneration of the Advocate a honorarium in Germany or is it a fixed charge?' 'It is fixed by law. His services are as fixed as the services of an Attorney are in this country.'

"'Is that subject to taxation?' 'Yes, certainly; the costs are generally taxed, but notwithstanding the charge being fixed by law, in cases of importance there is generally a honorarium given.'

"'Is it recoverable by law? Could an Advocate, if he wished it, bring an action?' 'Certainly not— not for the honorarium.'

"'But he could for that which is fixed?' 'Yes.'"*

"Can English certificated Conveyancers recover their fees?" asked Percival.

"Certificated Conveyancers, unlike Barristers, are legally entitled to recover remuneration for their services.† The business of Conveyancing is, I may also observe, in passing, carried on in some instances, in partnership: but every member of the firm must have a proper certificate,‡ and a general partnership between an Attorney and a certificated Conveyancer is illegal.§

---

* Minutes of Evidence ut supra, Questions 1293, 1294, 1295, and 1296.

† Poucher v. Norman, 3 B. and C. 744, overruling Jenkins v. Slade, 1 Car. and P. 270, contra. See also Davies v. Sibly, 6 D. and R. 4; Crammond v. Crouch, 3 Car. and P. 77.

‡ See Edmonson v. Davis, 4 Esp. 14.

§ See Re Jackson, 1 B. and C. 270, Scott v. Miller, 28. L. J. (Ch.) 584.

"If the Bar," continued Stephen, "were to adopt universally the practice recommended by Mr. Justice Bayley, and insist, as they have a perfect right to do, that the fees shall be paid when the brief is delivered, or case submitted for opinion, all the inconvenience and hardships that result from the rule that Counsel cannot sue his client for his fees would at once be obviated. In conveyancing practice, no doubt, where the documents prepared by Counsel are paid for by their length, prepayment would be impossible."

"Why not put Conveyancing Counsel in the same position as Certificated Conveyancers?" suggested Percival. "But, let me ask, are the English Attorneys and Solicitors satisfied with the present method of taxing their costs?"

"No. Great dissatisfaction exists among Attorneys and Solicitors with respect to the method in which their fees are reckoned.

"'The false and mischievous principle of paying for what is not done, by way of compensation for not paying for what is done, pervades the whole frame of the Law.' The *Law Times*, commenting on these words in Dr. Sadler's 'Memorial Sketch of Mr. Edwin Wilkins Field,'* observes : — 'A client thinks it witty to tell his friends that he paid six-and-eightpence for looking at an Attorney's clerk. . . The client, however, omits to inform his friends,

* London, Macmillan and Co., cited 'Law Times,' vol. lii. p. 421.

that he paid his Lawyer a miserable forty-two shillings for the whole of one day's hard and responsible work, involving, possibly, the happiness and prosperity of the client's children or his own safety in the purchase of property.'"

"I see that the Associated Provincial Law Societies have been agitating for the taxation of costs as between party and party upon the principle now applicable to costs as between Solicitor and client," said Percival; "and for a more liberal valuation of the time of Solicitors."

"Yes," replied Stephen; "but, then, Lord Hatherley was 'unable to satisfy himself' as to the propriety of the first proposal; and as to the second proposal he confessed that he was not 'in favour of the principle of payment by time,' and hinted that it was not the Solicitors, but their clerks, whose time was charged and paid for, and that the time of the clerks was not worth more than the present valuation."*

"Perhaps Lord Selborne will be more placable to the Solicitors," said Percival.

"Perhaps," echoed Stephen Starvington.

---

* See the Correspondence between the Associated Provincial Law Societies and the ex-Lord Chancellor in the Appendix to the last Report (1871-2) of the Incorporated Law Society.

§ 9. THE INCORPORATED LAW SOCIETY.

"When I am disposed," said Mr. Rich, one day to his junior partner, "to take a desponding view of the state of my own branch of the Legal Profession, I turn, for encouragement and relaxation, to the Reports of the Incorporated Law Society. From the splendid abode of the 'Students, Practisers, and Professors of the Laws of England,' which our munificence had contributed to rear, we were ungenerously expelled, as 'immaterial persons of an inferior nature,' unfit to sit at meat with the Inner and Outer Barristers—the successors of those Apprentices who had gradually appropriated our right of audience in the Superior Courts. We sought refuge in the Inns of Chancery, and sat patiently at the feet of the Readers, whom the Inns of Court sent to lecture in our Halls. But, in time, even these lectures ceased, for the Attorneys were no longer required to be members of the lesser Inns, which passed into private hands, and, while retaining many of the old names and customs, were entirely lost to the Legal Profession.* In the

---

* See Mr. Thorndike's Report on Staple's Inn, Appendix to Report of Royal Commission, 1854, p. 261.

case of Rex v. Barnard's Inn,* a rule for a mandamus to the Principal and Ancients of Barnard's Inn, requiring them to admit an Attorney into the Society, was discharged, it not appearing that the Court of King's Bench had the requisite authority over the Inn.

"At the commencement of the present century the Attorneys and Solicitors of England were destitute alike of a Hall of Assembly, Library, Office of Registry, Club, Rooms for Professional Conferences, and Fire-proof Rooms for the safe keeping of valuable muniments of title. The first quarter of the present century was drawing to a close, when Mr. Bryan Holme, of New Inn, Strand, together with several other leading Attorneys and Solicitors,† determined to found ' The London Law Institution,' afterwards known as ' *The* Law Institution,' in some part of Chancery Lane, or in the immediate neighbourhood of the Inns of Court. The Institution was designed to supply the want of a place of general meeting, and also of a Library, an Office of Registry, Rooms for Professional Conferences, and Fire-proof Rooms for the safe keeping of valuable muniments of title. This may be gathered from the ' Prospectus,' which bears date, January 23rd, 1825, and which attributed the ab-

* 5 A. and E. 17, 2 H. and W. 62 (1836).
† The original list of Subscribers contains 223 names, all London Practitioners.

sence of any previous effort of a like nature to the incessant labour and attention, bestowed by London Attorneys and Solicitors, on the concerns of their clients, which left them little leisure or inclination to attend even to their own private affairs, and still less to consider subjects relating to the Profession at large. The Prospectus affords us one little glimpse of the shifts to which we were driven before the Institution was founded. It refers to the time when the Attorneys resident in the City were accustomed in the evening to frequent the Coffee Houses in the neighbourhood for the purposes of business. I have alluded to the material comforts which the Institution was intended to secure. But its promoters aimed at a much higher and worthier object—the *moral elevation* of the Attorneys and Solicitors of London, and, eventually, of England. It is not without a feeling of pride that I have perused and reperused the following passage in the Prospectus:—' The members being placed under the constant observation of the whole body, the least tendency in any individual to ungentlemanly conduct or dishonorable or illiberal practice will be immediately noticed and checked; and, as they will be brought into frequent contact with each other, a familiar and friendly intercourse will be produced, the effect of which will be to correct the asperity of manner and personal hostility towards each other which the very nature of the Profession is too apt to produce.' . . . ' As a beneficial result from this division of the Profession—it being intended carefully to exclude all disreputable characters—it may be expected that individuals, whose past conduct shall have excluded them from becoming members of the Institution in the first instance, will begin to appreciate the advantages of good character, and be induced to alter their conduct, in order to obtain admittance at some future period; but if so desirable a change is scarcely to be hoped for in those whose characters are already formed, a powerful example will be held out to the rising generation of the value of character, which will not fail to have a salutary influence.'

" The first cost of establishment was thus to be provided for :—

" ' The expense of erecting the buildings, and of fitting up and furnishing them and of purchasing the library shall be defrayed out of moneys to be raised by a subscription—(in shares of £25 each) —amongst Attorneys and Solicitors, to whom the proprietary shall be confined, and from amongst whom a Committee of Management shall be chosen; no person shall hold more than two shares.' Future expenses were to be provided for by an annual subscription (1.) from proprietors: (2.) from Attorneys and Solicitors in town and country, not proprietors : (3.) from articled and managing clerks, admitted to the Institution.

" The first meeting for the purpose of considering

the advantages which would accrue to our branch of the Profession by the establishment of such an Institution, was held on the 29th March, 1825. At this meeting a Committee was appointed; and on the 2nd June, 1825, a general meeting of the Institution was held at Furnival's Inn Hall to consider their Report. It was resolved that a Society should be established to be called 'THE LAW INSTITUTION,' composed of Attorneys, Solicitors and Proctors in the United Kingdom, and Writers to the Signet, and Writers to the Courts in Scotland, and of gentlemen falling within any of these descriptions, who might have voluntarily retired from the Profession. The other Resolutions were an echo of the Prospectus, except that the number of Shares that each individual was to be permitted to hold was increased to twenty. The fund to be raised for the purposes of the Institution was fixed at £50,000 in 2,000 Shares at £25 each. The Committee of Management was to consist of 24 Proprietors of not less than 10 Shares each. To this Committee was entrusted the preparing of a proper deed of settlement, the purchase of a convenient site, the erection and fitting up of the building, the purchase of the library, the preparation of rules, the appointment of officers, the distribution of shares, and, in short, the general management of all the concerns of the Institution. Armed with these ample powers, the Committee of Management addressed itself with skill and energy to the formation of ' The Law Institution.' The Deed of Settlement bears date the 16th February, 1827. By this Deed it was provided that the first Committee of Management should continue in office for the space of three years from the date of the Deed, with power to fill up vacancies occurring in their number.* At the end of the three years, the general meetings of the members of the Association were to enjoy the power of choosing at each annual general meeting six new members of the Committee of Management.† Every four years there would be a new Committee. Thus wisely, the Institution, after the preliminary arrangements had been completed, was placed upon a *representative* basis, and to this must be largely attributed the confidence which it inspired. The Society is governed by a Representative Body.'"‡

" That's one pull, at all events, that we have over the Junior Bar," observed Mr. Readymoney.

" Certainly. Their governing body is 'self-elected.' The Committee of Management reserved to itself the right of dissolving the Association, in case, from the non-payment of calls, or otherwise, it might appear expedient, prior to the formation of a contract for a site. This right it was, happily, not necessary for the Committee to exercise. At the third Annual General Meeting,

* Deed of Settlement, § 32.
† Ibid. § 19, § 80.
‡ Report of the Select Committee of the House of Commons, 1846, p. xv; Maugham, Question, § 2075.

held on the 2nd June, 1829, the Committee of Management were able to announce that the proposed Capital of £50,000 might be considered as completed, a few shares only remaining unsubscribed, which they considered it desirable to reserve for special appropriation: that the purchase of the site of the intended building had been completed at a total expense of £13,400, under an Act of Parliament expressly obtained; that out of sixty-two sets of plans, many of them of great merit, for the new building, that of Mr. Lewis Vulliamy had been selected, and awarded a prize of 100 guineas; that Mr. Vulliamy had been appointed Architect to the Institution; and that the Committee looked forward to the completion of the building, in time to permit the members to assemble at the next Annual Meeting, 'in their *own* Hall.' The word '*own*' is italicised in the Report; and the word could not fail to awaken a feeling of justifiable exultation in the breasts of the members of our 'long proscribed caste,' reduced, by the arbitrary edicts of the Benchers, to the painful necessity of haunting coffee-houses 'for the purposes of business!'

" The site which the Committee purchased consisted of two houses in Chancery Lane, nearly opposite the Rolls Court; one formerly occupied by Sir John Silvester, (and then lately by Messieurs Collins and Wells,) and the other by Messieurs Clarke, Richards, and Medcalf, and of the house behind these houses, in Bell Yard, then lately in the possession of Mr. Maxwell. Thus the site had the advantage of two frontages, and from its contiguity to the Law Offices and Inns of Court was peculiarly adapted to the objects of the Institution. The late Mr. Roche's house in Bell Yard was purchased for £3,540 and added to the Institution prior to the presentation of the Fourth Report (June 7th, 1830). At this meeting the representative principle came into play, the three years having expired under the Deed of Settlement, and six new members of the Committee of Management were elected by ballot, in lieu of the six, who retired by rotation. It is hardly to be wondered at that at this meeting 'a cordial and grateful vote of thanks' was presented to the Committee of Management for 'their care and attention to the interests of the Institution.' The Country Practitioners had already begun to appreciate the benefits which the Institution was calculated to confer upon them. On the 17th July, 1830, the Institution comprised 79 Country members, holding 193 Shares, and 594 Town members holding 1,807 Shares, the Country members being thus one-seventh of the entire body. The original Charter of Incorporation of the Institution bears date the 22nd December, 1831,— (the second year of King William the Fourth). The name and style of the Institution was declared by the Charter to be 'The Society of Attorneys,

Solicitors, Proctors and others, *not being Barristers*, practising in the Courts of Law and Equity of the United Kingdom.'* The Shareholders were declared to be the proprietors of the Joint Stock of the Incorporated Society, and to be entitled to participate in its profits in proportion to the number of their respective shares,† the amount of each share being fixed at £25,‡ and no member being allowed to hold more than 20 shares.§ It was, very judiciously, provided,‖ that any shareholder rendered incapable of practising in consequence of the Order of any Court of competent judicature, should cease to be a proprietor, but be allowed to dispose of his shares to any qualified member, willing to purchase them. The Committee of Management was empowered to veto the admission of any new member.¶ The Charter required that a General Meeting of the Proprietors should be held, within six months, to frame 'Bye-laws.'** The most interesting of the Bye-laws framed in pursuance of this requirement relate to the Committee of Management. The Charter having vested the election of the Committee in the proprietors at the Annual General Meeting, the proprietors ordained that the six members who had been longest in office should retire from the Committee

---

* Charter, § 1. † Ibid. § 8. ‡ Ibid. § 7.
§ Ibid. 23. ‖ Ibid. § 11. ¶ Ibid. § 13, § 19.
** Ibid. § 21.

annually, and six new members be elected instead, retiring Committeemen being immediately eligible for re-election. Vacancies occasioned otherwise were to be filled up by the proprietors. It will thus be seen that the Institution was permanently placed upon a *representative* basis. The total number of Committeemen was fixed at 24, being the maximum number mentioned in the Charter.* The qualifications of a Committeeman were thus defined:—
'He shall be a practitioner of at least ten years standing and be a holder of at least ten shares in his own right.'† The property qualification was reduced, in 1841, to five shares.

" On the 5th July, 1842, a report was presented by the Committee, which contained some important reflections on the inexpediency of allowing the Society to continue any longer a Joint Stock Company. The respectability of the Society was stated to be compromised—its usefulness to be crippled by the interest of the members in the fees, rents and subscriptions payable to the Society, and by the right of the members to demand a division of the profits. A serious inconvenience also arose from the restriction of the right of holding shares to members of the Society. The shares of deceased members devolved upon their representatives, anxious to realize, but unable to do so, except at

* § 15, 6.
† Bye-laws ordained at a General Meeting of the Members held 29th May, 1832, § 29, § 30, § 31.

a loss, and incapacitated from enjoying any of the privileges or emoluments of the Society, *quâ* representatives. The Society was thus placed in the awkward predicament of having connected with it several persons not recognized as members, yet impossible to be overlooked; enjoying an interest in the capital, but not in the profits; holding 147 shares in the property, but not contributing to the support of the Society. These persons could have no interest in the welfare of the Profession. A Special General Meeting of the members was held on the 2nd August, 1842, to consider the expediency of remodelling the Constitution of the Society, as suggested in the Annual Report. At this meeting it was resolved, that it was expedient to alter the Constitution of the Society and remodel it on the principle of other professional, literary and scientific public bodies, by admitting members on payment of an entrance fee, and vesting the whole right of property in the Corporation. It was also resolved that the 147 shares held by persons not members of the Society should be bought up,—that each of the 1,229 members of the Corporation might become members of the new Corporation, without the payment of any admission fee, in consideration of his surrendering one share. A Committee was appointed to settle the proper mode of purchasing the 792 extra shares held by 249 members of the Society; and this Committee fixed the value of these extra shares at £15 a-piece.

"In the very next report (1842-3)—which announced that the total number of members had risen to 1,313,—it was also announced, with sincere satisfaction, that all of these 1,313 members, except about 22, had expressed their concurrence in the alteration of the Constitution of the Society proposed at the Special General Meeting, and that 420 out of the 792 'extra shares' had been offered by the owners of them as donations to the Society; equivalent to a present to its funds of £6,300! The Society did not appeal in vain to its members to forego their individual rights of property in its Joint Stock. Ultimately only 244 'extra shares' at £15 each, remained to be paid for, and the Council was enabled to buy them out of the Exchequer Bills, cash at bankers, annual subscriptions, rents, and fees of the Society, 'leaving its whole property entirely unincumbered.' Next to the foundation of the Institution itself in 1825 and the high moral tone, which its founders adopted, I regard with just pride the disinterested conduct—the self-sacrificing spirit—of the proprietors of its Joint Stock in 1843.

"A curious delay arose in the final settlement of the terms of the new Charter. The Report for 1843-4 announced that out of 1,328 members holding 2,168 shares, 12 members holding 14 shares withheld their concurrence to the Resolutions of the Special General Meeting of August 2, 1842. Two of these 'dissenting members' filed a

Bill against the Society in Chancery, praying an Injunction to restrain the Committee from surrendering the old Charter and accepting a new one; upon which an Interim Order was granted by Vice-Chancellor Knight Bruce, on May 25, 1844. The opposition of the 'dissenting members' was not altogether barren of good results. They obtained all that they asked for, viz.:—the adoption of the 11th clause of the old Charter, which declared that members who should be rendered by an Order of Court incapable of practising should cease to be members, and which had been struck out of the draft Charter: the exclusion from the proposed new Council of persons not in actual practice as Attorneys or Solicitors.* The last point was not conceded without a hard struggle: but it was evidently desirable that the governing body should be composed exclusively of men actively, *i.e.* pecuniarily, interested in the well-being of the Profession.

"While the negociations respecting the alteration in the Society's Constitution were in progress, an important accession of dignity and power was received by the Society in the passing of the Attorneys' and Solicitors' Act (6 & 7 Vict. c. 73). 'By that Act,' observe the Committee of Management (in their Report for 1843-4), 'the new and responsible office of Registrar of Attorneys and

---

* See Charter, 1845, § 6 and § 8.

Solicitors was established, and the performance of its duties was confided to this Society—a trust, which secured to the body not only a legislative recognition, but a continuance, during the whole of his professional career, of that superintendence over every practitioner, which, by his examination previous to admission, had already been reposed at his entrance into it.'

"On February 22, 1845, the Law Society, by a deed under the Corporate seal, surrendered into the hands of Her Majesty the Charter of Incorporation granted it by King William the Fourth; and this deed was enrolled on February 24 in the Court of Chancery.*

"The new Charter, which bears date February 26, 1845 (8th Victoria), recites that it had been represented to Her Majesty that the Constitution of the Society should be so modified that the members should not possess any individual right of property in its capital, rents, or income, but that these should be wholly applicable to the general purposes of the Society in *promoting professional improvement, and facilitating the acquisition of legal knowledge.*"

"The language of this recital reminds one of that of James I., in his Letters Patent, granting to the use 'of the Students and Professors of the Laws of the Realm,' 'the Inns of the Inner and Middle Temple, London, two of those four most

* Charter of 1845, Recitals.

famous Colleges of all Europe,' in which he 'strictly commands,' that these Inns should 'serve for the entertainment and *education* of the Students and Professors of the Laws of the Realm, residing in the same Inns, for ever.' "*

" The chief difference, I apprehend, between the Incorporated Law Society and the Temple, is not to be found in the objects for which they were severally designed, as in the persons for whose benefit these objects were to be carried out," observed Mr. Rich. "While the Patent of King James I. dedicates the Temple to the use of 'the Students and Professors of the Law,' in general, a form of expression which would clearly include Attorneys and Solicitors, and even their articled clerks, the Law Society is strictly tied by Her Majesty's Charter to 'Attorneys, Solicitors, Proctors, and others, *not being Barristers*, practising in the Courts of Law and Equity of the United Kingdom.' If an intercomity were established between the two branches of the Profession, and Attorneys and Solicitors were restored to their rightful position in the Inns of Court, the Incorporated Law Society would, I am sure, make no difficulty in expunging from the title of the Society the words 'not being,' and inserting the word 'Barristers' before 'Attorneys,' instead of leaving the word in its present forlorn position."

* See this Patent in the Appendix to the Report of the Inns of Court Commission, 1854, p. 207.

"Its present position is an *exclusive* one!" cried Readymoney, laughing, "and, therefore, one that the Bar is well accustomed to!"

"All mention of 'shares,' 'shareholders,' and 'proprietors,' is carefully omitted from the new Charter," continued Mr. Rich; "but in other respects the provisions of the old Charter are followed in the new one. The judicious provision that any member 'rendered incapable of practising in consequence of the Order of any Court of competent judicature' should cease to be a member, is retained, with this explanation that the incapacity must arise from 'malpractice or other professional misconduct.'* Retired legal practitioners ('not being Barristers') were in the old Charter and are in the new one expressly rendered eligible.†

"The sole and entire management of the Society and of its income and property, (subject to the powers of General Meetings,) are vested in the 'Council of the Society,'‡ a Body corresponding very closely with the old 'Committee of Management.' The maximum number of members of this Council is fixed at 30, the minimum at 20.§ The old Committee was limited to 24. The method of appointing the Council is left by the Charter to the General Meetings of the

---

* Charter, § 6.   † Ibid. § 10.
‡ Ibid. § 11.   § Ibid. § 8.

members,* the Charter simply stating that it is to be 'elected from the members of the Society practising in England.'†

"The Charter required that a General Meeting of the members of the Society should be held within six months to frame Bye-laws:‡—and power was given to subsequent General Meetings to make new Bye-laws, from time to time, and alter or annul old ones.§ Under the Bye-laws framed in pursuance of the old Charter, it was provided, as we have seen, that six members of the Council,—(that is to say, one-fourth,—the total number of members being 24,)—should retire annually. The direct *representative character* of the governing body was made still more pronounced by the new Bye-laws: the number of members of the Council required to retire annually being raised to ten‖— (that is to say, one-third of the Council,—the total number of Members being fixed at 30.)

"The election of the ten new members of the Council is directed to be by show of hands: but, in case ten of the members of the Society present desire it, the election is to be by ballot, taken on the spot, within the space of two hours. The only check imposed upon the nomination of new members of the Council is the requirement that their names shall be transmitted to the Secretary seven days, at least, before the day of

* Charter, § 12. † Ibid. § 8.
‡ Ibid. § 13. § Ibid. § 12. ‖ Bye-laws, No. 11.

election. A list of the persons so proposed is to be fixed up in the Hall six days before the day of election. These Bye-laws secure at once quietness and publicity for the elections. The property qualification for a seat on the Council is, of course, abolished: the qualification as to 'standing,' is, of course, retained.* The election of President and Vice-President is wisely placed upon a formal basis, so that all jealousy and strife in the Council are avoided. The names of the Councillors† 'who have not passed the chair' are formed into a rota according to the date of their election ; if two or more are elected on the same day, their names are to be placed on the rota alphabetically. The first member on the rota in each year is to be elected by the Council and to be submitted to the General Meeting of the Society as Vice-President for that year. The Vice-President of one year is the President of the next." ‡

"An admirable arrangement," said Mr. Readymoney.

"The freedom of discussion at the General Meetings is secured by the Bye-laws, but so as not to trench upon the transaction of the ordinary routine

* Bye-laws, Nos. 13, 25, 29, pp. 13, 17, 18.

† The Bye-law says "Council." But this is evidently a mistake for "Councillor." The phraseology is borrowed from the Mansion-House.

‡ Bye-laws, No. 42.

of business. After all business introduced by the Council has been disposed of, it is competent for *any* member of the Society to make *any* proposition, which may be legally entertained at the meeting: and the mover of any resolution is allowed to reply.*

"Such, in brief, are the leading principles and regulations, upon which the Incorporated Law Society takes its stand. The Council has uniformly sought to hold a course strictly within the range of its chartered powers. Other more elastic bodies claiming to represent the whole or a certain portion of our branch of the Profession have sprung up beside it. I may mention especially, 'The Associated Provincial Law Societies,' and 'The Metropolitan and Provincial Law Association'—excellent bodies, no doubt, in their way: but in any readjustment of the two branches of the Profession it is evident that the interests of our branch of it can better be represented by the Incorporated Law Society—recognized as it is by Act of Parliament, and including 2,450 of the leading Attorneys and Solicitors of the kingdom,—than by any other body whatever. I only regret that membership in the Society has not been made a condition precedent to permission to practise.

"In 1839 we are introduced to 'The Law Society Club.' The Club has from the first been

---

* Bye-laws, No. 13, (9), (10), pp. 14, 15.

strictly limited to members of the Law Society, from which it sprung. The entrance fee was fixed by the rules at five guineas for the first 400 members, and ten guineas for each member beyond that number. The annual subscription was fixed at five guineas for members residing within a distance of twenty miles of the the Society's Hall, and three guineas for members residing beyond that distance. This Club is still in existence, and quite equal to an average West End Club.

" The Annual Report of the Council for 1871-2 refers to two questions, with regard to one of which the Society has exercised a healthful influence from its very commencement in 1825; and with regard to the other, since the year 1841. The first question resolves itself into the abatement of two nuisances:—(1) The malpractices of qualified Attorneys and Solicitors, and (2) the invasion upon our rights of unqualified persons. The second question is the concentration of the Law Courts in the vicinity of the Law Society and the Inns of Court.

" With regard to the first question you will recollect the high moral tone which characterized the Prospectus of the original 'Law Institution.' The same tone is maintained in each of the Annual Reports. In the Report for the year 1837-8, and other subsequent Reports, the Committee of Management noticed instances of a combination of the two nuisances—qualified Attorneys and Solicitors encouraging an invasion of our rights by unqualified persons. Qualified Attorneys and Solicitors have, I am sorry to say, been found, mean enough and silly enough to shelter behind their names unqualified persons.

"In their last Report (1871-2) the Council mention that there had been, unhappily, no diminution in the number of complaints brought before the Council with regard to the misconduct of Attorneys and Solicitors; and that many communications had been received from the Profession with regard to unqualified persons assuming the functions of Attorneys and Solicitors. 'A rule nisi' had been obtained in the case of an unqualified person acting wrongfully as an Attorney. Four Attorneys and Solicitors had been removed from the Rolls, and one suspended for two years, at the instance of the Society. There is a class of *quack* Attorneys, who advertise, and who are as obscene a nuisance as the quack physicians, who advertise. Here is a recent sample. 'A lengthy advertisement is inserted in the country papers headed thus—Campbell and Co.'s Legal Offices: Reform your Lawyer's Bills. This advertisement states that for an annual subscription of two guineas a member receives *free* advice (!) in all matters of law and legal agency in the English, Scotch and Irish Courts of Common Law and Chancery. Should he be plaintiff or defendant in any litigation, *the Solicitors attached to the Office* will bring or defend any action or suit, upon agreed charges, at 50 per cent. below usual Attorney's costs.'* I should like to put the 'Solicitors attached to the Office' in the dock along with 'Campbell & Company.' They are the enemies of their Profession, and quite as much so of the public, and far worse than the quack Attorneys who hire them to do their dirty work."

"It is just possible," suggested Percival, "that, 'the Solicitors attached to the Office' are a myth."

"The following copy of a *printed* circular appeared in the *Law Journal* of the 2nd February, 1872, vol. vii. p. 85.

'Manchester, Jan. 23, 1872.

'The Manchester Prosecution Society for (*sic*) Fraudulent Debtors under the new Imprisonment for Debt Act (passed in the 10th year of the reign of Her Majesty Queen Victoria) hereby give you notice that, unless the account, viz., £ , you owe our member, Mr. of is not settled before Tuesday evening the 30th inst., we shall institute other (*sic*) proceedings against your goods and body, without further notice, and also at the expense of the said Society, your case being one which we can punish, as we have found, upon inquiry, that you are well qualified to pay, if

---

* Law Times, (Journal), Sept. 28th 1872, Vol. liii. p. 381.

willing, the said money forthwith.—I am, yours respectfully, (!)

'JOHN FINDLAY, Secretary.
' To Mr.   .'

" The correspondent who communicates this illiterate piece of braggadocio, calls attention to the fact that the ' Society' gives *no address*.

" In the *Law Journal* of the 19th January, 1872, (vol. vii. p. 44) a 'long firm' is exposed. This debt-collecting establishment issues various notices. No. 1. is a request for payment in full or by instalment, otherwise action. No. 2. is an 'arrear notice' for payment of an overdue instalment, under threat of immediate steps being taken to recover the entire debt. No. 3. is headed 'Final Notice, Collecting Department,' and threatens that unless the debt is immediately paid, it will (dreadful to relate) be passed over into the Legal Department. Last comes the notice headed ' Legal Department,' which intimates that on a day named the necessary steps will be taken for obtaining a warrant of execution against the goods and chattels of the debtor, and, failing that, a warrant of imprisonment for contempt of Court.*

* " Perhaps the most peculiar feature in this class of business," says the *Law Journal*, " is the presumption of ignorance among debtors. Otherwise how can we understand the repeated demands of fees and charges for issuing the several notices, not one of which could be recovered by process of law? Indeed the best course for a debtor to adopt when pressed by a

"The Incorporated Law Society in its last Report, 1871-2, (observes in self-defence for alleged inactivity in prosecuting such persons) that 'it does not seem to be generally understood, that, unless it can be proved that proceedings have actually been taken by unqualified persons in any Court, the Society has no power to interfere under the Attorneys and Solicitors Acts.'"

"Their hands ought certainly to be strengthened by the Legislature," said Mr. Readymoney. "The Public are the greatest losers by the depredations of these unscrupulous men." *

---

debt-collecting association is to pay the instalments as required and the expenses charged against him, until he has paid in all the amount of the original debt and no more, and then to hold his hand, as we are quite sure that no County Court judge would compel him to pay more than the amount of the debt itself."

* See the suggestion of the *Law Journal*, Vol. 6, 783. 'G. M. W.' in the *Law Times* of the 16th Sept. 1871, thinks that 'no proper authority exists to stop the touting for business by unqualified practitioners.' 'T. G.' in the *Law Times* of Sept. 9th, 1871, thinks that there does exist some 'authority,' and suggests to Attorneys and Solicitors 'energetic action.' 'I ask,' he says, ' through the medium of your Journal, for the names of five firms of Solicitors who will volunteer to co-operate with mine, in forming an Association, the chief object of which shall be, ' To enforce the laws against unqualified persons who act as Attorneys and Solicitors.' 'I trust,' he adds, ' that this appeal to the Profession will not be made in vain.' So far as I know, it has been ' made in vain.'

" I pass, now, to the second question. As long ago as the year 1841, the Law Society presented Petitions under its corporate seal to the Houses of Lords and Commons in support of the proposal for removing the Courts of Law and Equity from Palace Yard to the vicinity of the Inns of Court."

" Thirty-one years have since elapsed, and the only evidence of progress in that direction is a howling wilderness at the back of the Law Society, fit for dragons and satyrs to dance in," said Mr. Readymoney.

" A Select Committee of the House of Commons sat in 1841 to consider the subject," said Mr. Rich; " 'the evidence,' says the Report of the Society for 1841, ' fully justifies the interference of this Society.'"

" I wish the Society would ' interfere' in this matter now," said Mr. Readymoney. " I suppose the First Commissioner of Works is so absorbed in his revolutionary scheme for continentalizing us by the establishment of Tribunals of Commerce, that he has no time to consider the expediency of going on with the Law Courts. The Profession is beginning to prophesy that the Law Courts will take as long to finish as the Foreign Office—that is to say, an entire generation."

" The Council of the Incorporated Law Society, in its last Report (1871-2), not unnaturally, declare that it is ' very much to be regretted, that any difference of opinion as to the designs should further delay the *commencement* of a work of so much consequence to the public and to the Profession.' It must be disappointing to the members of this Society, which has, for 31 years, devoted its best energies to the erection of the new Law Courts, to find that the Building has not yet been *commenced*. Perhaps Mr. Lowe wants to have his own way as to the Thames Embankment Site, after all."

" The Incorporated Law Society would need to be up and doing," said Mr. Readymoney, "as I see that Mr. C. E. Lewis, the recently elected member for Londonderry, who is alike able and energetic, is heading an influential movement for infusing a little more vigour into its proceedings.* Two important meetings have been held at, I believe, his instance—one at the Hall of the Society on the 12th of January, 1872, and the other at the Freemasons' Tavern, on the 8th January last. At the former steps were taken to increase the number of Members of the Council from 30 to 40, by a Supplemental Charter, and also to empower the Society by a new Bye-law to raise the maximum limit, at any future time (should it seem expedient), to 50. It was also decided at this meeting that, as the country members have increased to one-fourth of the entire body of members, from one-fifth,—the proportion which they bore

* See Report of the Meeting at Freemasons' Hall, Law Times, Jan. 11, 1873.

in 1842, when the existing Charter was applied for, —and as it is expedient to make the Incorporated Law Society less of a mere Metropolitan and more of a National representation of our professional interests, the number of country Attorneys and Solicitors on the Council should be increased from 5 to 10 —thus preserving the relative proportions of town and country representatives, while increasing the total number of members of the Council. A very friendly feeling towards country practitioners seemed to pervade the meeting,—Mr. Lewis, if I recollect aright, proposing that the country members of the Society should be entitled to vote by proxy, which would certainly be a great boon to them. All collateral questions were, however, reserved for consideration until the Society proceeds to frame its Bye-laws under the Supplemental Charter."

" Of all these proposals," said Mr. Readymoney, " I heartily approve. They are steps in the right direction."

" The only retrograde movement that I noticed was a proposal that only a fourth of the Council of 40 should retire annually, instead of a third. Under the Charter of 1831, six out of 24, you will recollect, retired annually, that is, one-fourth ; while under the Charter of 1845 ten out of thirty retire annually—that is, one-third. If the maximum limit be raised to 40, thirteen, at least, ought to retire annually."

"It is impossible to fix an exact third, without a fraction; and when the Society is framing its new Bye-laws under the Supplemental Charter, I would strongly advise it to throw itself boldly and unreservedly on the representative principle, and elect an entirely new Council every year."

"That proposal would, I am sure, meet with the approval of the Committee, which Mr. Lewis succeeded in forming at the other meeting, to which I just now referred. The meeting unanimously resolved, that 'with a view to the increased efficiency of the Incorporated Law Society and to making that body and especially the Council *more thoroughly representative* of the Profession generally, it is desirable to secure at the forthcoming special election and at the subsequent elections, the introduction of thoroughly independent men, of good professional standing and character, who are prepared to take active steps to promote the welfare and protect the interests of the Profession, generally;' and a Committee was appointed to aid in selecting candidates.* At this meeting Mr. Lewis said that 'it would not be difficult to prove that the Council had been sluggish and apathetic;' and that if he were to affirm that the Law Society had accomplished the end and design, 'for which it was organized,' every one in the room would 'howl with

---

* Evening Standard, Jan. 9th, 1873. Law Times, Jan. 11th, 1873.

indignation.' I cannot but think that Mr. Lewis's language at this meeting was just a '*leetle*' too strong. It is impossible to read the Reports of the Law Society from its very commencement and not to feel that the governing body for the time being has fairly exercised the trust confided in it, within the limits of its chartered powers."

"We live, however," said Mr Readymoney, "in a sensational age, when *all* Institutions are put upon their trial for their lives, and required to vindicate their '*raison d'être*.'"

§ 10. NO TAXATION WITHOUT REPRESENTATION.

"The Benchers are excellent landlords," said Stephen Starvington, "but they sometimes direct the sub-treasurer to threaten us, if we don't pay up our dues, with all kinds of pains and penalties. 'I am directed by the Masters of the Bench of this Society to request the payment of the undermentioned duties and commons.' 'I am directed by the Finance Committee to request an early settlement;' these are couched in mild language: but, if you don't pay up, it gradually becomes stronger."

"I tell you what, Stephen," said Percival, laughing, "we must get up a Bencher's reform demonstration, and hire Beales, M.A. and Odger for the occasion. 'No taxation without representation!' will form an excellent war-cry."

"The Right Hon. Robert Lowe, too, might grace our platform. Have you read his evidence before the Royal Commission of 1854? 'I consider that the general feeling, which there is against self-elected bodies, applies with some force to the Inns of Court. I think the Inns of Court would be more in harmony with the feeling of the Bar generally, if the Benchers were not self-elected.'* Putting, however, Beales, M. A., Odger, the Chancellor of the Exchequer, and joking apart, I have no hesitation in saying that one of the salutary reforms, which the spirit of the age demands, is the introduction into the governing body of the Bar of *the principle of representation.* That principle has already been introduced into the Incorporated Law Society, the governing body of the other branch of the Profession. The President, Vice-President, and Council of that Society are elected at the Annual General Meetings—pursuant to its Charter."

"We must incorporate the Inns of Court,"† said Pennyless, "and elect Benchers at the Annual General Meeting. Have the Benchers always been, as Mr. Lowe says, 'self-elected'?"

"Before the Restoration, the Benchers were really self-elected. Now they are, for the most part, nominees of the Crown, that is, of the Lord Chancellor for the time being. Formerly the only avenue to the Bench was through the office of Reader or Lector, and the Readers were selected

---

* Royal Commission, 1854, Answer to Question 1622.

† "I would suggest that, if any alteration is made in the constitution of the Inns of Court, it is very desirable that they should be made a *Corporation.*" Evidence of Mr. Whitehurst, Q. C. (Question 576) before Inns of Court Commission, 1854.

by the Benchers. Students of the Inns of Court are puzzled by the number of 'Lectors' whose names and insignia adorn the panels on the walls of the Inns. These Readers were the raw material of which Benchers were made. The Readers maintained a splendid, sometimes a ruinous hospitality, and presided over the meetings and disputations in which students, Barristers, and Benchers used to sharpen their wits for the more serious business of the Courts of Law. The Reader had a right of precedence at Westminster, the privilege of calling Students to the Bar, the first claim to be made a Judge, and it was from the Readers that the King's Attorneys General and Solicitors General were chosen. Hence there was no lack of candidates for the burdensome office, which only lasted, indeed, for half a year. At the end of the half year the Reader ascended the 'Bench of his Inn.' The Serjeants were originally the only King's Counsel, as distinct from the Privy Council and the Judges. Mr. North, afterwards Lord Keeper Guilford, is generally considered to have been the first 'King's Counsel' in the modern acceptation of the term. He was made King's Counsel in the time of Charles II., over the heads of many who were his seniors at the Bar, and applied to the Benchers of the Middle Temple to be made a Bencher. The Benchers refused his application—'insisting, that if young men, by favour preferred, came up straight to the Bench, and by their precedence were allowed to top their more ancient brethren, the Constitution and independence of the Society would be destroyed.' These objections the then servile Court of King's Bench overruled; they enforced compliance; and Mr. North was invited to take his seat as a Bencher. Similar applications were subsequently made by Barristers similarly promoted, and the Benches of the Inns of Court became gradually filled almost exclusively by the nominees of the Crown.* The Junior Bar were shut out from all hope of promotion to the governing bodies of the Inns of Court, and the form of election to the Bench became almost as unreal as the ceremony of congé d'elire. Mr. Whitehurst, Q.C., Treasurer of the Middle Temple, told the Royal Commissioners of 1854, that stuff-gowns are 'seldom called to the Bench of that Inn under 40 years standing, or before approaching 70 years of age!' Mr. Whateley, Q.C., Treasurer of the Inner Temple, intimated that the stuff-gownsmen invited to the Bench of that Inn, are 'far advanced in life.'† On the other hand, almost every gentleman who receives a silk gown from the Lord Chancellor, notifies the fact to the Bench of his Inn, and is elected, as a matter of course, a

---

* An interesting account of the former "Readings" and of the change effected at the Restoration will be found in Mr. Macqueen's Lecture on the Inns of Court.

† Mr. Gathorne Hardy is a distinguished exception. See to the above Evidence, Questions 477 and 239.

Bencher. When, therefore, it is said, that the Benchers are 'self-elected,' it must be remembered that their choice is restricted, by an iron and inflexible custom of two hundred years standing, to 'Juniors' of 70 and nominees of the Crown! I have referred to the extravagant sums spent by 'Readers.' Dugdale tells us that in ten days one Reader spent £600, (a large sum in those days), in feasting his visitors. Nobles, Prelates, Ministers of State, Judges, Serjeants, Royal favourites, civic functionaries, enjoyed the Reader's hospitality during his half-year of office.* When a Barrister was called upon to be a Reader he paid, if he refused, a heavy fine, variously estimated at from £100 to £300. When the readings ceased, it became customary for Benchers to pay a fine for non-reading:† and this fine is retained till the present day. At Gray's Inn the fine amounts to £150, which every Barrister pays, who is called to the Bench. This is the account given of this payment by the Treasurer of Gray's Inn. At the Middle Temple the payment, on admission to the Bench, varies according to the position of the applicant. If he is a Queen's Counsel, he pays £331: if he is a stuff gownsman, he pays £100 less:—and the Treasurer of the Middle Temple attributes the difference in amount to the circum-

---

* See Mr. Macqueen's Lecture, pp. 18, 20.
† See Questions § 590-600, Royal Commission, 1854.

stance that the Queen's Counsel stand in the shoes of the ancient Readers, in relation to the right of call to the Bench.* At the Inner Temple the silk gownsmen pay £310, the stuff gownsmen £210, on admission to the Bench. Between 1823 and 1839 the amount paid by each Barrister on admission to the Bench of this Inn appears to have amounted only to £100. The larger amounts, varying according to the rank of the applicant, were fixed by resolution of the Benchers, only so recently as 1839. Mr. Justice Crompton paid £210 for a fortnight's enjoyment of the dignity of Bencher; he ceased to be a Bencher of the Inner Temple, immediately after his admission, owing to his becoming a Common Law Judge.† The reason, no doubt, why the fine was increased in the case of Queen's Counsel, was, probably, this:— The etiquette of the Bar requires that an Utter Barrister, on becoming a Queen's Counsel, shall notify the fact of his having obtained silk to the Inn, to which he belongs, and seek admission to the Bench. Here, then, was an opportunity afforded to the Benchers of rendering their several Clubs (for such they really are) more select.‡ Every Q.C. was, therefore, required to pay a heavy fine as a con-

* Questions § 474-477, Royal Commission, 1854.

† Evidence of Mr. Whateley, Q. C., Treasurer of the Inner Temple, Questions 226 and 227, before Inns of Court Commissioners, 1854.

‡ *E. g.*? the late Mr. Stephen Temple, Q. C. ?

dition of admission. This entrance fee operates so as to exclude poor men, and creates a kind of vested interest in the office of Bencher. One effect of introducing the representative system into the governing bodies of the Inns of Court would be to do away with this obnoxious fine."

" Fair play, however, would oblige us to compensate the existing Benchers for the loss of their office, to the extent, at least, of their admission-money."

" I have little doubt," said Stephen, " that the existing Benchers would all be re-elected under the new system. They are, for the most part, an honour to their Profession, and *facilè principes* in the daily hand-to-hand struggle for wealth and fame. There can, I think, be little doubt, however, that the creation of such costly vested interests is highly inexpedient. At Lincoln's Inn it appears from the tabular statement of the Steward* that only £26 6s is paid by each Barrister of that Inn upon his call to the Bench, and of this amount, £21 is paid in respect of a 'Library-fine '—no doubt in respect of the superior advantages which Benchers enjoy in taking out books,—a fine which is quite unobjectionable.

" In remodelling the Inns of Court on a representative basis, we need not want for examples

* Appendix to Report of Royal Commissioners, 1854, p. 248.

within the British empire. In Lower Canada a perfect system of representation of the general body of Legal Practitioners exists. By the 72nd Chapter of the Consolidated Statutes of that Colony, Section 1, 'all Advocates, Barristers, Attorneys, Solicitors, and Proctors at law in Lower Canada' are formed into 'a Corporation, under the name of 'THE BAR OF LOWER CANADA.'* 'The powers conferred upon the Corporation,' by that enactment, are 'exercised by a *General* Council, composed of all the officers and members forming the Councils of sections;' and the Council 'nominates and appoints from' its own body 'by ballot, a President, a Secretary and a Treasurer of the General Council of the Corporation' (s 4).† The 'Council of each section' consists of a Batonnier, a Syndic, a Treasurer and a Secretary, and certain other members whose numbers vary in different sections; comprising eight in the section of the district of Quebec; a similar number in the section of the district of Montreal; three in the section of the district of Three Rivers, and five in the section of the district of Saint Francis (s. 5).‡ The election of the Council in each section is by ballot among the mem-

* 12 Vict. c. 46, s. 1.; 16 Vict. c. 130, s. 4 (Lower Canada Statutes).

† 12 Vict. c. 46, s. 4, (Lower Canada Statutes).

‡ 12 Vict. c. 46, s. 5 ; 16 Vict. c. 130, s. 5 (Lower Canada Statutes).

bers of the Corporation belonging to the section.*
The quorum of the General Council is fixed at 15;
and all questions are determined by a majority of
the members of the General Council present."†

" The proportion of the members representing
the several sections, might almost be said," remarked Percival, " to fit exactly the strength of
the several Inns of Courts—eight for Lincoln's
Inn, eight for the Inner Temple, five for the
Middle Temple and three for Gray's Inn. The
scheme, however, would involve the formation of
the Solicitors and Attorneys, through the Incorporated Law Society, into an integral part of the
new Corporation, eh, Stephen?"

" No doubt. But if it be thought desirable to
adopt the plan of incorporating the Legal Profession as a whole, while keeping the members of
each branch of the Profession separate, this could
be obtained by uniting together the four Inns of
Court—(the Inns of Chancery are now private
property, unaffected by any known trusts)—under
one representative body, the Incorporated Law Society,—(membership of which should be made compulsory)—retaining its own representative body,
and by then incorporating the entire Profession. The
General Council could be selected from the mem-

---

* 12 Vict. c. 46, s. 8 ; 16 Vict. c. 130, s. 5 (Lower Canada
Statutes)

† 12 Vict. c. 46, s. 12 (Lower Canada Statutes).

bers of the two representative bodies, without interfering with their disciplinary powers over the branches of the Profession which they respectively would represent. I submit this modest suggestion as a via media."

"Spoken like an oracle!" said the Honourable Percival Pennyless. "But this scheme of a 'Bar' which is to include, like that of Lower Canada, 'all Advocates, Barristers, Attorneys, Solicitors and Proctors-at-Law' would frighten Sir George Jessel, and his faithful followers, into fits."

"Let us turn, then, to some more Conservative model.—In France, as you are probably aware, every town has its own Bar. Foremost, in point of reputation, is the Bar of Paris. Let us turn from Lower Canada, which was originally a French colony, to the capital of its mother country. We are introduced at once to a complete system of representation of the Bar of Paris. The Council of the Order of Advocates is elected annually in the first fortnight of April.* The Bâtonnier, or President of the Order, convenes the Assembly of the Order by circular letter.† Notices are also posted up in the Library.‡ The Bâtonnier presides over the Meeting, at which the election takes place,§ and is assisted by two Members of the

* "Règles de la Profession d'Avocat:" par M. Mollot, 1866, 2me. Edition, Tome II. 8.
† II. 7.   ‡ II. 21.   § II. 9.

Council: the three together constitute the tribunal, which decides upon the validity of the election.* The election takes place by universal suffrage. All the Advocates inscribed upon the 'tableau' have the right of voting.† In 1842 the 'tableau' contained the names of 904 Advocates. In 1865 the number inscribed was 691.‡ Each person, who is elected, must have an absolute majority of the electors present at the election in his favour.§ The Council retires every year *en masse*, and the old Council, with three or four exceptions, is generally re-elected.‖ All attempts to arrange that a certain number should retire annually, have hitherto proved unsuccessful.¶ The Council consists of 21 Members.** Each ballot paper must contain as many numbers printed upon it, and must be filled up with as many names, as there are Members to elect, otherwise it is void. The Ballot papers are supplied by the Bâtonnier. If the votes for two or more Candidates are equal, the Senior in standing at the Bar is elected.†† There is only one restraint upon the choice of the electors. The Candidates must have been inscribed upon the 'tableau' as Advocates of the Parisian Bar for 10 years.‡‡ The new Council

---

* Mollot, II. 21. † II. 7. ‡ II. 161-2. § I. 531: II. 8.
‖ II. 12. ¶ II. 12-20. ** II. 7. †† II. 21.
‡‡ I. 536. Five years standing is sufficient in other towns.

at a special meeting, summoned within 8 days after its election, selects the Bâtonnier of the Order by secret ballot and by an absolute majority, from their own number.* Since 1830 the Bâtonnier has always been re-elected for a second year.† A Treasurer, Secretary, Keeper of the Archives, and Librarian, are selected by the Council from among themselves in the same manner.‡

"There is a striking resemblance between the powers vested in the Benchers of the Inns of Court and those vested in the Council of the Order of Advocates. Both are the rulers of 'voluntary societies recognised by the law.' Both have the power of admitting or refusing to admit as students, persons who seek to qualify for exercising the profession of Advocate. Both have the power of admitting or refusing to admit students to be Advocates, after the necessary preliminaries have all been complied with. Both have the right of suspending the Advocate from practice and of excluding him from it altogether. From the decision of the Benchers, in certain cases, an appeal lies to the Judges, and from the decision of the Council, in certain cases, an appeal lies to the Court."

"Why is the authority of the Council of Discipline cheerfully obeyed by the Bar of Paris, while

* II. 8, 22.   † II. 11, 16, 27.   ‡ II. 23.

that of the Benchers is viewed with aversion by the Bar of England? The answer, I think, is simple.. The Council is fortified in its decisions by the suffrages of the entire Order of Advocates. But what do the Benchers represent?"

"Themselves," answered Percival, "and the Chancellor for the time being."

§ 11. EXCLUSION OF ATTORNEYS FROM LEGAL APPOINTMENTS.

"'There has been gradually rising,'" observed Mr. Rich, citing the words of Mr. C. E. Lewis, the newly elected member for Londonderry, at the meeting of the 8th of January last, 'to consider certain proposals with reference to the Incorporated Law Society,'* "'there has been gradually rising in the mind of the Legislature an assumption that a Barrister of seven years standing, whether he knows anything or nothing, is qualified for every place, and that an Attorney of thirty years standing, although he knows everything, is qualified for none.'

"Mr. Jevons,† an Attorney of great ability and energy, is scarcely less emphatic in his exposure of the injustice of excluding Attorneys from Legal Appointments, only he doesn't lay the blame of it on the Incorporated Law Society. 'The only offices,' he says, 'exclusively given to Attorneys are the offices of the Chief Clerks to the Chancery Judges, Taxing Masters in Chancery, and Regis-

* Law Times, 11th Jan. 1873. (Vol. liv. pp. 197, 198.)
† Legal Profession, pp. 1, 6, 7.

trars of the County Courts.' . . . 'All the higher judicial officers at home and in the Colonies, County Court Judges, Commissioners in Bankruptcy, Recorders, and Judges of all Inferior Courts of Record, Examiners in Chancery, Associates, Stipendiary Magistrates, and Revising Barristers, are exclusively appointed from Members of the Bar; who, besides, monopolise a number of minor appointments, on special or permanent Commissions, and even the Solicitorships to some of the great public departments.' . . . 'From the social standing supposed to be conferred by the degree of Barrister, and from the monopoly by the Bar of all judicial offices and of numerous other appointments not judicial, many persons are induced to join the Bar, without any reasonable prospect of success in practice, and even without any serious intention of practising.'"

"That is perfectly true," said Mr. Readymoney. "It is a pitiable thing to see the number of middle-aged Barristers who 'hang on by their eyelids' to Circuit, without the ghost of a chance, or even of an expectation, of a brief. They have been hanging on in this way any time within the last quarter of a century, waiting for some friend to get into power and give them legal appointments. By the time they have forgotten all their law (if they ever knew any!) they'll disappear, one by one, from the Circuit, and reappear as Colonial Judges, Indian Magistrates, Stipendiaries, Chairmen of

Quarter Sessions, Attorneys and Solicitors General, Lord Chief Justices of distant settlements, Commissioners, Secretaries of State, Recorders, County Court Judges. What is the knowledge of Littleton's 'Tenures,' or Fearne's 'Contingent Remainders,' compared with the reputation at a circuit-mess of being a right down 'jolly good fellow'?"

"What indeed?" repeated Mr. Rich, rather absently. "'Attorneys and Solicitors are in fact, equally fit with Barristers, for many of the offices to which Barristers exclusively are appointed; and,' indeed, 'from their greater acquaintance with the practical details of the Profession, are better qualified.' And again:—' Owing to the superior prizes of wealth and distinction offered to the Members of the Bar, who succeed in practice, the inferior appointments do not as a rule command a choice of the highest talent of the Bar, whilst they would be readily accepted by able Solicitors.' Such are the enlightened conclusions of Mr. Jevons. A highly intelligent periodical, the *Spectator*, says,* 'The injustice of excluding Attorneys from all the chief legal appointments is, no doubt, felt by them alone; but it is none the less real, and it carries with it a diminution of social status, which is a clog upon the whole of that branch of the Profession.' 'By holding out,' says Mr. Saunders,† 'the great prizes of the Profession,' to the Attorneys,

* Article cited by Mr. Saunders, p. 26.
† P. 31.

'as the legitimate reward of ability and hard work,' you would 'stimulate them to greater excellence.'

"The very names of some of the legal appointments now exclusively given to the Bar indicate that these appointments originally belonged to us. Not to speak of the offices of Attorney-General and Solicitor-General, there are offices like the Solicitorship to the Treasury, held by Mr. Gray, Q.C. ;—the Assistant Solicitorship to the Treasury, held by Mr. Stephenson, Barrister-at-law ;—the Solicitorship to the War Office, held by Mr. Clode, Barrister-at-law ;—the Solicitorship to the Commissioners of Woods and Forests, held by Mr. Watson, Barrister-at-law ; the Assistant Solicitorship to the Customs, held by Mr. Rumsay, Barrister-at-law; the Solicitorship to the Commissioners of Works, held by Mr. Lawrence, Barrister-at-law, called, apparently, last year (1872) ; the Solicitorship to the Admiralty, held by Mr. Bristow, Barrister-at-law, called, 1868, and 'instructing' Mr. Huddleston, Q.C., the 'Counsel'—called 1839 ! !"

"That will do, I think," said Mr. Readymoney. "The 'reign of Barristerdom'—a new phrase ingeniously coined by Mr. Lewis,—must be overthrown. 'The cup of' our 'wrath and indignation, is,' I quite agree with him, 'filled to the brim!'"*

"And this," added Mr. Rich, 'is our *third* grievance."

* See Law Times, Jan. 11th, 1873, Mr. Lewis's Speech.

§ 12. HOW NOT TO BECOME AN INNER OR OUTER BARRISTER.

"What are 'Inner' Barristers?" enquired Percival. "I know that you and I are 'Utter' Barristers: (a corruption of 'Outer' Barristers, I suppose:) but 'Inner' Barristers, what are they, I wonder? Perhaps Q.C.'s, called within the Bar?"

"'Inner' Barristers are 'students' of the Inns of Court," replied Stephen. "The term 'Inner' Barrister is used in the Order of Queen Bess, A.D. 1574, as synonymous with 'student'—a 'student or Inner Barrister.'"*

"Do cases arise sometimes in which the Benchers decline to admit persons who wish to study for the Bar, to the degree of 'Inner' Barrister?"

"Occasionally such cases arise. Thus in Michaelmas Term, 1824, Mr. T. J. Wooller applied for admission to Lincoln's Inn. In Hilary Term he received an official letter from the steward in-

---

* See note to Doe d. Bennett *v.* Hale, 15 Q. B. 225, and Dugdale's "Origines," p. 312.

forming him that the Benchers had rejected his application: no reason was assigned. After vainly petitioning the Benchers to be heard on his own behalf, Mr. Wooller on the 9th April, 1825, petitioned the twelve Judges, as Visitors of the Inns of Court, for redress. On the 20th of April, the clerk to the Lord Chief Justice of England informed him, by letter, that the Judges had no power to interfere. After another vain attempt to elicit from the Benchers of Lincoln's Inn some reason for his rejection, Mr. Wooller, on November 26th, 1825, applied to the Court of King's Bench, upon an affidavit of the facts, for a rule, calling upon the Masters, Treasurer, and Benchers of Lincoln's Inn to shew cause why a writ of Mandamus should not issue commanding them to admit him as a member of their Society for the purpose of qualifying himself to be called to the Bar. The Rule was unanimously refused.* The Lord Chief Justice of England, (Abbott, afterwards Lord Tenterden) laid down the principle that, as Visitors, the Judges only have jurisdiction over *actually admitted* members of the Inns of Court. He also declared that an individual had *no inchoate right* to be admitted a member of one of these Societies for the purpose of qualifying himself for the Bar. 'Even if these Societies act capriciously upon the subject,' observed Mr. Justice Bayley, 'this

* Rex v. Lincoln's Inn, 4 B. and C. 855 : 7 D. and R. 351.

Court can give no remedy, because, in fact, there has been no violation of a right.'

"'The four Inns of Court,' observe the Common Law Commissioners of 1834, in their sixth Report, 'severally enjoy the privilege of conferring the rank of Barrister-at-law, a rank which constitutes an indispensable qualification for practice in the Superior Courts. No other means of obtaining that rank exist, but that of becoming enrolled a student in one or other of these Inns, and afterwards applying to its principal Officers (or Benchers) for a call to the Bar.' . . . 'If a person be refused admission as a student by any of the four Inns of Court, he has no means either by appeal to the Judges, or otherwise, of bringing under revision the propriety of the rejection; and a certificate of the rejection is transmitted to each of the other Societies.'

"'Would you hear a person who applied to be admitted to the Inn, by Counsel?' enquired the Common Law Commissioners of 1834, of Sir Launcelot Shadwell, V.C.

"'It never has been the practice,' replied Sir Launcelot.*

"I may add that Candidates for admission must produce a Certificate of character signed by a Bencher or by two Barristers.

"This being the state of practice with reference

* Sixth Report of Common Law Commissioners, 1834, pp. 5, 7, 74.

to *admission* to the Inns of Court, let us next consider the state of practice with reference to the *call* to the Bar.

"'Where any of the Societies refuse to call a student to the Bar, the Benchers will hear him personally or by Counsel, and allow him to give evidence to rebut the charges made against him; and, if he be dissatisfied with their decision, he may appeal to the Judges. On such appeal the Benchers send to the Judges a certificate stating the reasons of their refusal to call him to the Bar.'* I shall have occasion presently to refer to the unsatisfactory method of hearing adopted by the Benchers.

"On the 21st April, 1780, (20 Geo. III.), Mr. William Hart, instead of appealing to the twelve Judges, which is the 'ancient and usual way of redress for any grievance in the Inns of Court,'† moved, by his Counsel, Mr. Dunning, for a Rule to shew cause why a Mandamus should not issue to the Benchers of Gray's Inn, to compel them to' call him to the Bar. In this case the Benchers had stated their reason for their refusal, which was that Mr. Hart had been 'discharged under an Insolvent Debtor's Act.' The Rule was unanimously refused, Lord Mansfield observing that

---

* Sixth Report of the Common Law Commissioners, 1834, p. 8.

† Booreman's case, March's Rep. 177, (17 Car. I.).

'. the party must take the ancient course of appealing to the twelve Judges.'*

" 'In 1793 it was resolved,' said Mr. Eldred, for nearly half a century Under Treasurer of the Middle Temple,† (in reply to the Common Law Commissioners of 1834,) 'that the applicant was improper to be called to the Bar on the ground of character.'

" ' Was any evidence taken on that occasion, with regard to the respectability or character of the party?' 'No. It was known to one of the Benchers, and he communicated it to the rest.'

" The most celebrated case illustrative of the refusal of the Benchers to call to the Bar a student of an Inn of Court is that of Mr. Daniel Whittle Harvey, M.P., who commenced life as an Attorney, and was admitted a member of the Inner Temple in 1810, while still upon the Roll. In 1819 he was struck off the Roll of Attorneys at his own request. In 1821 (after the then usual interval of two years) he applied to be called to the Bar. The Benchers informed him that he must first explain his conduct in connection with two cases, in which he had been respectively plaintiff and defendant, Harvey v. Andrew, and Frost v. Harvey. In one he was accused of 'purloining a paper,' and in the other of realizing for himself a large profit on the

* Rex v. Gray's Inn, 1 Douglas's Rep. 353.
† Sixth Report of the Common Law Commissioners, 1834, p. 73.

sale of the estate of a gentleman for whom he was
Attorney. The Benchers refused to call Mr. Harvey to the Bar, and the Judges 'confirmed the
certificate of the Benchers *instanter*,' without receiving the evidence of a single witness, although
' several witnesses to meet and explain points of
objection set forth in the certificate' were in attendance. A Select Committee of the House of
Commons, over which the late Mr. Daniel O'Connell
presided, and which included Mr. Gladstone, Sir
Robert Peel, General Peel, Lord Lytton, Mr. Grote,
Mr. Serjeant Spankie, Mr. Hume, the then Solicitor-
General, and other well-known members of the
House of Commons, *entirely exonerated* Mr. Harvey
from the charges brought against him. They said:—

"'As your Committee have arrived at conclusions directly at variance with those of the Benchers,
they feel themselves bound to express their conviction, that the opinion formed of those two cases
by that learned body should be attributed to the
imperfect reports of the trials, and, still more, to
the *total absence of* ' any ' *authority to compel the
attendance of necessary witnesses, or to enforce the
production of essentially important documents;* which
defects have, in this inquiry, been remedied by the
powers of the Committee; and they beg leave to
state to the House their regret that the circumstances last alluded to should have produced consequences to Mr. Harvey, which, especially in the
sacrifice of a great deal of valuable time, are

irreparable; but the Committee, therefore, express their confident hope, that after the examination of the whole of the evidence, the Benchers will be induced to give Mr. Harvey the full benefit of the present inquiry.'*

" The Common Law Commissioners of 1834† in their sixth Report, already cited, make the following weighty observations :—‡

" ' It appears that there is vested in the Benchers of the several Inns of Court an uncontrolled and irresponsible power of debarring any person from admission into their Societies, though that admission forms the first entrance into a Profession occupying a most prominent and important rank among our civil institutions; and even when this entrance has been gained, and the party has consequently been led to devote himself for a period of three or of five years to the studies which are to qualify him for practice, the discretionary power of refusing that call to the Bar, without which his further progress is impossible, is again vested (subject, indeed, to appeal) in the same bodies of persons. It should be remarked, too, that the Benchers derive from those privileges, not only the means of excluding from the Bar any particular individual whose admission they disapprove, but the right also of laying down such general

---

* Second Report of the Select Committee on the Inns of Court, 1834, p. 7.

† Sir Frederick Pollock, Mr. Serjt. Stephen, Mr. Starkie and Mr. Justice Wightman.   ‡ Report, pp. 8, 9.

regulations as from time to time they may think fit, applicable to the case of all persons desirous of becoming Barristers. THIS STATE OF THINGS DOES NOT APPEAR TO US TO BE SATISFACTORY. Though the probity and honour of the persons who now fill the Benches of the different Societies are well known—and though the number of the rejected candidates has within the last twenty years been extremely small,—yet we cannot think that a power, in the right use of which society is so deeply interested, ought to be left without control in the hands of persons whose functions are not of a public and responsible kind.' . . . ' In point of expediency, the ordinary immunities of a voluntary Society ought not to be allowed to any body of persons claiming to be the medium of admission into one of the learned Professions. If a body is to enjoy this privilege, *it is no longer a private Association, but one in which* THE PUBLIC HAS A DEEP INTEREST, and the proceedings of which, if not adapted to the purposes of general utility, ought to be made so by the interposition of law.

"' Under these circumstances we deem it right humbly to recommend in the first place, that, either BY ACT OF PARLIAMENT, or by authority of Your Majesty in Council, the Societies be enjoined to allow, and the *Judges* of the Courts of Westminster to receive, an appeal from any act of the Benchers of any Inn of Court, rejecting *an application for admission* into their Society.

"'It would be right, also, in our opinion, to establish, by way of positive regulation, that in all cases where an application is rejected, whether it relates to admission as a Student, or to the Call to the Bar, the party applying shall have notice in writing of the cause of rejection, shall be allowed to clear himself from any charge of misconduct which it may involve, and for that purpose shall be at liberty to make his defence either in person or by Counsel, and to produce evidence; and that a full Report of the whole evidence and other proceedings before the Benchers shall (in the event of an appeal) be laid before the Judges. We have further humbly to recommend that by PARLIAMENTARY or Royal Authority, it should be ordained that no general Rules or Orders in future to be made by any of the Societies, on the subject of the admission of students or the Call to the Bar, shall be of any force, until they shall have been laid before all the Judges of the Superior Courts at Westminster, to be assembled for that purpose, and approved and subscribed by such Judges, or any eight or more of them. It may be useful to remark, that, while obvious advantages would be derived from requiring this additional sanction to the Rules, no objection can be made to such a course on the ground of innovation. It is, in fact, a partial return to the ancient usage ; as it appears by the extracts from Dugdale contained in the Appendix, that the admission of Students, as well as of Barristers was, at a remote period, a matter on which the Judges at Westminster possessed (either by themselves or jointly with other authorities) a power of regulation.

"'With respect to the regulation which relates to practising as Special Pleaders or Conveyancers, and the necessity of obtaining for that purpose the permission of the Societies, it appears to us to be objectionable. Its apparent object is to prevent uneducated and incompetent persons from practising in those capacities; but its effect is to make all persons, however well qualified, hold their profession of Special Pleader or Conveyancer by the precarious tenure of the pleasure of the Benchers, and to vest in these gentlemen a discretion, very liable to abuse. To subject Special Pleaders, in particular, to a regulation so arbitrary, is to expose to inconvenience and disadvantage a body of persons whose prosperity is of great importance to the general interests of the Profession, and to the science of the Law itself.

"'Another regulation which appears to us to require revision, is that which relates to the manner in which candidates for admission to the Societies are to be proposed. The recommendation of one Bencher or two Barristers (comprising a certificate of character) is indispensable. Now it is a case of no improbable occurrence, that a young man, respectably connected, may be without any acquaintance among the Profession, and therefore, without the means of easily complying with this condition. On a person so circumstanced the Rule might operate with considerable hardship; and we think it right, therefore, to suggest the propriety of providing that, in a case like this, the certificate of two graduated members of any of the Universities, or of two respectable householders should suffice.'

"In 1863, twenty-nine years after these recommendations were made by such weighty authority, Mr. Shaw Lefevre* called attention to the circumstance that no attempt had been made to carry them into effect: and now, after a further interval of ten years, (making in all thirty-nine years), I respectfully," said Stephen, with emphasis, "invite attention to the same circumstance."

* P. 7.

§ 13. DISCIPLINE.

" Whatever reforms may be effected in the Legal Profession," said Singleton, one day, to Marchmont, " I trust the discipline of the Bar will undergo substantial improvement."

" It is, indeed, a reproach to our branch of the Profession," replied Marchmont. " The Judges exercise, at the instance of the Incorporated Law Society, or of aggrieved parties, a stringent surveillance over the Attorneys and Solicitors: but the Judges exercise and, indeed, can exercise none over the Bar, unless the Benchers choose to take the initiative."

" It appears, however," said Singleton, " that the Courts formerly did exercise some kind of discipline over the Bar, in the first instance, and that aggrieved clients had some remedy against it. The Court of Chancery has summarily ordered Chancery Barristers, guilty of misconduct, never to practise again in that Court.* ' Numerous instances,' say the Special Committee of the Law

---

* See Re Mitchell, 2 Atkyns, 173; Butler *v.* Freeman, Ambler, 304: Viner's Abr. Counsellor, A. 5; Hill's Case, Cary's Rep. 38; Mitford on Pleading, 48. See Emerson *v.* Dallison, 1 Rep. in Ch. 103. (£5 fine only).

Amendment Society, 'are mentioned in the old books where the principle is clearly admitted that Counsel are liable for misconduct on the ground either of *crassa negligentia*, of breach of confidence, or of breach of contract to attend to a client's cause, and where detriment arises to the client from such misconduct, an action of deceit or assumpsit lies.'* The Committee cites a curious case mentioned in Viner's Abridgment†:—'If I retain a man of the law to be of my Counsel at Guildhall in London on such a day, at which day he does not come, by which my cause is lost, I shall have a writ of deceit against him. 20 Hen. VI. 34 b.' On looking out, however, the case cited by Viner, I find that the words which he cites as a solemn decision of a Court of Justice are merely an obiter dictum of Stokes, one of the Counsel engaged in the case!

"The Statute Westminster the First renders Counsel guilty of deceit liable to be put to silence in the Court and imprisoned for a year and a day.

"In an anonymous case‡ in the third year of Queen Anne, Lord Chief·Justice Holt and the other Justices of the Queen's Bench enquired, somewhat negatively, 'does anybody think but a Counsellor-at-law is a kind of minister of justice and right,

---

* Report, p. 22.
† Viner's Abr. Action (assumpsit) (P.) 6.
‡ 6 Modern Rep. 137.

and as such, punishable for misbehaviour in his Profession?' And the Lord Chief Justice said to a 'Counsellor accused of foul practice in his Profession,' 'Will you have the question tried, whether a Counsellor-at-law may commit extortion?' This 'Counsellor' had been an Attorney.

"Mr. Serjeant Hawkins lays it down in his famous work on 'Pleas of the Crown,' that 'Counsellors' are punishable by attachment 'for any foul practice,' 'inasmuch as they have a special privilege to practise the law, and their misbehaviour tends to bring disgrace upon the law itself,' and that, 'notwithstanding they are neither officers of any Court, nor invested with any judicial office.'* The anonymous case in 3 Anne is cited in the margin, in proof of this.

"It must be taken, however, as pretty well settled at the present day, that, except in cases of contempt of Court, the Judges have delegated the right of exercising discipline, in the first instance, over the Bar to the Benchers of the Inns of Court, and that, as a rule, aggrieved clients have no remedy against Counsel by action-at-law, either of tort or of contract.

"The nature of the jurisdiction exercised by the Benchers, and the glaring defects by which it is unfortunately disfigured, were described in forcible

* Book II. chap. 22. p. 219. This method of punishment, however, is more applicable to Attorneys, who *are* " officers of the Courts." See instances, ubi supra, pp. 207, 210, 211, 212.

terms by Sir Alexander Cockburn, in the case of Hudson v. Slade, (3 F. and F. 390). In that case Mr. Digby Seymour, Q.C., was charged with having misappropriated certain shares in a Gold Mining Company. A Parliament was held by the Benchers of the Middle Temple, to enquire into these charges, Mr. Seymour being a member of that Society. This action was brought by a former director of the Company, whom Mr. Seymour called as a witness for the defence, for an assault and battery committed upon him by order of the Benchers.

"Cockburn, C.J. said (inter alia) :—'We cannot over-estimate the importance of an inquiry such as that which was going on before the Benchers upon this occasion. A gentleman—a Queen's Counsel — holding rank in the Profession—holding a judicial office — one whose ability entitled him to the confidence of suitors of our Courts—was charged with acts of fraud so discreditable that if they were brought home to him, the Benchers, in the exercise of their important functions, would have been bound to disbar him and to expel him from the Profession. *It is true that the Parliament of an Inn of Court, sitting on a question like this, is not a Court armed with the powers which a Court of Justice possesses for compelling persons to attend as witnesses, or to produce documents essential to the investigation of the truth.* But when it is said that the Benchers of an Inn of Court, sitting on-the trial of alleged delinquencies on the part of a member of the Bar, is a merely 'friendly tribunal,' I cannot assent to that description of it. It is a good deal more than a mere 'friendly tribunal,' *though it is not armed with powers of procedure coextensive with its jurisdiction.* THAT, NO DOUBT, IS AN INHERENT DEFECT IN ITS NATURE AND CONSTITUTION. By a friendly tribunal we mean one which by the consent of both parties sits for the adjustment of mutual differences; that is not the case with the Parliament of an Inn of Court in a case such as this. The Benchers, on a charge being preferred against a member of the Bar, are armed with the power to disbar him—that is, to deprive him of his professional position and existence. Indeed, short of those heavy consequences which would attach to the greater and more heinous offences, I own I can conceive of no jurisdiction more serious than that by which a man may be deprived of his degree and status as a Barrister, and which, in such a case,—perhaps after he has devoted the best years of his life to this arduous Profession,—deprives him of his position as a member of that Profession and throws him back upon the world to commence a new career as best he may, stamped with dishonour and disgrace.'

"Compare with this nervous language of Sir Alexander Cockburn, the evidence given by Mr. W. S. Cookson, before the Commission on the Inns of Court and Chancery, 1854, respecting the power of depriving an Attorney and Solicitor of his position in the Legal Profession.

" ' You have no mode, have you, of excluding a person from the Roll (of Attorneys), who has shown great ignorance ? '

" ' Not after he is once admitted on the Rolls ; his removal must be the act of the Judges.'

" ' Nor for bad conduct ? '

" ' Several cases have occurred, in which we have thought it necessary to bring the misconduct of Attorneys before the Court.'

" ' It is a difficult proceeding even then, is it not? It is not easy to get an Attorney struck off the Rolls ? '

" ' No ; and *it ought not to be so.*'

" ' It is not easy to get a man of bad character struck off the Rolls ? '

" ' If you establish that he has been guilty of gross misconduct, then the Judges will remove him from the Rolls.'

" ' Would it be better in your opinion, to invest the body of Attorneys at large with a power to regulate the admission or exclusion of their own members? '

" ' Although I have no doubt that if such a power were vested in the Council of the Incorporated Law Society, they would exercise that power with care, caution, and strict impartiality, yet I think it is desirable *so important and serious a question as that of depriving a professional man of his means of livelihood, should be submitted to the highest* *authorities.* The proceeding is a more solemn one, and carries greater weight.'*

" The defects inherent in the mode of inquiry pursued by the Benchers are well illustrated by a case now pending.

" The Petition of Mr. Edwin James, addressed to 'the Judges of Her Majesty's Supreme (?) Courts of Common Law,' grounds the appeal, lodged eleven years after his disbarment, on the following 'Reasons':
—1. That 'no *charge* or accusation was ever made or preferred before the Benchers against' him. 2. That 'there was *no evidence* adduced before the Benchers of any misconduct, professional or otherwise, sufficient to support' the order vacating his call to the Bar. 3. That ' the Benchers constituted themselves *both accusers and judges* throughout the whole proceedings.' 4. That 'the Benchers at the conclusion of the proceedings, refused to allow' his 'Counsel a reasonable time to address them on his behalf.' 5. That 'the *order* is invalid and unjust, and *does not* properly *inform*' him 'upon *what charge* or charges of misconduct he has been disbarred.' 6. That the ' *decision* pronounced by the Benchers was *hasty* and not considered with due justice to' him. 7. That he ' was *never* afforded the *opportunity of explaining* or rebutting a large amount of the testimony *which the Benchers brought*

* Questions 1552, 1553, 1554, 1555 and 1556. Report of the Royal Commission, 1854, on the Inns of Court and Chancery.

against' him. 8. That, 'upon the inquiry the Benchers allowed *irrelevant and hearsay evidence* to be given.' 9. That the inquiry was conducted by the Benchers themselves in an unjust, unfair and *inquisitorial* manner; that private transactions of the Petitioner, not within the proper jurisdiction and cognizance of the Benchers, were inquired into; that charges and accusations were made by the Benchers, who afterwards acted as Judges against the Petitioner, which had no foundation, and which unjustly and unfairly prejudiced the Benchers, and (?) the majority of them against him.*

"It is not a little curious that only one charge of 'professional delinquency' was even attempted to be made against Mr. Edwin James,† viz.:—'placing himself under a pecuniary obligation to one to whom he was professionally opposed.' Mr. James's contention is, that this was the only charge 'with which the Benchers were really competent to deal.' The other charges were founded entirely on money-lending transactions.

"The forum of the Bench, as sketched in this petition is certainly a very 'domestic' one, and contains many elements, which savour more of continental than of English forms of procedure, such as interrogating the accused, with a view to getting him to criminate himself‡—forming con-

---

* Petition of Edwin J. James, pp. 20, 21.
† Ibid. p. 10.   ‡ Ibid. p. 6.

clusions from *mala fama*, hints, surmises, and hearsay evidence,—which would be utterly inadmissible in an English Court of Justice—his accusers sitting in judgment on their own accusations—and not allowing the accused sufficient opportunity of preparing his defence."

" But is it not just possible that the Judges may confirm the certificate of the Benchers?" enquired Marchmont.

" It is not only possible, but probable," replied Singleton. " But the Judges confirmed the Certificate of the Bench in Mr. Daniel Whittle Harvey's case, and yet a Select Committee of the House of Commons found that the accusations against him were utterly groundless."

" There can be little doubt that the Judges would bestow much more pains on the investigation of charges against members of the Bar if the facts were brought before them in the first instance, and not by way of appeal from the Benchers. Most of the Judges have been Benchers themselves, and it is not unnatural that they should rely implicitly on the facts as stated in the certificates, instead of going into the allegations of malpractice *de novo*."

" Mr. Coryton suggests* that disbarment should follow upon malpractices 'proved, not, as now, before a body of Barristers, however high in

* Letter to Editor of the Post, Jan. 14, 1873.

standing, but before a Judge in open Court. The discipline of the Bar is confided in Germany to the Courts. Mr. Adolphus Bach gave the following evidence before the Royal Commission of 1854*:—

"' Is there any control over the moral conduct of a member of the Profession, supposing a man conducts himself, unfortunately, in a manner discreditable to an Advocate?' 'The control lies with the Court.' But then the Advocate in Germany is also an Attorney.†

"A power of putting an Advocate on his trial, as it were, in open Court for his Professional life, would be degrading to the Bar. If Barristers could be dragged as criminals, on mere suspicion of malpractice, before the Judges, what would become of 'the habitual respect, which all Judges pay to the opinion of the Profession,' and which Mr. Justice Blackburn assures us,‡ is 'the only real practical check on' their Lordships?— The independence of the Bar would be sacrificed to the petty spite of disappointed clients and the malice and envy of rival Advocates. I am decidedly in favour of the exercise of discipline over the Bar by a domestic forum."

"On what model would you form it?" enquired Marchmont.

"In Lower Canada," replied Singleton, "a well-

* Question 1273, Royal Commission, 1854.
† Saunders, p. 13.
‡ Second Report of the Judicature Commission, p. 26.

ordered code of discipline has been prescribed by the local legislature.* The Corporation of the Bar is empowered to 'make all such bye-laws, rules, and orders, as it deems necessary, for the interior discipline and honour of the members of the Bar,' and to 'change, alter, and modify them, whenever it shall deem it necessary.' 'In all cases, where a member of the Bar is accused of any offence before the Council of the Section to which he belongs,' the accusation is to be 'decided by the absolute majority of the Council of the Section,' who are to 'declare vivâ voce whether the member accused is guilty or not guilty.' *Each Council is to have the right to require witnesses to appear before it by subpœnas,'* in a prescribed form, in the name of the Batonnier under the Seal of the Section, and signed by the Secretary; and *'the same powers with respect to compelling the attendance of witnesses to give evidence, as are exercised by the Civil Courts in Lower Canada.*

"'The Secretary, or any other member of the Section' may 'administer the oaths to the witnesses or to any other person, and any person guilty of any wilful false statement in any oath, is to be *liable to the penalties by law imposed upon perjury.'*

"The Royal Commission of 1854 recommended, 'as well worthy of consideration,' the question

* See the Consolidated Statutes of Lower Canada, chap. 74.

whether similar powers should not be conferred upon the governing bodies of the Inns of Court, 'when proceeding to examine judicially as to the admission of Students to the Bar, or the disbarring of Barristers.' 'Great hardships,' they added, 'might arise to the party whose conduct is in question for want of any power to compel the attendance of witnesses and production of documents.'* Any thing more ludicrous than the raid on Mr. Hudson's book could not well be conceived.

" If we turn from Lower Canada to its mother-country, France, we are introduced to the most perfect code of discipline that probably the world has ever seen. The bare recapitulation of its details occupies two stout volumes of the Avocat, M. Mollot. The fundamental principle upon which the exercise of discipline by the Council of the Order of Advocates of the Bar of Paris is based, is the omnipotence of the Bar over its own members. '*L'Ordre est maitre de son tableau.*'† The Code of Discipline extends from the paternal admonition‡ to the erasure of the Advocate's name from the tableau,§ which may be compared to the power, possessed by the Benchers of our Inns of Court, of disbarring. The Council have the power

* Report of Royal Commission, 1854, p. 14.
† Mollot, t. ii. p. 136.
‡ Ibid. t. ii. 234. § Ibid. t. ii. 376.

of admonishing, reprimanding, suspending, and erasing. An appeal from the decision of the Council in the cases of suspension and erasure lies to the Court.* This somewhat resembles the visitorial powers exercised by the Judges over the Inns of Court.

"In addition to the control exercised by the Council of the Order over the Advocates inscribed upon the tableau, it also occasionally inflicts the penalties of suspension and erasure upon 'stagiaires,' or individuals undergoing the 'stage,' or period of probation,† who answer, in some degree, to our students of the Inns of Court. A student erased from the list of 'stagiaires' cannot be admitted to the tableau‡ (or called to the Bar). I may mention, *en passant*, that if an Avoué wishes to become an Avocat he must undergo the 'stage' like an ordinary student,§ *i.e.* for three years.|| The surveillance of the Council of Discipline extends to the most minute points of etiquette on the part of Counsel—such as the inscription on the door-plate of his house¶; the distribution by Counsel of professional 'cartes'**; restoration to the client of the excess of a fee over and above the ordinary 'honorarium'††; Counsel writing leading

---

* Mollot, t. i. 425.   † Ib. t. ii. 104, 410.   ‡ Ib. t. ii. 411.
§ Ib. t. i. 449, (Ordon. du 20 Nov. 1822, Art. 37); t. ii. 106. || Ordon. du 20 Nov. 1822, Art. 30.
¶ Ibid. t. ii. p. 233.   ** Ib. 202, 233.   †† Ibid. 235.

articles in the newspapers*; or writing 'avec trop de vivacité,' to a Magistrate, with whom he had had an altercation in Court†; the sudden announcement, in the course of a speech for the defence of a prisoner, of the death of the prisoner's wife‡; Counsel getting business through the 'garçons' of the Court§, exacting from clients fees fixed by himself ǁ; frequenting prisons and getting 'en rapport' with the prisoners¶; asking payment of fees in advance (!)**; bringing an action against a Railway Company for services rendered††; stipulating for a lump sum in each case, irrespective of its importance‡‡; allowing himself to be described as acting under the direction of a Society of which he was standing Counsel§§; Counsel writing to ask for his feesǁǁ; &c., &c. Some interesting cases relate to the Rule of Etiquette, which requires the Counsel to be at his post when the case is called on, unless he has *previously* given the client an opportunity of selecting another Counsel. An Avocat, for keeping to the evening before the trial the brief for a prisoner, accused of a capital crime, and leaving him without any Counsel to defend him, received an 'avertissement' from the Council¶¶.

---

* Mollot, t. ii. 236.   † Ib. 238.
‡ Ib. 247. "Sa femme, dechirée par la douleur que lui a donnée ce fatal procès, elle est morte hier ! et c'est moi qui lui en apporte aujourd'hui la nouvelle !"   § Mollot, t. ii. 254.
ǁ Ib. 255.   ¶ Ib. 256.   ** Ibid.   †† Ib. 257.
‡‡ Ib. 258.   §§ Ibid.   ǁǁ Ibid. 260.   ¶¶ Ib. 238.

So did another Avocat, who mistook the 13th July for the 14th, and consequently left a prisoner charged with theft at the Assizes undefended, although the alleged thief was acquitted.* It is not therefore surprising that Mr. Lefevre† should look to the establishment of a Council of Discipline, as the best means of relieving clients from their grievances against the Bar, as well as of enforcing rules of etiquette and superintending the discipline of the Bar generally. After referring to the Joint Committee of the Benchers of the four Inns of Court, which it was then (1863) proposed to form, and which has since been formed, Mr. Lefevre observes:—' I cannot but think that it would be better to adopt a system founded on the example of the French Bar.' "

" The discipline at present exercised by the Benchers," said Marchmont, "is, at once, too lax and too severe.—It is too lax, because the Benchers rarely, if ever, hold an inquiry, except when the accused Barrister is charged with acts of fraud so discreditable that, if brought home to him, they would be bound to suspend or disbar him. Minor offences escape notice altogether; and this is not at all surprising: the only wonder is that the distinguished men who fill the Benches of the Inns can find time to attend the lengthy inquiries into the more serious charges. The dis-

* Mollot, t. ii. 241.   † P. 28.   ‡ P. 36.

cipline, which the Benchers exercise, is, on the other hand, too severe; because they go upon hearsay, and *mala fama* chiefly, and not upon facts proved by sworn testimony and according to well-established rules of evidence."

" Minor offences on circuit, you must recollect, are left," said Singleton, " to that august tribunal, the Bar Mess of each Circuit. The Bar Mess at Quarter Sessions takes cognizance of minor offences at Sessions."

" Yes, but these ante-convivial and post-prandial vehmgerichts don't exist at the Chancery Bar or at Westminster. However, we must be careful what we say of them. If we venture to lift the veil from these awful and mysterious 'Courts,' we might, perhaps, have to do penance in white sheets, like some of their unhappy victims. Mr. Lefevre has pointed out that the Bar Mess can inflict no higher penalty than expulsion from itself: it cannot inflict expulsion from the Circuit; the penalty is social, and similar to expulsion from a Club, which, indeed, the Bar Mess very closely resembles. The Bar Messes, also, have no means of communicating directly with the Benchers, who take no notice of their censures and expulsions."

" The Benchers would be conferring a great benefit on the Legal Profession, if they set to work to define and codify the rules of etiquette," said Singleton. " Unscrupulous men violate with impunity rules, which possess no authoritative sanction, while, as Mr. Lefevre observes,* 'men of high feeling are sometimes over-punctilious in the observance of supposed rules, which have no real existence.'"

" Mr. Lefevre†, however, is of opinion that the Rules of Etiquette can best be settled by a Council of Discipline, elected by the entire Bar of England, whose 'decisions,' also, would 'form precedents for the future.' The rules which govern the etiquette of the Order of Advocates at Paris are 153 in number; and M. Mollot, who has collected them, expresses a hope‡ that these rules of the Parisian Bar may spread into the neighbouring States and become international."

" If the Benchers of the Inns of Court," said Marchmont, "were a representative body elected by the Bar of England, I feel persuaded that the Bar would hail with satisfaction the introduction of a system of discipline similar to that exercised by the Council of the Order of Advocates over its members. But so long as the Benchers are a self-elected body, it can hardly be expected, I fear, that the Bar will assist to enhance their powers."

* P. 15.   † P. 38.   ‡ Introduction, p. xxii.

§ 14. DOE ON THE DEMISE OF SIR ROUNDELL PALMER v. THE INNS OF COURT.

I.—WHAT CERTAIN ATTORNEYS SAID ABOUT IT.

"The action of ejectment brought by Sir Roundell Palmer, now Lord High Chancellor of England, against the Inns of Court, last Session, unfortunately fell through," said Mr. Smith, "because the jury could not agree."

"The argument of the Attorney General had, I think, considerable weight with many honorable members," said Mr. Jones. "If you turn to the debate in Hansard*, you will see that he said:—

"'It would be a mistake and a failure to raise up by the side of the Inns of Court a shadowy Institution that would in vain attempt to rival their wealth, reputation, and influence.' The conservative instincts of the lawyers in the House were offended at the sweeping and severe character of Sir Roundell Palmer's scheme."

"Sweeping and severe measures are now the order of the day," said Mr. Smith, with emphasis. "We demand that they shall be applied to 'these four Colleges,' once 'the most famous of all

* Vol. ccix. p. 1247 (March 1, 1872).

Europe,'* but now, as the Chancellor of the Exchequer told the Royal Commissioners on the Inns of Court, 'in a state of decay'†. Instead of 'raising up by their side a shadowy Institution,' we must dismantle their 'tumble-down Chambers,' and 'scatter the very walls of the old Inns themselves,' to borrow the fierce language of the *Law Times*‡. We will build upon the old foundations, but the old foundations must first be cleared of their superincumbent rubbish—the accumulations of centuries of abuse and neglect. Our 'School of Law' shall arise, like a Phœnix, from the ashes of its former self. Its rejuvenescence shall be the signal for the restoration of our branch of the Profession to its ancient, but long-estreated rights. 'The small remnant of the prestige of the Bar' must 'disappear'"§.

"If the Inns of Court decline to co-operate in the formation of the Central School of Law—if they refuse to put their hands into their pockets and assist us, why, all that remains to be done, no doubt," said Mr. Jones, "is for the 'State' to 'take them in hand' as Sir Roundell Palmer suggested"‖.

"'I regard them,'" said Mr. Smith, "like the

---

* Patent of James I., set out in the Appendix to the Report of the Royal Commission of 1854, p. 207.

† Question 1617, minutes of same Commission, p. 135.

‡ Vol. li, p. 189 (July 15, 1871).

§ Ibid.

‖ Hansard, ubi supra, 1237-8.

Editor of the *Law Times**, 'as traitors to their trust,' and 'would rejoice,' like him, ' to see these shams swept away to-morrow.'"

" Mr. Macqueen"†, said Mr. Jones, "indignantly repudiates the notion that the Inns of Court were originally either a 'private work' or 'a jobbing speculation,' but 'a great, a wise, and a *national* contrivance.' The Common Law Commissioners of 1834 do not scruple to recommend that if the Inns of Court are 'not adapted to the purposes of general utility,' they 'ought to be made so by the interposition of Royal or Parliamentary authority'‡. The language of the Letters Patent of James I. clearly imply that the Benchers of the Inner and Middle Temple hold their property in a fiduciary character. Mr. Whateley, in his evidence before the Royal Commissioners in 1854, interpreted this language to mean that the Benchers of the Inner and Middle Temple hold their property in a fiduciary character. The ex-Lord Chancellor, who was in the Chair, asked him, 'Is there, in your judgment, any expression of Trust with reference to the property?' Mr. Whatcley replied: —' Yes, there is. It is a point which, of course, the Commissioners will consider, whether, having accepted this grant, we are not bound by the Trust ; *we consider ourselves bound by it as a*

---

* Law Times, ubi supra.   † P. 11.
‡ 6th Report, p. 8.

Trust'*. The Commissioners did consider the matter and came to the same conclusion. This view is borne out by the language of the Deed of Partition, by which the joint-estate of the two Temples was severed, A.D. 1732. The Inner Temple and Middle Temple were then severally conveyed '*in trust* for the purposes appointed by the said letters patent, to serve and be employed for the entertaining, education, and habitation of the Students and Professors of the law residing within' the same.† From the year 1687 Gray's Inn appears to have been held by the Benchers of the Inn ' to and for the common profit, benefit, and utility of the Society of Gray's Inn, and the members of the same for the time being, for ever, *according to the true, ancient, and laudable government thereof*, and for none other use, trust, intent, or purpose whatsoever '‡. The Conveyances to the trustees of Lincoln's Inn, in 1580, appear to have been in fee§; but there must evidently have been some arrangement between the Trustees and the Society, defining the trusts."

---

* Royal Commission, 1854, p. 47, question 190.
† See the Letters Patent, ibid. pp. 215, 216.
‡ F. Whitmarsh, Q. C., Treasurer of Gray's Inn, ibid. p. 77
§ Ibid. p. 242.

II.—WHAT CERTAIN BARRISTERS SAID ABOUT IT.

"I am glad, Singleton, that our new Chancellor failed in his effort, last Session, to cŕeate, as he said, 'a Central Authority superior to the Inns of Court*,' or, as the Attorney General said, 'to raise up by their side a shadowy institution that would in vain attempt to rival their wealth, reputation and influence†.' I am for *reconstruction*—not *destruction*. I entirely agree with the Attorney-General‡ that 'the Inns of Court ought to do the work, which' Lord Selborne 'proposed should be done by this new Institution. Those great and ancient bodies are in possession of ample funds for the purpose. I grant you that they have not done their duty: but they ought to be made to do their duty.' Mr. Gregory mentioned § a point, also worthy of consideration. The existence of the Incorporated Law Society, as well as the Inns of Court, would be imperilled by the creation of this School of Law: and I am not surprised that the Council of the Society was, at first, opposed to the scheme, although, overwhelmed by the desire of 6,000 Attorneys ‖ 'to raise their social status'¶, it was forced to give way.—' The new College' as

---

* Hansard, vol. ccix. 1231.   † Ibid. 1247.
‡ Ibid. 1246.   § Ibid. 1249.
‖ Ibid. 1236.   ¶ Ibid. 1248 (per Mr. Gregory).

Mr. Locke observed*, 'certainly was intended to absorb all the powers now vested in the Inns of Court, *and also*, in the Incorporated Law Society in Chancery Lane.' It would 'improve them' both 'off the face of the earth †!' Sir Richard Baggallay rightly contended‡ that "there are elements in existence, which if properly applied and energetically developed would do all that is necessary.' 'We have already got within the metropolis Schools of Law.' These views as to reconstruction are entirely in accordance with those of the Select Committee of 1846. 'A College of Law is not less important to the lawyer, than a College of Surgery or of Medicine to the Surgeon or Physician. This institution is to be sought rather in *the application*, if possible, *of old establishments*, than in the erection of new ones, from the guarantee, which the former give, of order, efficiency, and permanency; and such an Institution is, to a great degree, to be met with in the Inns of Court. In direct connection with the Bar, under the superintendence of its highest authorities, the Judges, or of its most distinguished members, the Benchers, with old prescription, ancient privileges, very large accommodations, ample funds, and venerable associations, immediately interested in the progress, and honourably jealous of the fame of the Profession, no bodies could be more appropriately

---

* Hansard, vol. ccix. 1250. † Ibid. 1253. ‡ Ibid. 1258-9.

selected, if willing, or likely to be more willing, when once they shall have entered upon the task, than the Inns of Court. No violent or inappropriate innovation is attempted to be forced upon them. They resort only to their own ancient Statutes and practices, and *resume anew* the original objects of their Institution '*.

" The *Law Journal* has taken precisely the same view of the question. 'The policy,' it says, referring to the debate on Sir Roundell Palmer's Resolutions last Session, 'which did find acceptance with the House of Commons, was, in effect, this: — Here are the Inns of Court, the Societies in whom have been vested for centuries the education of students for the Bar, the prerogative of calling to the Bar, and the control over the members of the Bar. These Societies enjoy considerable revenues, to be used for the purposes for which the Societies were founded and exist. It is argued, and to a large extent admitted, that these Societies have not done all their duty, within the province committed to their charge. What, then, is to be done ? Abolish them ? Certainly not. That is against the traditional and universal policy of this country. They *can* be reformed, and they must be reformed '†.

" The Prime Minister himself capped these views

* Report of the Select Committee on Legal Education, p. lix.
- † Law Journal, March 8th, 1872.

to some extent by declaring * that 'a Committee and a Commission had reported that it was from and through the Inns of Court and the Incorporated Law Society that the proposed reform must come, and the Government wished to act upon that principle.'

" Still, I think that, if I had been in the House, I should, probably, have voted for Sir Roundell Palmer's Resolutions," said Singleton, "as a protest against the existing state of things. This was practically the course pursued by Mr. Spencer Walpole, than whom there is no one better entitled to speak upon the subject. He was a member of the Select Committee of the House of Commons on Legal Education, which sat in 1846, and is, I believe, Vice-Chairman of the Joint Committee of the Inns of Court. 'The four Inns of Court,' he said,† 'can only by agreement act concurrently, and if they were to take different views on the subject of education [and discipline],‡ there is no power by which they could jointly and concurrently be required to extend that education, or enforce that discipline. . . . . There must be an Act of Parliament' (*i.e.* a 'public authority') 'as well as a Royal Charter. *The Inns of Court should be empowered by Act of Parliament to act concurrently in the two great matters of extended education and professional discipline:* and I do not see how that object is to be

---

* Hansard, vol. ccix. 1293.   † Ibid. 1270-2.
‡ These words seem necessary to fill out the sense.

effected, unless proposals something like the present Resolutions are assented to by the House.'

"Mr. Walpole's *via media* seems to me the best solution of the difficulty. Mr. Denman (now Mr. Justice Denman), who supported the Resolutions, evidently concurred in Mr. Walpole's view, for he grounded his support on the fact that 'the Inns of Court have not the machinery for *combining* into one great central Body.'* A good illustration of the antagonism which sometimes exists between the four Societies may be gathered from Mr. Locke's taunt that Lincoln's Inn—the Inn to which Lord Selborne himself belongs—refused in 1859, and until 1871, to assent to 'the principle of Compulsory Examination,' which the other three Inns were then prepared to adopt†. The Inner Temple, indeed, decided in favour of it forty-four years ago. On the 11th February, 1829, the Benchers of the Inner Temple came to a unanimous Resolution 'that it is expedient to exclude, as far as may be possible, from admission to the Bar persons, whose education and previous habits of life do not afford sufficient testimony of the integrity and learning, which are essential to the dignity of a liberal profession, and the best titles to the respect and confidence of the public. With a view to effect this desirable object no person' shall 'be hereafter admitted a student of this Society without a previous examination, first,

* Hansard, vol. ccix. 1276. † Ibid. 1252.

by one Barrister of the Society, to be named for that purpose by the Masters of the Bench, and, secondly, by two of the Masters of the Bench, and a certificate to be respectively signed by the Examiners of the competency of the candidate for admission in classical attainments and the general subjects of a liberal Education. Such examination shall include the Greek and Latin languages, or one of them at least, together with such subjects of history and general literature as the Examiners may think suited to the age of the candidate. In like manner before any student be admitted to the Bar, it shall be proved to the satisfaction of the Masters of the Bench, by a like examination and certificate, that he has continued to prosecute the same studies.'* The Resolution, it was agreed, should 'be submitted to the Masters of the Bench of the other' Inns, with an invitation to them to 'concur therein': but it does not appear that any of them accepted the invitation."

"The present Bench of the Inner Temple," said Mr. Marchmont, "has worthily followed in the footsteps of the framers of the Resolution you have cited. It has, 'at a cost of something over £2000 a year,'† restored the Collegiate character of the Inn, by providing Tutorships for its students and

---

* Appendix to Sixth Report of the Common Law Commissioners, 1834, p. 61.

† Per Mr. Staveley Hill, Q. C., Hansard, vol. ccix. 1265.

admitting them to the lectures of the College Tutors free of all expense."

"I confess," said Singleton, "that I don't think the new scheme of the Joint Committee of Benchers at all adequate to the educational wants of the Profession, much less of the Public. The *Times* turns it into ridicule, and says it provides 'something less than the average teaching staff of the Law Faculty in a third-rate German University' *. Anything more preposterous than requiring the same Professor to teach Jurisprudence, International Law, Roman Law, Constitutional Law and Legal History, could not well be conceived! The increase in the value of the Studentships is good, but why are Studentships, Exhibitions and Certificates of Honor for proficiency in *five* subjects to be 'given up' and Studentships for proficiency in *one* subject only to be substituted for them? The Benchers are rushing from one extreme to another. We have neglected Roman Law and Jurisprudence. Now we are to neglect every other Legal study but these!" †

"The new rule sanctioning the admission of the Public to the lectures is a concession to the Legal Education Association," said Marchmont, "and is a step in the right direction. Revive the ancient

---

* Times, Jan. 13, 1873.
† See the last Report of the Legal Education Association, pp. 11 and 12.

splendours of this National School of Law. In the days of Henry VI. 2,000 students frequented the Inns of Court and Chancery, equal, according to Lord Brougham's calculation, to 10,000 students at the present day. Besides the students, designed for Legal practice, as Counsel and Attorneys, who resorted to this Legal University, 'Barons and Knights with other grandees and noblemen of the kingdom,' says Chief Justice Fortescue, 'place their sons there, though they do not desire to have them thoroughly learned in the law, or to get their living by its practice.'"*

"I am entirely opposed to calling to the Bar, any students who have not passed a severe compulsory examination, and I would be glad to see the race of 'ornamental Barristers' consigned to merited oblivion, but it is not at all necessary that the sons of noblemen and gentlemen resorting to the Inns of Court, as in the days of Fortescue, to acquire an essential part of a liberal education, should be required or expected to do more than enter themselves as *students* for a definite term."

"Sir George Jessel, in the course of the debate on the Resolutions of Sir Roundell Palmer, took a similar view. He remarked:—' It was said to be desirable that not only students of the Inns of

*- " Neither at Orleans nor at Angiers, Caen, nor any other University of France, Paris excepted, are there so many students who have passed their minority as in the Inns of Court." Fortescue, cap. 49.

Court, *but gentlemen not intending to follow the law as a profession*, and even Members of Parliament, should have an opportunity of studying the science of law. He by no means dissented from that, and there was a very easy way of attaining it. *Any one could become a student of an Inn of Court*, and if the Chancellor of the Exchequer would be kind enough to remit the tax so far as regarded those students who made a *declaration that they did not intend to follow the law* as a profession, they might, for £8. 11s 6d become forthwith members of an Inn of Court and attend lectures'*. The *Law Journal*, commenting on the debate, observes:—'We welcome heartily the hint thrown out by the Solicitor General that the Chancellor of the Exchequer should remit the tax of £25. 2s 6d imposed on students admitted to an Inn of Court, in any case where the student should declare that he did not intend to become a member of the profession. . . . We should be glad to see the knowledge of law in its outlines and leading principles widely disseminated among the educated classes.' "†

* Hansard, vol. ccix, 1284.
† Law Journal, March 8th, 1872.

§ 15. A "MOOT" POINT.

"How did you like my Call-party the other night?" enquired Percival.

"O, awfully jolly!" exclaimed his friend. "Wines of the finest vintage; songs and speeches worthy of the occasion."

"Your speech was the gem of the evening," said Percival, "what a brilliant picture you drew of the students 'bolting' and 'mooting' and eating their way to the Utter Bar!"

"Alas! the eating is all that remains of the good old days! I think it is Henry VIII. who says that students (or Inner Barristers) who have profited by the study of the law, are called to plead, argue, and dispute some doubtful matter before certain of the Benchers; these pleadings, arguments and disputations are called 'mootings:' and the degree of Utter Barrister is conferred by the Benchers as a reward for the learning displayed on these momentous occasions.* These 'mootings' degenerated into an

* See 5 Foss's Judges, 108, 109, citing Dugdale's Orig. 194, and Mr. Macqueen's Lecture.

idle ceremony—'I say that the widow shall have her dower.'* Dr. Broom once tried to revive them by holding discussions on decided cases in his class-room. Why should the other Lecturers not follow his example? Mr. Locke said, in the debate on Sir Roundell Palmer's Resolutions last Session, that the discussion of legal questions at debating societies was 'a better mode of advancing one in the study of the law than simply attending lectures:'† and surely if the debate were carried on under the eye of a Professor, it would be greatly enhanced in value?"

* Per Lord Brougham, Q. 3,774, 1846.
† Hansard, vol. ccix. p. 1253-4.

§ 16. AMALGAMATION.

The Honourable Percival Pennyless's absence from the side of his faithful friend and Mentor, Stephen Starvington, had, of late, become more frequent, and, on one occasion, he was "missing" for a week. Shall we draw the curtain back, and disclose the truant playing a new part?

The scene opens at Mansfield Court, in the County of Wessex; the actors are the Honourable Percival Pennyless and our old friend, Mr. Robinson Rich, the proprietor of the stately mansion in which Percival was an honored guest. The young Barrister had been lately introduced to the second daughter of the wealthy Solicitor at the house of a mutual friend in the West End. The young lady, though not beautiful, was accomplished; she sang and played the piano to perfection. The Honourable Percival Pennyless sang and played the flute. What more natural than that he should accompany her on that instrument? Duets and glees followed as a matter of course, and so did an invitation to Mansfield Court.

The gentlemen were seated over their wine, and the wealthy Solicitor, who was never so happy as when discussing a legal topic, introduced the subject

Y

of the amalgamation of the two branches of the Legal Profession. He had hardly broached it, however, when he rose and rang the bell. To him enter John, the portly butler.

" John, fetch me my note-book. You will find it on my study-table."—Exit John.

Re-enter John with the note-book.

" Here, Mr. Pennyless," said Mr. Rich, " are a few notes that I have made upon the constitution of the Legal Profession in foreign countries. We will take first, if you please, *the United States.*" (Clever old gentleman, was he not?) " Two American Lawyers, Mr. Horace Binney, junior, and General Thomas, were examined before the Royal Commission on the Inns of Court and Chancery, in 1854. Mr. Binney was examined as follows:—

" ' 359. You are a citizen of the United States?'—' I am, and a Member of the Bar of Philadelphia, practising in the State of Pennsylvania. . . . My father was one of the leaders of the Bar of Philadelphia.'

" ' 362. You have been some time in practice yourself, have you not?'—'I have been in practice about 23 years. I was admitted in 1831, being then 22 years of age, and I have been practising since that time.'

" ' 364-5. Will you state, first of all, the course of proceeding for admission to the Bar of Pennsylvania?'—' In Pennsylvania there is no distinction of *grades* in the profession. The term Barrister is not used. We are all Attorneys-at-law, and the Attorney, as such, does all the duties of the Profession, that is to say, from the first institution of the suit, through the preparation of the pleadings, the trial at Nisi Prius, the argument in Banco, and, if necessary, the issuing of final process. The Judges of our Courts select seven Members of the Bar, and those seven (the senior acting as Chairman and the junior as Secretary) are called the Board of Examiners. A Student-at-law must read law in the office of a practising Attorney for three years, if he commence under 21 years of age; and for two years, if he begins after 21 years of age. He is attended to by his Professional Instructor during that period, but does not serve as an articled clerk. At the outset he is registered on the dockets of the Court as a candidate for admission to the Bar. Three months before the expiration of the probationary period, he gives notice of application for admission to the Bar, which is published in the *Legal Intelligencer*. He then presents himself, at a stated time, before the Board of Examiners, and brings with him a certificate of good moral character from his Instructor. The examination is vivâ voce and lasts, perhaps, an hour. The examination being favourable and the certificate satisfactory, some gentleman at the Bar makes a motion for his admission in open Court. He swears allegiance to the Constitution and the State and fidelity to the Court and his client, and is then admitted to practise.' '389. There is at Philadelphia, an association of gentlemen of the Bar, called the Law Association of Philadelphia. That Association has some little capital, though nothing at all to be compared with that of the Inns of Court, which I see around me. It has also some small invested fund for the relief of unfortunate Members of the Bar. This Law Association is supposed to represent the honor of the Bar. We have a Committee of Censors, which would, if properly applied to, take strict cognizance of any malpractice alleged against a member of the Association. Such a thing as a censure from the Law Association would be very formidable to any member of the Bar.'

"'393. Can they expel a member?'—'Yes, I certainly think so.'

"'403. Supposing you had a case that was to come to Nisi Prius, would you examine the witnesses yourself, beforehand?'— 'In general, we should. We would see the witnesses personally.'

"'419. Do the Attorneys assume the character of Advocates in any causes except those in their own office, or are they like our Barristers, who receive causes from others?'—'Attorneys do not confine themselves to causes originating in their own office. A member of the Bar will be called in as senior or junior colleague in a case *from any office.*'

"Subsequently General Thomas was examined:—

" '994. Are you conversant with the practice of Law in the United States?'—'I am.'

" '995. In what State are you most conversant with the practice of Law?'—'New York. I have lived in three or four States.'

" '998-9. What was the original course of proceeding in the State of New York, with reference to any gentleman who wished to become an Advocate?'—'He was required to have graduated at some College, and to have entered his name in an Attorney's office, and pursued there, under the direction of an Attorney, the study of Law for three years. He was then examined before three persons, appointed by the Supreme Court of the State, and if he passed a satisfactory examination, he was then, by the Supreme Court, licensed to practise Law *as an Attorney.* He was required to practise as an Attorney for three years..... At the end of three years of practice as an Attorney, he was required to undergo an examination on the Principles of Law. The first examination was chiefly upon the Practice. On the second examination, previously to being admitted *as a Counsellor*, he was examined upon the Principles of Law very thoroughly by three Counsellors appointed by the Supreme Court, and, if that examination proved satisfactory he was admitted to practise as a Counsellor, and could then appear and argue cases in Court, and not till then. Previously, he could only appear as an Attorney.'

" '1005. When a person is admitted as a Counsellor, does he still continue to practise as an Attorney, does he combine the two?'—'He may practise either as an Attorney or as a Counsellor.'

" '1006. What change in the system has taken place since 1846?'—'Since that period the examination has been for admission to *the Bar*, and a person, once admitted, is admitted to practise in all the Courts of the State. There are no degrees, therefore, of Attorney and Counsellor recognized by the Law. A candidate for admission to *the Bar* is required to be examined by three Counsellors appointed by the Supreme Court, and [is] licensed by the Supreme Court to practise Law as before; but, after having obtained this license, he is then admitted to practise *as an Attorney, or Solicitor, or Counsellor, as he may get employment.* It is not necessary that he should have attended an Advocate's office, or any other office whatever.' '1010. I think I may say that there is as much free trade allowed in the law as it is possible one can conceive.' '1015. The examination is confined chiefly to the practise of the Law, the mode of bringing actions, their nature, and generally those questions with which an Attorney is supposed to be familiar.'

"'1057. You approve very much of the amalgamation of the two branches of the Profession in one person?'—'Yes.'

"'1060. How is the evidence hunted up?'—'That is done by the Attorney and Client, but Counsel sees personally the leading witnesses.'

"'1061. Who is the Attorney, as distinct from the Counsel?'—'The offices are divided according to the nature of the business. A man begins to practise law in New York, for instance, and he has one or two cases. He then does all the business himself; but his business increases, and he has more than he can do himself, and he then employs a clerk, who takes a part off his hands; then *he employs an Attorney*, and the cases that require no investigation, such as bringing a common action, would be commenced by the Attorney, without seeing the Counsellor, unless there was a special request made in the matter.'

"'1062. So that the Attorney is nominated and employed by the Counsel?'—'Yes; he *generally belongs to his office.*'

"'1063. And, generally speaking, there is a partnership,

is there not ?'—' Yes. The moment the business becomes sufficiently important to justify the taking a partner, the Counsel takes in this man, *whom he has employed* as Attorney, or some one else, as his partner, and who does the ordinary business of the office, while he goes into Court.'

"' 1065. Practically, in all important cases, there is the same division of labour between the Counsel and the Attorney in the United States, as exists in this country ?' 'Exactly so; but it is rendered so by circumstances. If you go into States that are new, where the population is sparc, there are few law-suits, and the Counsel will sit in his office half the day and talk with a client, for he has nothing else to do. Of course, in that case, he needs no Attorney.'

"' 1066. *Is not the effect of this system, that in all simple causes, only* ONE AGENT *is employed ?'*—' *Yes.*'

"' 1067. *Therefore it is* MUCH CHEAPER *in practice than the system pursued in this country, of having* TWO AGENTS *in every case.?'*—' YES ; this is certainly true.'

" If we turn from the United States to Germany, we find that (in the language of the Report of the Select Committee of the House of Commons, which sat in 1846)*,

"'The distinction in the Profession is not, in Germany, as [it is] with us, between the Advocate, Barrister, or Pleader, on the one side, and the Solicitor or Attorney, on the other, but between the State servant and the free Practitioner. . . . The Profession does not branch off into the recipient of instructions from the client (or the Solicitor), and the forensic Advocate (or Barrister) ; they are identified, and form one body.'

" Mr. Adolphus Bach gave the following evidence respecting the constitution of the Legal Profession in Germany, before the Royal Commission of 1854:—

* Report, p. xxv., referring to Question § 3, 242.

"'1232. You have for some time resided in England?'—
'Yes.'

"'1233. You are yourself a member of the Legal Profession in Germany?'—'I am.'

"'1260. *Is the Profession divided in Germany, as it is in this country, into Advocates and Solicitors?*'—'It is not; not even in those parts of Germany where the French Law prevails.'

"'1261. The same people take all departments of practice; for instance, they would serve processes and summon witnesses personally, and at the same time conduct a cause in Court?'—'Not quite so; the Courts serve all the processes by their own Officers.'

"Mr. Greenwood, in his Report to this Commission upon 'the different Systems of Legal Education pursued in the different States of Germany'*, observes:—

"'24. Throughout Germany the Advocate performs most of the duties of the Attorney in England, and of the Avoué in the French Courts. A scale of fees is established in all the Courts for his remuneration, and beyond that he has no claim upon his client. But these fees he may recover by process of Law. . . . A stated number of Advocates is appointed to each Court, among whom all the business must be divided out. In general, throughout the Courts, the number of Advocates is below that of Judges; but this is in a measure accounted for by the fact that a great deal of the business, which in other countries is performed by the office clerk, the Attorney, or the Barrister, is done by the Judges *ex officio.*'

"'36. The decision of causes in these Courts is very prompt, the most difficult and complicated suits very rarely lasting more than six months, and actions at law are attended with less expense in Prussia Proper than in any other part of Germany,

* Appendix to Report, 1854, p. 272.

or, perhaps, in Europe. The functions of the Courts of Appeal seem directed rather to correct the errors than to reverse the decisions of the Inferior Courts.'

" Mr. Saunders assures us* that 'in Sweden and Denmark, in Italy, Spain, and Portugal, the functions of the Attorney and Advocate are combined.' He adds, 'that in *all* our colonial dependencies no severance of the two branches of the Legal Profession exists.' It would, of course, be impossible in a brief space to enumerate the regulations which govern the constitution of the Profession in 'all our colonial dependencies,' but I will select a few colonies by way of illustration.

" By an 'Ordinance respecting Barristers and Attorneys-at-Law,'† the Legislative Council of British Columbia, in 1868, empowered 'Barristers to practise as Attorneys and Solicitors, and Attorneys and Solicitors as Barristers,' 'in *all* the Courts of Civil and Criminal Jurisdiction' within the 'former Colony of Vancouver's Island and its Dependencies.'

" The 'Journals of the Legislative Council'‡ inform us that

* " Amalgamation of the two Branches of the Legal Profession," p. 13.

† No. 7 of Ordinances of the Legislative Council of British Columbia, Session March to May, 1868: New Westminster, printed at the Government Office.

‡ Journals of the Legislative Council of British Columbia, 22 April, 1868, p. 21.

" On the order of the day being read for the second reading of the Barristers and Attorneys' Bill, the Hon. Mr. Wood moved that the Bill be read a second time that day six months : whereupon a debate arose, which having terminated, and the amendment being put, the Council divided: Ayes 3 ; Noes 14. So the amendment was lost."

"Among the 'Sessional Papers, 1868,' will be found the following interesting

"' Petition of certain members of the Legal Profession ':—

"' That we, the undersigned Barristers and Attorneys of the Supreme Court of British Columbia and Vancouver Island, humbly pray :—

"' 1. That in view of the Bill being passed, entitled, "An Ordinance respecting Barristers and Attorneys-at-Law,' *which practically amalgamates the two professions of Barrister and Attorney*, such amalgamation cannot justly be carried out with respect to the existing practitioners of such Courts, unless they can in every respect be placed on an equality as regards their status as Officers of such Courts; and this desirable object can only be obtained by allowing every Barrister forthwith to be admitted as an Attorney in addition to his character of a Barrister, if he should so wish ; and, in the same way, by allowing every Attorney to be called to the Bar, if he should so wish, of such Courts, and admitted to practise as a Barrister, in addition to his existing character of an Attorney.

"' 2. With respect to future practitioners, they cannot complain, if, whilst allowed to practise in both capacities of Barrister and Attorney, they cannot attain the status of both in this colony, unless they have either been already admitted in both capacities elsewhere, or have shown themselves qualified to fill such capacities, and as prescribed by the 'Legal Practitioners' Ordinance, 1867,' and complied with its conditions.

"' We, therefore, pray your Honourable House, that the annexed clause may be passed, so that the objects of the Bill may be obtained without injustice to either branch of the Profession, considering, as we do, that in its present state it is open to that objection.' "—(Here follow 8 Signatures).

" The suggested clause was as follows:—

" 'Every Barrister now entitled to practise as a Barrister in the Supreme Courts of British Columbia and Vancouver Island, or either of them, shall, on his Petition to either of the said Courts to be admitted as an Attorney, be forthwith admitted as an Attorney of such Courts; and be entitled to all the privileges of an Attorney of such Courts; and every Attorney now entitled to practise as an Attorney of such Courts or either of them, shall, on his Petition to either of the said Courts to be admitted as a Barrister, be forthwith called to the Bar, and admitted as a Barrister of such Courts, and entitled to all the rights and privileges of a Barrister of such Courts.'*

" This Petition was presented by the Hon. Mr. de Cosmos, who introduced the Barristers and Attorneys' Bill, on the same day on which the debate took place on the second reading of that Bill; but no notice appears to have been taken by the Council either of the Petition or of the proposed clause, beyond ordering it to 'lie on the Table.'

" By an Act of the Legislature of the Islands of Bermuda, (dated as long ago as the 4th June, 1831.)

"'No person, except those already admitted, shall be admitted to plead or practise *as Counsel or Attorney*, in the Courts of Common Law in these Islands, unless such person shall have been admitted *a Barrister-at-law* in England or Ireland, *or* a member of the faculty of Advocates in Scotland, *or* shall have kept at least twelve terms in one of the Inns of Court in England or Ireland, or shall have served three years

* Sessional Papers, 1868, No. 12, p. xi.

or longer as a pupil under *some Barrister or Attorney*, practising in the said Islands of Bermuda.' A penalty of £50 is imposed on 'any person presuming, to plead or practise as aforesaid without first being admitted.'*

" A still older precedent is furnished by the law of Dominica. By an Act passed on the 5th May, 1803, the Legislature of Dominica enacted that

"'No person shall be admitted to *practise the law* in this island until he shall have proved to the satisfaction of the Justices of the Court of Common Pleas, that he hath been admitted *a Barrister* in England or Ireland, or hath kept such a number of terms at one of the Inns of Court in England, as would have entitled him to be called to the Bar there; or hath been regularly admitted and sworn *an Attorney* of one of His Majesty's Courts at Westminster; or hath practised as a *Barrister* in any of His Majesty's Colonies in America, for the space of five years at least; or hath been bound by contract in writing, to serve as a clerk for five years to *a Barrister and Attorney* in this Island, and caused an affidavit to be made and placed in the Secretary's office, of the due execution of such contract, within three months next after the date thereof, and shall, during the whole time and term of service continue actually employed by *a Barrister and Attorney* in the proper business, practice and employment of an *Attorney*.'

" A penalty of £50 is imposed on 'any person presuming to *plead or practice the law*,' in the Island, ' or *give advice in any law matter, or draw conveyances* of land for any fee, present, or reward, until he shall have been admitted and qualified himself as aforesaid.' †

* Bermuda Acts: p. 179 (1831: No. 8, s. 30). Edition 1862, edited by Chief Justice Darrell.

† Laws of the Colony of Dominica: Roseau, 1818: p. 179 (No. 37, clause 3).

"By another clause* writs were directed to be 'served by the Provost Marshal, or by some person authorized by him.'

"The regulations governing the Legal Profession in the *Bahamas* are still older. The leading enact-ment was passed in the last century (39 Geo. III. c. 2, 1798, intituled 'An Act for the better regulation of Counsel, Attorneys, Solicitors and Proctors').

"'Whereas it is requisite and expedient that proper qualifications and due regulations should be attended to, in the admission of all persons hereafter to be admitted as Counsel, Attorneys, Solicitors and Proctors, in the several Courts of Law and Equity within the Islands; no person who had not before the 1st day of March, 1798, been sworn, admitted and enrolled, *a Counsel and Attorney* of the General Court, shall be permitted to act as a Counsel, Attorney, Solicitor or Proctor, or to sue out any writ or process, or to commence, carry on, or defend any action or suit, or other proceedings whatever, in any Court, either of Law or Equity, within these Islands, unless such persons shall have been *called to the Bar*, either in Great Britain or Ireland, or shall have been sworn and admitted *an Attorney* in the Court of King's Bench or Common Pleas, in England, or in Ireland, or shall have been bound by contract in writing to serve and shall actually have served, as a clerk, for and during the space of five years, to *a Counsel and Attorney* of the General Court of these Islands, duly and legally sworn, admitted, enrolled, and practising as such, and also unless such person shall have been sworn, enrolled and admitted in manner hereinafter directed.'

"'II. It shall and may be lawful for *the Judges* of the General Court and they are hereby authorized and required *to examine* and inquire, by such reasonable ways and means as they shall think proper, touching the qualification, fitness and capacity of all persons who shall hereafter apply to be admitted

* Clause 5.

Counsel and Attorneys of the General Court; and if such Judges (of whom the Chief Justice shall always be one) shall be satisfied that any person applying for admission is duly qualified as *a Counsel and Attorney*, then and not otherwise the Judges shall and they are hereby authorised to administer to such person the oath hereafter directed to be taken and shall cause him to be *enrolled and admitted a Counsel and Attorney of the General Court.*' *

"In the first Schedule to the 'Act respecting the Bar of Lower Canada' will be found the form of diploma which is granted by the Bâtonnier when admitting a Candidate to the Bar:—

"' I, the undersigned, Bâtonnier of the Bar of Lower Canada, Section of the District of . . . . in conformity with the provisions of the 72nd cap. of the Consolidated Statutes of Lower Canada, in pursuance of the certificate to me delivered by three of the Examiners of the said section dated the . . . , whereby it appears that A. B. of . . . . under the requirements of the said Act, after having served a regular clerkship, as prescribed by law, has undergone before them on the . . . . day of . . . . the examination necessary to his admission to the profession of Advocate : and that from such examination it appears that he is in all respects worthy and qualified to be so admitted, have given and granted to him, and do, by these presents, give and grant to him, according to the provisions of the said Act, the present Diploma, conferring on him the right of practising as an *Advocate, Barrister, Attorney, Solicitor and Proctor-at-law in all Courts of Law* in Lower Canada.'†

"I might multiply almost *in infinitum* these illustrations of the constitution of the Legal Profes-

* Statute Law of the Bahamas. London: Sweet: 1862, p. 262. (Part II. class 7, No. 1.)

† Consolidated Statutes of Lower Canada : 1861. Cap. 72 (Schedule 1.)

sion within Her Majesty's dominions, on which the sun never sets; but I forbear.

"Let us now consider the advantages and disadvantages of amalgamating the functions of Advocate and Attorney, and thus assimilating our system to that of the rest of the civilized world."

"France always excepted," said the Honourable Percival Pennyless.

"France always excepted," repeated Mr. Rich. "I give you the full benefit of that exception. Suppose I state the advantages, and you the disadvantages?"

"By all means," said Percival.

"I will take first the advantages to your Branch of the Profession," said Mr. Rich, "and then the advantages to ours; and then the advantages to the Public. In the first place, the amalgamation of the two branches of the Profession will bring the Bar into immediate contact with the Public, by excluding the intervention between them of the middle-man, the Attorney."

The Honourable Percival Pennyless winced. Do you enquire the reason, gentle reader? He was about to "form a connection!" Concealing his disgust at his future father-in-law's first reason, he boldly grappled with it. "The Bar would gain nothing by that; the intervention of the Attorney is merely a rule of etiquette, which the common consent of the Bar may, at any moment, abrogate. There is no rule of Law that prevents the Barrister from taking instructions, in all cases, direct from the Public."

"As for the rules of etiquette," observed Mr. Rich, catching at the expression, "the amalgamation of the two branches of the Profession would consign them *en masse* to the waste-paper basket; and certainly a greater tissue of absurdities could not well be devised."

"Mr. Jevons, however, thinks* that these rules have 'been necessarily and properly established,' although, 'at first sight,' they may 'appear absurd.' They 'preserve,' he says, 'the independence of the Bar.'"

"Independence of the Bar!" exclaimed Mr. Rich, contemptuously. "Why, Sir, a more pitiable object than a member of the Junior Bar 'hugging an Attorney' cannot well be conceived. One extraordinary result of the present 'division of labour' is, that the civil business of a Circuit of 200 Barristers, with a constituency of more than 700 Attorneys, is done by about a dozen Barristers: say six Seniors, and an equal number of Juniors. These are over-worked, while the remaining 188 Barristers have the privilege of looking on, till death or promotion removes their successful rivals out of the way. The temptation to supplant the men in business by 'hugging Attorneys' is very great. I have often thought that a Barrister must feel, as Swift did at the house of Sir William Temple, a sense of deep humiliation, and almost of agonizing self-abasement, in the presence of the patron upon whose favour his future success in life—

* P. 11.

his future livelihood—depends! Let him but utter an offensive word, or give a cross look, and he may bid farewell to his hopes. It strikes me that the successful silk frequently takes his revenge for the state of vassalage in which he was held, when a struggling Junior, by seizing every opportunity to snub the patrons of his youth!* When fortune smiles upon him, he gives full rein to the scorn and rage which were held in check, in less fortunate days, by self-interest."

This picture of the Bar was so graphic and so true withal that Pennyless winced again; but taking up his parable, he said, " What you say is quite true; but, then, the Bar has the compensating advantage of high social status—of *existimatio*, so to speak, in Society. A Barrister undergoes a *capitis deminutio* if he leaves the Bar and takes to 'practising Attorneyship,' as Philip and Mary phrase it."

" You are touching now on one of the grievances of our branch of the Profession," observed Mr. Rich, rather testily. " We are dealing now, Sir, with your grievances. Hear what the late Mr. J. G. Phillimore (whom Mr. Saunders, by the way, has confounded with Sir Robert Phillimore) says about it. I am quoting from the Royal Commission of 1854:—

* "' We should recollect that it too often has been in time past, and will be *again*, our lot to be slighted and overlooked by those who soon forget the guineas, which, with thanks, they once took out of our hands.'—" A Registrar," in the *Law Times*, March 2nd, 1872.

" 'The circumstance of the more highly educated branch of the Profession depending for distinction and profit upon a class quite inferior to it in education and sentiment, has a very pernicious effect upon the higher class. The great evil that our Profession has to struggle against is, and has been, the narrowing and illiberal tendency, which must be the result, where men look for encouragement and reputation to persons of inferior education; I speak, of course, generally. It is not likely such persons should encourage qualities they do not understand and cannot appreciate.'

" ' To what do you attribute the superiority you suppose to exist in the French Bar over the English ?'—' Principally to the study of the Roman Law and of the theory of Jurisprudence, added to *the absence of the evil* I have noticed, *in the almost absolute power of Attorneys over the English Bar.*' 'The way to raise the Profession, I think, is by obliging people to acquire a certain amount of knowledge before they enter it, and *by holding out other motives than the favour of Attorneys to them.*' ' I venture to repeat that the evil we are now suffering from is that to which Lord Bacon refers when he says, 'The rewards of learning are in the hands of the unlearned.' The more you can correct that the better, and diminish the overwhelming and *malignant* influence of Attorneys on our branch of the Profession.'*

" This language is, I agree with Mr. Saunders,† ' rather strong;' but it is the opinion of a highly accomplished scholar and of a former member of Parliament."

" A far more feasible way out of this state of things, if it really exists," said Percival, " than the

* Questions 1485, 1504, 1514, and 1515: Minutes of Evidence before the Royal Commission on the Inns of Court and Chancery, 1854.

† P. 28.

suggested amalgamation, is to restore to the Bar the privilege that it formerly possessed of advising clients directly, without the intervention of Attorneys. Let the Public go to the Attorneys, if the Public pleases, and ask their advice in the first instance; and let the Attorney then, if necessary, instruct Counsel; or, let the Public go to Counsel, if the Public pleases, and ask their advice in the first instance, and let the Counsel, if they think that judicial proceedings are necessary, instruct Attorney. I was once told that in a certain town the Barristers' Chambers had become a resort for clients, like Attorneys' Offices. Recognize this practice, which is sanctioned by constitutional precedent, and in which there is nothing whatever that is dishonorable, but rather the reverse. You would thus give us free trade in Law, in the best sense of the term."

"You are obliged," said Mr. Rich, "to stop short, in your scheme for the aggrandizement of the Bar, with the initiation of 'judicial proceedings.' Counsel, you say, must *then*, at all events, 'instruct Attorney.' But if 'the Statutory privileges of the Attorneys and Solicitors' were 'abolished'—and it would require little more than the repeal of the Statute 6 and 7 of the Queen, cap. 73 (saving the repeal by that Act of former enactments,) to abolish them *—the Bar might employ experienced

* Report of the Special Committee of the Law Amendment Society, 1852, pp. 12 and 19.

clerks (just as the Attorneys and Solicitors do now), to conduct suits through the forms of the Courts; while process might be served, as in some of the States of North America and countries on the Continent of Europe, by State officials, at a trifling expense. The Bar would thus obtain a monopoly of all legal business."

"Would it not be more likely," said Percival, "that the Attorneys, admitted to a right of audience in the Superior Courts, would obtain a monopoly of all legal business? 'By a judicious distribution of duties among the different members of an Attorney-partnership, the firm would be enabled to dispense entirely with the assistance of the Bar.'"*

"The arguments, I admit, *pro and con*, from the point of view of the Bar, are pretty evenly balanced," said Mr. Rich. "The advantages of amalgamation to our branch of the Profession are, on the other hand, obvious. Regarding the fusion of the two branches of the Profession as a logical consequence of the creation of a School of Law, on the governing body of which the leaders of both branches, and in the class-rooms of which the students of both branches, are to be placed, side by side, on a footing of social equality, 6,000 Attorneys and Solicitors—more than one-half of the entire number of Attorneys and Solicitors—petitioned, last Session, in favour of Sir Roundell Palmer's motion, while only 900 Barristers—less than one-fourth of

* Ibid, p. 19.

the entire Bar—petitioned in its favour. The social grievance lies at the root of the agitation. Sir Charles Lyell has stated this grievance very clearly. 'An artificial line of demarcation,' he says, 'is erected between Attorneys and Advocates marked enough to depress their social rank, and to deter many young men of good families from entering in reality the most important branch of the Profession.'* Mr. Jevons alludes † with some bitterness to 'the social standing *supposed* to be conferred by the degree of Barrister,' and points out that 'Barristers and Attorneys and Solicitors are practically taken from the same classes of Society, different members of the same family in many cases, practising in the different branches.' Not only does the 'artificial line of demarcation' tend to 'deter young men of good family' from entering our branch of the Profession,' but it attracts them into yours, and so swells your numbers with many ornamental but far from useful Barristers, 'without any serious intention of practising.' Amalgamate the two branches of the Profession, and this social grievance will disappear."

"I firmly believe," said Percival, "that this amalgamation, instead of raising the tone and status of the Attorneys, would only lower the tone and status of the Bar. I believe Mr. Jevons to be totally in error in supposing that the tone and status of the

* Cited by Mr. Saunders, p. 18.
† Pp. 3, 6, and see Saunders, p. 31.

Bar in the United States is higher than it is in England.* Let him ask Mr. Benjamin : I am willing to abide by the decision of that distinguished Statesman and lawyer. Let him turn to the Bars of France—to the Berryers, the Favres, the Dupins, and other ex-Bâtonniers of the Parisian Order of Advocates, aye, to the Dictator Gambetta himself, for instances of 'political power' wielded by Advocates, where the Advocate is distinct from the Attorney. ' Lawyers,' forsooth, ' don't succeed in Parliament'! Shades of More, Bacon, Somers, Hyde, Lyndhurst, and Brougham !—guardian angels of Palmer, Cairns, Cockburn, Thesiger, Whiteside, Keogh, Coleridge, Henry James, aye, and Vernon Harcourt, refute the astounding assertion! As for ornamental Barristers, the compulsory examinations will, I hope, exclude the wealthy bourgeoisie who wish to be elevated, by the simple process of eating a few dinners, into a kind of lower order of nobility with access to the *salons* of the higher order of nobility at the West End, and to obtain an artificial precedence on the magisterial bench. Our practice, I trust, will become assimilated to that of the French Bars. ' No one can be inscribed upon the tableau of a Court, or of a tribunal, unless he actually practises before it.' † This regulation ' tends, and with reason, to remove from the Order

* Pp. 14, 15.
† Mollot: Tome I. 309, 310. Ordon. du 20 Nov. 1822, Article 5.

of Advocates and to exclude from the tableau individuals, who, provided with the necessary degrees and sworn, do, not actually practise as Advocates, and wish, by the possession of a naked title, without giving themselves up habitually and exclusively to the duties of the Bar, or to Chamber-practice, to enjoy the prerogatives which only belong to hardworking men, really devoted to the Profession, which they have embraced.' *

" Amalgamation," said Mr. Rich, "will give Attorneys and Solicitors access to the Inns of Court, and also to judicial appointments. Are these not advantages?"

" They would be advantages to your branch of the Profession, I admit, but you have some prospect of getting them, without amalgamation, and your gain would, in any event, be our loss: the increased competition for chambers in the Inns of Court, would lead to an increase in our rents, and each appointment conferred upon you would be one more opportunity of earning a decent livelihood gone—irrevocably gone from us."

" After all," said Mr. Rich, "the real point to be considered is the public interest; and 'it is amalgamation,' say sthe *Spectator*,† 'that the public interest demands.' The argument that will weigh most with the Public will, I think, be the diminution in

* Circular of the Keeper of the Seals to the Procureurs Généraux, dated 6th Jan. 1823, cited by Mollot, ubi supra.

† Article cited by Mr. Saunders, pp. 26, 27.

the expenses of suitors. Instead of consulting an Attorney, who instructs Counsel, the client would consult Counsel, himself. It is all the difference between the expense of two agents and one. Time would be saved by the substitution of a direct for a roundabout proceeding. Facts will be clearly ascertained by Counsel—"

" My dear Sir, your three reasons are the very ones that the Special Committee of the Law Amendment Society* urges in favour of clients consulting Counsel, without the intervention of an Attorney. Cheapness, expedition, and accuracy may all be secured, without fusing the two branches of the Profession, by the simple abrogation of a rule of etiquette."

* * * * * * *

" And now," said the Honourable Percival Pennyless, " that our friendly disputation is over, permit me to assure you, my dear Sir, that I am perfectly satisfied with THE LEGAL PROFESSION *as it is.*"

" Well," thought Mr. Rich, " Cornelius Brown and Sir George Jessel may, perhaps, be right, after all! The son of my new friend the Earl of Pauperborough is a clever fellow: Mrs. Rich will be introduced by the Hon. Mrs. Percival Pennyless into the best Society, and, I shall take care that her husband has no cause to regret his alliance with the great house of Rich & Readymoney."

* Pp. 14, 15, 16. And see Saunders, p. 12.

§ 17. "WOO'D AN' MARRIED AN' A."

"Mansfield Court, Wessex,
"Feb. 20th, 1873.
"Dear Starvington,
"I beg to give you notice that I shall quit your Chambers next quarter-day. I have taken a large set in Applepie Court.

"Yours faithfully,

"PERCIVAL PENNYLESS."

This is a letter which Stephen received on February 21st.

*　*　*　*　*　*　*

Stephen, from hints that Percival had let fall, had some dim notion that, 'there was a lady in the case.' The mystery was soon made clear by the following announcement, which appeared in the leading Journal:—

"Married, on the 1st day of March, 1873, at St. Jacob's Church, Piccadilly, the Hon. Percival Pennyless, of No. 21, Applepie Court, Temple, second son of the Earl of Pauperborough, to Angelica, second daughter of Robinson Rich, of Lincoln's Inn Fields and Mansfield Court, in the County of Wessex, Esquire."

§ 18. A GLOOMY PROSPECT.

"And so Percival has 'formed a connection!'" exclaimed Stephen Starvington, on reading this announcement; "a partnership for life. He will become 'seized of' innumerable 'briefs in right of his wife.'* 'The business of the' great 'firm' of Rich and Readymoney will 'flow in upon him.'† He will be, in short, its 'talking member.' And this, not because he took honors at the Bar Examinations—(bah! honors; the Attorneys, as a rule, dislike them, and so do the Benchers, for they prefer as Tutors men who never obtained them)—but solely because he has 'fallen in luck's way, and married a Solicitor's daughter.'‡ And I, in this boasted nineteenth century, with a fair share of industry and ability, which are, I am told, the certain passports to wealth and fame—I must 'sit alone in my Chambers and languish from inaction.'§ Colossal fortunes may be made by sheer dint of industry and ability in every calling, *save one*—and that one is the Bar; the Profession that I have chosen! And many, many another is supporting,

* Article in *Times*, cited by Mr. Coryton, late Recorder of Rangoon, in his letter to the *Post*, Jan. 14, 1873.

† *Globe*, 18 Jan., 1872: article on "Briefless Barristers."

‡ Ibid. § Ibid.

like myself, the position of a member of the aristocracy with the income of a pauper!"

And Stephen threw himself back in his armchair, and remained buried in thought.

* * * * *

Then, along the vista of coming years, he saw expanding before him the downward course of a comparatively briefless Barrister's existence—the wasting struggle between an ingenuous pride and a degrading pauperism—the heartsickness of hope deferred—the descent of the " golden shower of fortune" upon his less worthy competitors; and Stephen Starvington bowed his head, and covering his face with his hands . . . . pity, but do not think harshly of him, gentle reader . . . . wept like a child.

* * * * *

One gleam of comfort flits across the gloomy vision of the future . . . He will, one day, be saved from entering the Union Workhouse, through the timely aid of the Benevolent Society, which the generous sympathies of a few of the leaders of his noble Profession, rising superior to pedantic prejudices, have founded . . . He will not be left, like poor Haddy, to die of absolute want—"ALONE IN LONDON."

APPENDIX.

CASES CITED.

	PAGE
A's case	121
A. v. B.	121
A. v. B.	121, 122

Anonymous cases, 40, 41, 44, 45, 92, 99, 100, 101, 110, 119, 120, 122, 152, 290, 291

B. and C's case	121
Banks v. Allen	184
Bateman, In Re	151, 152, 153
Blagreve v. Belne	62, 115
Booreman's case	281
Butler v. Freeman	289
Canterbury, Archbishop of, v. Bishop of Rochester	62
Cotton, Ex parte	255
Crammond v. Crouch	229
Curle's case	185
Cuts v. Pickering	172, 173, 174
D'Arcy v. the Abbot of Rowham	120
Davies v. Sibly	229
Dean's case	218

Doe d. Bennett v. Hale, 50, 56, 58, 68, 74, 75, 89, 115, 122, 168, 169, 176, 278

Doig's case	290
Edmonson v. Davis	229
Edmund v. Grandcourt	39, 94, 95, 96
Egan v. the Kensington Guardians	217
Evans, Ex parte	29
Fell v. Brown	160, 161
Fundenhale, De, v. De Helgeton	72
Hill's case	289
Hudson v. Slade	292

	PAGE
Jackson, In Re	229
Jenkins v. Slade	229
John and Isabel's case	97
Kennedy v. Brown	215, 216, 217, 219, 226
Marsh v. Rainsford	217
Mitchell, In Re	289
Montgomery, De, v. De C.	109
Moor v. Row	217, 218
Morris v. Hunt	219
Mortimer, De v. De Toune	107
Mortymer v. Mortymer	104, 105
Moscati v. Lawson	178
Mulligan v. McDonagh, Q.C.	161
Paston v. Genney	124
Pourice v. Parker	218
Poucher v. Norman	229
Redvers v. Bardolf	117, 118
Regina v. the Derbyshire Justices	29
Rex v. B.	106, 107
Rex v. Barnard's Inn	233
Rex v. Giffard	107
Rex v. Gray's Inn	281, 282
Rex v. Hubert De Burgh, Earl of Kent	54
Rex v. Le Mortimer et uxor	106, 107
Rex v. Lincoln's Inn	279
Rex v. Thomas Le Mareschal and others	54
Roberts' case	111
Scales, De v. Wichend et uxor	72
Scott v. Miller	229
Serjeants' case, The	53, 76, 128
Shuttleworth v. Nicholson	178
Standish v. Langeton	39, 93, 94, 104
Swinfen v. Lord Chelmsford	225, 226
T.'s case	97, 98, 99
Talker v. B.	114, 115

Thomas the Notary's case	101, 102, 103
Tovyn v. William	105, 106, 112
Turner v. Phillips.	161
Val, De v. Le Mortimer.	107
Verdoun and another, v. the Abbot of Combermere.	93
Willet v. Chambers	185, 186
Wysard et uxor v. B.	38, 91, 92, 104

STATUTES CITED.

9 Hen. III. c. 11	79
3 Edw. I. (Westminster I.) c. 29	55, 58
13 Edw. I. (Westminster II.) c. 3	102
13 Edw. I. (Westminster II.) c. 10	68, 75, 102, 168
28 Edw. I. c. 11	88
15 Edw. II. (Statute [?] of Carlisle)	37, 80, 81, 82, 83
36 Edw. III. c. 15	71
4 Hen. IV. c. 18	84, 87
2 Hen. VI. c. 3	70
33 Hen. VI. c. 7	89
11 Hen. VII. c. 12	85
2 Geo. II. c. 23	90
6 and 7 Vict. c. 73	90, 244
6 and 7 Vict. c. 73, s. 1	84
6 and 7 Vict. c. 73, s. 2	90
6 and 7 Vict. c. 73, s. 6	154
12 and 13 Vict. c. 106, s. 247	32
15 and 16 Vict. c. 54	27, 32
23 and 24 Vict. c. 127	145
24 and 25 Vict. c. 134, s. 212	32
32 and 33 Vict. c. 71	32

COLONIAL STATUTES CITED.

	PAGE
Consolidated Statutes of Lower Canada, c. 72	268, 269, 299, 33
Ordinances of the Legislative Council of British Columbia, Session March to May, 1868, No. 7	328
Bermuda Acts, 1831, No. 8	331
Laws of the Colony of Dominica, No. 38, Clause 3	331
Statute Law of the Bahamas, Part II. Class 7, No. 1	333

FRENCH ORDINANCES CITED.

Ordon. du 20 Nov. 1822, Art. 5	341
Ordon. du 20 Nov. 1822, Art. 30	301
Ordon. du 20 Nov. 1822, Art. 37	301

TREATISES CITED.

Grand Coustumier de Normandie
Glanville
Bracton
Matthew Paris
Assizes of Jerusalem
Fleta
Fortescue's De Laudibus Legum Angliæ
Liber Albus of the City of London
Coke's Institutes
Spelman's Glossary
Viner's Abridgment
Selden's Notes to Fleta and Fortescue
Dugdale's Origines
North's Life of Guilford

Whitelock's Memorials
Blackstone's Commentaries
Stephen's Blackstone
Reeves' History of the English Law
Maddox's History of the Exchequer
Hawkins' Pleas of the Crown.
Mitford on Pleading.
Stephen on Pleading.
Manning's Serviens ad Legem.
Herbert's Inns of Court.
Pearce's Inns of Court.
Pulling's Law of Attorneys.
Lord Campbell's Lives of the Chief Justices.
Foss's Judges.
Jones's History of the French Bar.
Mollot's Régles de la Profession d'Avocat, &c. &c.

PARLIAMENTARY PAPERS CITED.

The Placitorum Abbreviatio.
The Rolls of Parliament.
First Report (1829) of the Common Law Commissioners.
Sixth Report (1834) of the Common Law Commissioners.
Report of the Select Committee of the House of Commons
  (1834) on the Inns of Court.
Report of the Select Committee of the House of Commons
  (1846) on Legal Education.
Report of the Royal Commission (1854) on the Inns of
  Court and Chancery.
Second Report of the Judicature Commission.

www.ingramcontent.com/pod-product-compliance
Lightning Source LLC
Chambersburg PA
CBHW020235240426
43672CB00006B/536